For Hélène
"E sem si pien d' amor che, per piacerti,
Non fia men dolce un poco di quiete."

VITA

Donald H. Reiman has since 1965 been editor of SHELLEY AND HIS CIRCLE, the multivolume edition of the manuscripts of Shelley, Byron, Hunt, Godwin, Wollstonecraft, Mary Shelley, and their associates in The Carl H. Pforzheimer Library in New York. Born in Erie, Pennsylvania (1934), Reiman took his B.A. at the College of Wooster and his M.A. and Ph.D. at the University of Illinois. He has held full-time teaching appointments at Duke University and the University of Wisconsin-Milwaukee and has served as visiting or adjunct professor in the graduate programs at Illinois, City University of New York, Columbia, and St. John's University. Though Dr. Reiman has always specialized in the writings of the British Romantics, his sixty essays, notes, and reviews cover topics from BEOWULF, Chaucer, and Shakespeare to G.M. Hopkins, Henry James, and J.D. Salinger. His books include SHELLEY'S "THE TRIUMPH OF LIFE" (1965); PERCY BYSSHE SHELLEY (1969; Griffin paperback, 1974); THE ROMANTICS REVIEWED (9 vols., 1972); SHELLEY AND HIS CIRCLE, Volumes V-VI (1973); BYRON ON THE CONTINENT (with Doucet Devin Fischer, 1974); THE ROMANTIC CONTEXT: POETRY (128 vols., 1976-78); and SHELLEY'S POETRY AND PROSE: A NORTON CRITICAL EDITION (with Sharon B. Powers, 1977). A founder of English 9: New York and the Wordsworth-Coleridge Association of America and formerly a member of the editorial boards of PMLA and KEATS-SHELLEY JOURNAL, Reiman now serves as Treasurer and executive officer of the Keats-Shelley Association of America, Inc. and as a member of the advisory board of STUDIES IN ROMANTICISM.

English Romantic Poetry, 1800-1835

AMERICAN LITERATURE, ENGLISH LITERATURE, AND WORLD LITERATURES IN ENGLISH: AN INFORMATION GUIDE SERIES

Series Editor: Theodore Grieder, Curator, Division of Special Collections, Fales Library, New York University

Associate Editor: Duane DeVries, Associate Professor, Polytechnic Institute of New York, Brooklyn

Other books on English literature in this series:

ENGLISH DRAMA TO 1660 (EXCLUDING SHAKESPEARE)—*Edited by Frieda Elaine Penninger*

ENGLISH DRAMA, 1660-1800—*Edited by Frederick M. Link*

ENGLISH DRAMA AND THEATRE, 1800-1900—*Edited by L.W. Conolly and J.P. Wearing*

ENGLISH DRAMA, 1900-1950—*Edited by E.H. Mikhail*

ENGLISH FICTION, 1660-1800—*Edited by Jerry C. Beasley*

CONTEMPORARY FICTION IN AMERICA AND ENGLAND, 1950-1970—*Edited by Alfred F. Rosa and Paul A. Echholz*

OLD AND MIDDLE ENGLISH POETRY TO 1500—*Edited by Walter H. Beale*

ENGLISH POETRY, 1500-1660—*Edited by S.K. Heninger, Jr.**

ENGLISH POETRY, 1660-1800—*Edited by Donald C. Mell**

VICTORIAN POETRY, 1835-1900—*Edited by Ronald E. Freeman**

ENGLISH POETRY, 1900-1950—*Edited by Emily Ann Anderson**

CONTEMPORARY POETRY IN AMERICA AND ENGLAND, 1950-1970—*Edited by Martin E. Gingerich**

ENGLISH PROSE, PROSE FICTION, AND CRITICISM TO 1660—*Edited by S.K. Heninger, Jr.*

ENGLISH PROSE AND CRITICISM IN THE NINETEENTH CENTURY—*Edited by Harris W. Wilson and Diane Long Hoeveler*

ENGLISH LITERARY JOURNAL TO 1900—*Edited by Robert B. White, Jr.*

AUTHOR NEWSLETTERS AND JOURNALS—*Edited by Margaret C. Patterson*

*in preparation

The above series is part of the
GALE INFORMATION GUIDE LIBRARY

The Library consists of a number of separate series of guides covering major areas in the social sciences, humanities, and current affairs.

General Editor: Paul Wasserman, Professor and former Dean, School of Library and Information Services, University of Maryland

Managing Editor: Denise Allard Adzigian, Gale Research Company

English Romantic Poetry, 1800-1835

A GUIDE TO INFORMATION SOURCES

*Volume 27 in the American Literature, English
Literature, and World Literatures in English
Information Guide Series*

Donald H. Reiman

*Editor, SHELLEY AND HIS CIRCLE
The Carl H. Pforzheimer Library*

Gale Research Company
Book Tower, Detroit, Michigan 48226

Library of Congress Cataloging in Publication Data

Reiman, Donald H.
   English romantic poetry, 1800-1835.

   (American literature, English literature, and
world literatures in English ; v. 27) (Gale
information guide library)
     Includes indexes.
     1. English poetry—19th century—Bibliography.
2. Romanticism—Bibliography. I. Title.
Z2014.P7R46   [PR590]   016.821'7'09
ISBN 0-8103-1231-X   74-11527

CONTENTS

Contents

Contents

Contents

PREFACE

Though they all wear "their rue with a difference" (to paraphrase Shakespeare via Peacock), enumerative bibliographers--like brides--tend to display something old, something new, something borrowed, and something blue. They draw on the work of their predecessors and, therefore, repeat the names of familiar authors and titles, some because the writers and works are classic and must be included, but others merely because to omit them would draw from reviewers (or from the authors of titles omitted or their students) charges of carelessness or ignorance. In the same way, the new bibliography usually acquires "something borrowed," because the new laborer, if he is to make an original contribution in other areas, usually must rely on his predecessors for data on a few publications that he is unable to verify personally (because of the inaccessibility of the first editions of some of the titles listed) or for descriptive details and evaluative comments from reviewers and other earlier commentators (because life is too short to permit continual reading and rereading and because knowledge is too specialized for one human being to evaluate accurately each item of the several hundreds or thousands with which he must deal). This unsatisfactory necessity--as much as the harmless drudgery of the work itself--leaves the conscientious bibliographer feeling "something blue," because he remains all too sharply aware of the limitations of both his method and his results. In some kinds of compilations there may be "ghosts," for no matter how many separate secondary sources the individual bibliographer checks, he has no certainty that they did not all copy misinformation originating in a common source. He will undoubted carry over from others a certain number of errors in titles, dates, and other information, as well as (alas!) introducing a few of his own. He will fail to do full justice to particular authors and publications because they were unfairly or mistakenly described and evaluated by the reviewers, scholars, and earlier bibliographers on whose judgment he has relied.

The reward--as well as the justification--of the latest enumerative and critical bibliographer is the "something new" he can add to the discipline or area covered by his work. He corrects errors present in earlier compilations. He calls to the attention of his colleagues essential aids to research that are familiar to students in other disciplines and specializations, but not in his. He highlights works which, though known and used by a few in his field, have not generally been perceptively described or strongly recommended to his colleagues and their students. He reevaluates a few works that were unjustly attacked or neglected by earlier scholars. And, of course, he adds recent works not included in previous compilations. Beyond these useful services, he may devise a method of organizing or presenting his material that increases its usefulness to the various readers for whom it is intended.

I herewith confess to decking out the present work with some feathers borrowed from such older compendiums as the NEW CAMBRIDGE BIBLIOGRAPHY OF ENGLISH LITERATURE (NCBEL); from the MLA-sponsored volumes reviewing "research and criticism" entitled THE ENGLISH ROMANTIC POETS (3rd ed., ed. Frank Jordan, Jr.) and THE ENGLISH ROMANTIC POETS AND ESSAYISTS (ed. C.W. Houtchens and L.H. Houtchens); from the annual international bibliography in PMLA and that of the Romantic movement found (at various dates) in ELH, PQ, and currently ELN; from the annual bibliography of Keats, Shelley, Byron, Hunt and their circles in KEATS-SHELLEY JOURNAL (K-SJ); from various bibliographical articles on the elder Romantics in THE WORDSWORTH CIRCLE (WC); from detailed scholarly reviews of various works--particularly from K-SJ, WC, JEGP, and SiR; from the excellent author bibliographies of Wordsworth by Logan, Stam, and Henley, of Coleridge by Haven, Haven, and Adams, of Byron by Santucho, of Shelley by Dunbar, and of Keats by MacGillivray; from many excellent specialized bibliographies appended to such scholarly works as Leslie A. Marchand's BYRON: A BIOGRAPHY and Bernice Slote's KEATS AND THE DRAMATIC PRINCIPLE; and from various "short title" lists (such as that included in each two-volume set of SHELLEY AND HIS CIRCLE). To the authors, compilers, editors, and indexers of these and other, comparable works, I owe debts beyond calculation, which I here gratefully acknowledge.

But thanks in part to new features, the present Information Guide performs functions that none of the above-named works can (or was designed to) perform. The readers at whom I aim are these:

1. Acquisitions librarians at universities, liberal arts colleges, and junior colleges with literature programs, and at central public libraries (as well as branch libraries) that attempt to serve the needs of students beyond the high school level.

2. Teachers of English literature at the undergraduate and graduate levels who conduct courses in which any of the major Romantic poets is taught.

3. Graduate and advanced undergraduate students taking courses in which the Romantics are featured.

4. Reference librarians or specialized humanities or English literature librarians in university and large public libraries.

For these disparate (though symbiotically interdependent) constituencies, the Gale Information Guide to ENGLISH ROMANTIC POETRY: 1800–1935 provides the following features:

1. By means of prominently displayed symbols, all users will be able to pick out easily those titles that (in judgments based on my personal knowledge and/or a consensus of expert opinion) rate top priority (*) for purchase, cataloging, and consultation on their particular subjects; those works of considerable importance (#) for the serious scholar's or advanced student's investigation of each topic; and those works of value with wide popular or general appeal to beginning students and general readers (@). Those titles receiving the asterisk (*) denoting primary value, include, for example, the best collective edition of the poems or complete writings of each author, as well as critical editions of individual titles or portions of the poet's works that surpass in authority the comparable section of that collected edition. They include the best descriptive bibliography of the poet's original editions (and/or manuscripts), the most detailed bibliography of secondary sources, the best critical biographies, and other works of scholarship and criticism deemed indispensable to understanding the poet's works. Those considered of high scholarly importance (designated by #) include other critical editions with texts or notes not totally superseded or encompassed by the primary works starred (*), as well as important biographical sources, scholarly and critical studies providing significant information or interpretations not incorporated into the primary, starred studies. Those works marked "@" include good popular biographies, handbooks, excellent student texts, the best introductions to an author's life and works, and well-written studies of wide range and interest.

   Though the usefulness of these indicators will decrease as new publications in the field supersede some items, librarians and teachers can keep their copies of this Information Guide up to date for years simply by interlining or interleaving data on the mere handful of extraordinarily significant new books in this field that appear each year, as evaluated in the reviews and specialized annual bibliographies.

2. Besides providing easy guidance to the cream of the publications in the field, this Information Guide offers expert guidance to the teacher, student, and reference librarian on how to master a particular subject or where to begin the search for a specific piece of information. Both the arrangement by subjects (subdivided as much as seems to be generally useful) and the descriptive and evaluative comments supplement the Index and facilitate the beginning (though they do not lead down every byway) of specific research.

3. Finally, the compact format of the Information Guide encourages
a judicious selectivity that, in itself, saves the user's time and
permits him to direct his energies to making bread from the wheat,
rather than threshing away the chaff, of a prolific century and a
half of writing on the Romantics. The specialist scholar may need--
or desire-- to read everything that was written on a particular
subject. The teacher, student, and general reader may wish to
confine their limited time to the best that has been known and
thought about Wordsworth's PRELUDE, Keats's life, or Shelley's
symbolism.

BOOKS IN PRINT, PAPERBACK BOOKS IN PRINT, and similar
directories will guide librarians and teachers to those titles currently available for purchase either by the library or for use as
classroom texts. (Some of these works have been in and out of
print several times and will be reprinted again if demand warrants
it.) I have usually recorded simply the first place and date of
publication, and the publisher at that location. In cases where a
title was published the same year by two or more publishers in different countries, I have given the place of publication more nearly
corresponding to the nationality of the author. Thus Thomas L.
Ashton's edition of BYRON'S HEBREW MELODIES is listed as being
published by the University of Texas Press, even though (as I know
from Ashton) Routledge and Kegan Paul of London were the primary
publishers, because Ashton is an American academic and the im-
print of the American university press gives the teacher and student a clearer idea of what to expect from the book. In the interest of simplicity--though many publishers have at various dates
had sales offices, or listed themselves as originating, in more than
one city (e.g., "Madison and Milwaukee: The University of Wisconsin Press," or "New Haven and London: Yale University
Press")--I have confined myself to recording as the place only the
location of the editorial office through which the MS of the book
finally passed. Thus, though with an Oxford University Press book,
I distinguish among "Oxford: Clarendon Press," "London: Oxford
University Press," and "New York: Oxford University Press," with
most other imprints I confine my record to the location of the
single editorial office ("Madison" or "New Haven"). This practice saves space and spares the reader confusion about meaningless
changes in publishers' imprints. Many publishers have, of course,
moved, merged, or gone out of business since the publication of
titles listed here, but to record and coordinate such changes would
involve a history of publishing in Britain and America. LITERARY
MARKET PLACE and other annual reference books will help the
interested user of this guide locate the present owners of the imprints listed here.

Donald H. Reiman
June 20, 1978
New York, New York

PLAN OF THIS VOLUME

A. SCOPE

This volume includes important modern studies of all kinds devoted primarily to or containing significant discussions of five major poets--Wordsworth, Coleridge, Byron, Shelley, and Keats--and twelve secondary poets. (As explained below, Blake and Crabbe have been excluded on chronological grounds.) It also includes works substantially devoted to historical or philosophical discussions of Romanticism in England during the early nineteenth century, and reference works, bibliographies, and major secondary studies of the historical, social, economic, political, intellectual, cultural, and literary background, a knowledge of which is requisite for full understanding and appreciation of English Romantic poetry.

Since this Information Guide is intended primarily for American teachers, students, and librarians, I have concentrated on works in English, listing only a few studies in French, German, and Italian that go substantially beyond anything available in English on the same topic. Considerable valuable work has been published over the years in these and other languages (including Dutch, Russian, and Japanese), but this material is both physically and linguistically inaccessible to all but a relatively few students and scholars.

Editions and studies devoted primarily or exclusively to William Blake (1757-1827) and George Crabbe (1754-1832) are not included in this volume because they (unlike the other English Romantic poets) both lived the greater part of their lives before 1800 and had developed their characteristic styles of poetry before that date; both were claimed for the volume that precedes this one chronologically in Gale Research's Information Guide Series partly on the pragmatic grounds that they are grouped in the eighteenth-century volume of such standard reference works as the NEW CAMBRIDGE BIBLIOGRAPHY OF ENGLISH LITERATURE. The critical judgment that Blake resembles Wordsworth and Shelley more than he does Cowper and Burns probably must (even if true) be disregarded in a series of reference books, lest the author of the bibliography of modern American poetry try to claim Blake by arguing for a family resemblance with those poets. The arbitrary calendar provides an objective point of division; no primary or secondary poet is treated here whose birthdate antedates that of Samuel Rogers (1763).

Many of the writers surveyed here wrote both poetry and prose; in some cases (notably Coleridge, Landor, Scott, James Hogg, Hunt, and Peacock), the significance of their fiction or other prose greatly outweighs that of their poetry. In the case of Coleridge and the other four major poets, I have included all major editions and criticism of their prose as well as their poetry, but for the secondary figures, I have been more selective, omitting (for example) all specialized bibliographies, editions, and studies confined to the novels of Scott and including only a few titles of or about Peacock's prose (with which his best poetry is more intimately intertwined). Naturally, I include important general bibliographies, biographies, and studies relevant to the total work of such authors.

In appropriate sections I list those periodicals I consider to be of exceptional value for the study of Romantic poetry in particular. Among individual titles, I list chiefly books (some of them reprinting significant periodical essays and studies), but I also include a select number of periodical articles (and portions of books not otherwise listed) in the following categories: (1) articles (most of them quite recent) that contain significant information and/or interpretations not yet embodied in the leading books on their subjects; (2) representative periodical publications by knowledgeable scholar-critics (many of them young) who have yet to publish a book on the subject of the periodical publication listed; (3) articles and essays representative of important trends (past or current) in the scholarship or criticism on the writer(s) under discussion (these essays are often written by creative writers or generalist critics who have never devoted an entire book to the Romantics); (4) useful articles and essays on subjects that are not treated sufficiently in the other publications listed.

B. ARRANGEMENT

The first chapter lists general background reference books and authoritative studies of proven value to students of English Romantic poetry at one level or another; some of these titles will prove more useful to teachers, graduate students, and scholars, while other works will better fill the needs of undergraduates who require a quick introduction to the historical setting, facts on a historical (or mythical) character who appears in a poem, or a survey of another area of life or art during the lifetimes of the Romantic poets. Within this chapter, books and articles are first classified by subject and listed alphabetically by author within each category or subcategory. For example, all books specifically on Turner and his art appear together within the subsection Painting, Sculpture, and Graphic Arts (Chap. 1.B.5), those on Malthus and Malthusian theory as a subcategory of the subsection on British sociopolitical background (Chap. 1.A.2.a).

Section C of Chapter 1, Literary Background, includes some general histories and reference works treating British and Western literature generally, as well as studies specifically devoted to the influence of earlier and foreign literatures (and other literary genres) on English Romantic poetry. Obviously a number of these more general works contain very valuable scholarship and criticism specifically devoted to particular English Romantic poets, and these studies should be consulted in research on more confined topics.

Chapter 2 includes all reference works, periodicals, editions, and studies that, though confined solely or chiefly to the historical period 1800-35, give about equal space or emphasis to two or more of the major poets treated in this volume. This chapter also includes theoretical and comparative studies of Romanticism as a historical movement in England, as a European phenomenon, or as a recurring philosophical perspective. Again, the student should consult relevant sections of this chapter, as well as the chapters on individual authors, when pursuing a specific research topic. Books and articles in this chapter are arranged alphabetically by author or editor within each numbered and lettered subdivision.

Chapters 3-7 are devoted to the five major English Romantic poets, arranged chronologically in order of birth: Wordsworth, Coleridge, Byron, Shelley, and Keats. Works in these five chapters are arranged according to a single plan, with individual works listed alphabetically by author or editor within each category.

Chapter 8, Secondary and Minor Poets, includes studies of twelve poets who, by virtue of either their recognition as significant poets in their own day or the attention given them by subsequent scholars and critics, have been raised above the crowd of lesser poets writing during the period. The parts of this chapter devoted to individual poets are arranged on the same organizational principle as chapters 3-7, though without as many subdivisions.

C. ANNOTATION

My comments serve two purposes: (1) to supplement the title's description of each work's subject matter and scope; (2) to evaluate its completeness, accuracy, and importance in relation to other studies, published or known to be forthcoming. A work accurately described by its title and subtitle and not competing directly with other works may require no comment at all. Sometimes—especially on critical works in areas where my own opinions are not fully fixed—I will not venture complete evaluation but merely indicate whether the work is of major or minor scope, or whether it is directed at an elementary or advanced audience. All my judgments that a work is the best, or more complete on a topic are (obviously) subject to revision as new works appear. Like time and distance records in track and field, some will be surpassed almost immediately, whereas others will stand through competitive generations. At the time this manuscript goes to press, these opinions represent my best information and judgment.

SYMBOLS, ABBREVIATIONS, AND SHORT TITLES

AES	ABSTRACTS OR ENGLISH STUDIES
BJ	BYRON JOURNAL
BNYPL	BULLETIN OF THE NEW YORK PUBLIC LIBRARY
DNB	DICTIONARY OF NATIONAL BIOGRAPHY
ELH	ELH: A JOURNAL OF ENGLISH LITERARY HISTORY
ELN	ENGLISH LANGUAGE NOTES
JEGP	JOURNAL OF ENGLISH AND GERMANIC PHILOLOGY
JK	John Keats
K-SJ	KEATS-SHELLEY JOURNAL
LB	Lord Byron
MLQ	MODERN LANGUAGE QUARTERLY
MLR	MODERN LANGUAGE REVIEW
MP	MODERN PHILOLOGY
MS, MSS	Manuscript, manuscripts
NCBEL	NEW CAMBRIDGE BIBLIOGRAPHY OF ENGLISH LITERATURE
OED	OXFORD ENGLISH DICTIONARY
PBS	Percy Bysshe Shelley
PMLA	PUBLICATIONS OF THE MODERN LANGUAGE ASSOCIATION OF AMERICA
PQ	PHILOLOGICAL QUARTERLY
SEL	STUDIES IN ENGLISH LITERATURE
SiR	STUDIES IN ROMANTICISM
SP	STUDIES IN PHILOLOGY
STC	Samuel Taylor Coleridge

Symbols, Abbreviations, and Short Titles

TSLL   TEXAS STUDIES IN LITERATURE AND LANGUAGE

WC   THE WORDSWORTH CIRCLE

WW   William Wordsworth

*   A work of the highest value to all readers.

\#   A work of high secondary importance, especially valuable for scholars and advanced students.

@   A work of high secondary importance, especially valuable for beginning students and general readers.

Chapter 1
GENERAL AND BACKGROUND STUDIES

In a specialized information guide of this kind it is possible only to suggest some of the kinds of general reference works and studies in related fields that are available to the scholar pursuing study of the English Romantic poets. I have included a number of detailed studies that I have found useful, as well as bibliographies and general surveys of various topics. The advanced student and teacher will be able to pursue their research through use of the bibliographies and footnotes in the books mentioned here, as well as in other studies housed in the same parts of the library in which these books are to be found.

A. SOCIAL, ECONOMIC, AND POLITICAL BACKGROUND

1. Reference Works

a. BIBLIOGRAPHIES

Batts, John Stuart. BRITISH MANUSCRIPT DIAIRES OF THE NINETEENTH CENTURY: AN ANNOTATED LISTING. London: Centaur Press, 1976.

> Though not as inclusive or as carefully done as Matthews' BRITISH DIARIES (below), this adds items to Matthews' listing of unpublished materials.

#Besterman, Theodore. A WORLD BIBLIOGRAPHY OF BIBLIOGRAPHIES AND OF BIBLIOGRAPHICAL CATALOGUES, CALENDARS, ABSTRACTS, DIGESTS, INDEXES, AND THE LIKE. 4th ed., rev. and enl. 5 vols. Lausanne, Switzerland: Societas Bibliographica, 1965-66.

> This enormously valuable and comprehensive work is relatively complete through 1963 for bibliographies on subjects ranging from Birmingham (England) to Birth Control and from Diderot to Druids.

*Brown, Lucy M., and Ian R. Christie. BIBLIOGRAPHY OF BRITISH HISTORY, 1789-1851. Oxford: Clarendon Press, 1977.

The new standard guide; arranged by subject, with an exhaustive
index of authors.

Bruce, A.P.C. AN ANNOTATED BIBLIOGRAPHY OF THE BRITISH ARMY,
1660-1914. New York: Garland, 1975.

The fullest survey of materials, published and unpublished, on the
British army during the period indicated.

*Elton, G[eoffrey] R. MODERN HISTORIANS ON BRITISH HISTORY, 1485-
1945: A CRITICAL BIBLIOGRAPHY, 1945-1969. Ithaca, N.Y.: Cornell University Press, 1970.

A brief, manageable overview, in essay form, with bibliographical
details given in footnotes.

Gross, Charles. A BIBLIOGRAPHY OF BRITISH MUNICIPAL HISTORY, IN-
CLUDING GILDS AND PARLIAMENTARY REPRESENTATION. 2nd ed. Pref.
G.H. Martin. Leicester, Engl.: Leicester University Press, 1966.

Essentially a reprint of the 1897 edition in Harvard Historical
Studies; chapters 6 and 7 are relevant to the Romantic period.

*Matthews, William. BRITISH AUTOBIOGRAPHIES: AN ANNOTATED BIBLIOG-
RAPHY OF BRITISH AUTOBIOGRAPHIES PUBLISHED OR WRITTEN BEFORE 1951.
Berkeley: University of California Press, 1955.

A basic source of information about hundreds of published autobiographies of all periods and from all walks of life.

* . BRITISH DIARIES: AN ANNOTATED BIBLIOGRAPHY OF BRITISH
DIARIES WRITTEN BETWEEN 1442 and 1942. Berkeley: University of California Press, 1950.

A useful chronological list of diaries, published or in manuscript,
with an alphabetical index by author.

Sheehy, Eugene P., et al. See under Winchell, below.

#Slocum, Robert B. BIOGRAPHICAL DICTIONARIES AND RELATED WORKS.
Detroit: Gale Research, 1967.

A general guide to biographical reference works of all countries
and periods. "Great Britain" occupies pages 155-78; the back of
the book contains a list of books arranged by vocation; there are
separate indexes to authors, titles, and subjects.

Williams, Judith Blow. A GUIDE TO THE PRINTED MATERIALS FOR ENGLISH
SOCIAL AND ECONOMIC HISTORY, 1750-1850. 2 vols. New York: Columbia University Press, 1924.

Valuable annotated and indexed bibliography of materials published through 1923.

*Winchell, Constance M.   GUIDE TO REFERENCE BOOKS.   8th ed.   Chicago: American Library Association, 1967.

This bible of reference librarians is divided into five main sections--A. General; B. Humanities; C. Social Studies; D. History and Area Studies; E. "Pure and Applied Sciences." The listing, frequently revised, is more up to date but less comprehensive than Besterman's multivolume work so far as bibliographies per se are concerned.   But it includes histories, dictionaries, and other standard reference tools.

The ninth edition (1976) is by Eugene P. Sheehy, Rita A. Keckeissen, and Eileen McIlvaine, with Winchell's name dropped from the title page.   Prefatory remarks explain the new arrangement of this revised basic title, which in its new form will doubtless become known as "Sheehy."

b. HISTORIES

#ANNUAL REGISTER, OR A VIEW OF THE HISTORY, POLITICS, AND LITERATURE. London: Various publishers, 1758-- .

Issued annually, a few months into the year following the one covered, from 1758 to date; there is an index volume covering 1758-1819. (GENERAL INDEX TO DODSLEY'S "ANNUAL REGISTER").

The ANNUAL REGISTER for a particular year provides the quickest way of ascertaining what people, crimes, legal cases, and historical events had loomed largest in the minds of the general British reading public during the year in question.   It often provides the scholar with data to understand allusions by writers in their literary works as well as letters.

Derry, John W.   REACTION AND REFORM, 1793-1868.   London: Blanford, 1963.

Reprinted in paperback in the United States under the title A SHORT HISTORY OF NINETEENTH-CENTURY ENGLAND, 1793-1868, this is a general survey of English history from the beginning of the first post-revolutionary war with France through the passage of the second reform bill.

#Fremantle, A.F.   ENGLAND IN THE NINETEENTH CENTURY: 1801-1810. 2 vols.   London: George Allen and Unwin, 1929-30.

An extremely detailed and vital account of a crucial decade.

General and Background Studies

@Hobsbawn, E[ric] J.E. THE AGE OF REVOLUTION: EUROPE, 1789-1848.
London: Weidenfeld and Nicolson, 1962.

> The industrial revolution, French Revolution, and their aftermath
> viewed from an academic Marxist point of view.

@Plumb, J[ohn] H. ENGLAND IN THE EIGHTEENTH CENTURY (1714-1815).
The Pelican History of England, Vol. 7. Harmondsworth, Engl.: Penguin
Books, 1950 (bibliography rev., 1963).

> This volume and David Thomson's, below, cover the same period
> treated by Trevelyan but with more modern attitudes toward the
> limitations of nineteenth-century British capitalism.

Rose, J. Holland; A.P. Newton; and E.A. Benians, eds. THE CAMBRIDGE
HISTORY OF THE BRITISH EMPIRE. Vol. 2: THE GROWTH OF THE NEW
EMPIRE, 1783-1870. Cambridge: Cambridge University Press, 1961.

> A standard account of the British colonies and their interactions
> with English and European politics.

Smart, William. ECONOMIC ANNALS OF THE NINETEENTH CENTURY.
Vol. 1: 1801-1820; Vol. 2: 1821-1830. London: Macmillan, 1910-17.

> This valuable work was cut short by Smart's death in 1915.

@Thomson, David. ENGLAND IN THE NINETEENTH CENTURY (1815-1914).
Harmondsworth, Engl.: Penguin Books, 1950.

> See Plumb, above.

Trevelyan, G[eorge] M. HISTORY OF ENGLAND; VOLUME 3: FROM
UTRECHT TO MODERN TIMES: THE INDUSTRIAL REVOLUTION AND THE
TRANSITION TO DEMOCRACY. London: Longmans, 1926.

> Revised, corrected, and reissued at various dates, through 1952.
> This standard, factually accurate account celebrates the virtues
> of liberal, democratic capitalism.

*Watson, J. Steven. THE REIGN OF GEORGE III, 1760-1815. The Oxford
History of England, Vol. 12. Oxford: Clarendon Press, 1960.

> A standard overview, continued in the volume by Woodward, be-
> low.

*Woodward, E[rnest] L. THE AGE OF REFORM, 1815-1870. The Oxford History
of England, Vol. 13. Oxford: Clarendon Press, 1938.

> A standard overview, preceded in the chronological series by Wat-
> son's volume, above.

c. BIOGRAPHICAL AND GENERAL REFERENCE WORKS

Arnault, A.V., et al. BIOGRAPHIE NOUVELLE DES CONTEMPORAINS OU DICTIONNAIRE HISTORIQUE ET RAISONNÉ DE TOUS LES HOMMES QUI, DEPUIS LA RÉVOLUTION FRANÇAISE, ONT ACQUIS DE LA CÉLÉBRITÉ PAR LEUR ACTIONS, LEURS ÉCRITS, LEURS ERREURS OU LEURS CRIMES, SOIT EN FRANCE, SOIT DANS LES PAYS ÉSTRANGERS. 20 vols. Paris: Librairie Historique, 1820-25.

Boase, Frederic. MODERN BRITISH BIOGRAPHY, CONTAINING MANY THOUSAND CONCISE MEMOIRS OF PERSONS WHO HAVE DIED BETWEEN THE YEARS 1851-1900, WITH AN INDEX. 7 vols. Cornwall: Privately printed, 1892-1921.

> Contains some 30,000 short biographies, including many details not elsewhere available.

#BURKE'S GENEALOGICAL AND HERALDIC HISTORY OF THE PEERAGE, BARONETAGE, AND KNIGHTAGE. London: Burke's Peerage, 1826--.

> This and DEBRETT'S PEERAGE (1713 to date), its great rival, together with BURKE'S DORMANT AND EXTINCT PEERAGES (1883), supply a wealth of information about those who were born into or founded an aristocratic family (e.g., LB, PBS, as well as most political figures of the Romantic period). The peerages are supplemented by BURKE'S LANDED GENTRY (1847 to date).

*ENCYCLOPAEDIA BRITANNICA. Edinburgh: Bell and Macfarquhar, 1768--.

> Along with its chief rivals CHAMBERS' ENCYCLOPAEDIA and the ENCYCLOPEDIA AMERICANA and similar works in other languages, the BRITANNICA provides a wealth of information on almost every topic known. To learn the knowledge and thought in the lifetimes of the Romantic poets themselves, the first three editions are especially useful, but often the same article, as rewritten by another expert contributor in another edition, will yield new and valuable information.

Foster, John. ALUMNI OXONIENSIS: THE MEMBERS OF THE UNIVERSITY OF OXFORD, 1715-1886. 4 vols. Oxford: Parker, 1888-91.

> This listing, together with the Venns' ALUMNI CANTABRIDGIEN-SIS (below), can be supplemented from lists of alumni of various secondary schools and Scottish and Irish universities and colleges, as well as lists of army and navy officers and professional and ecclesiastical directories.

Haydn, Joseph. HAYDN'S DICTIONARY OF DATES, RELATING TO ALL AGES AND NATIONS FOR UNIVERSAL REFERENCE. Ed. Benjamin Vincent and Revised for the Use of American Readers. New York: Harper and Brothers, 1869.

This extremely useful work, originally published in London in 1841 (and in this edition revised for Americans from Vincent's twelfth London edition of 1866) is especially strong on the basic facts of British history and European history of the eighteenth and early nineteenth centuries. Alphabetically arranged, it gives the exact date of Waterloo under both Battles and Waterloo, in the latter article giving the exact number of men and officers engaged on each side, the allied losses, and a synopsis of the battle.

*Stephen, Leslie, and Sidney Lee, eds. DICTIONARY OF NATIONAL BIOG-RAPHY. 22 vols. London: Oxford University Press, 1922.

Invaluable for giving rounded pictures of British figures encountered in studying the works and lives of the Romantic poets.

Venn, J[ohn], and J[ohn] A[rchibald] Venn. ALUMNI CANTABRIDGIENSIS: A BIOGRAPHICAL LIST OF ALL KNOWN STUDENTS, GRADUATES AND HOLDERS OF OFFICE AT THE UNIVERSITY OF CAMBRIDGE FROM THE EAR-LIEST TIMES TO 1900. Cambridge: Cambridge University Press, 1922-54.

Part 1 (4 vols.) covers the period from the beginnings through 1751 in alphabetical arrangement; Part 2 (6 vols.) covers 1752-1900.

2. Special Studies of Sociopolitical Background

a. BRITISH

#Aspinall, A[rthur], and E. Anthony Smith. ENGLISH HISTORICAL DOCU-MENTS. Vol. 11: 1783-1832. London: Eyre and Spottiswoode, 1959.

Significant acts of Parliament, speeches, government reports, and correspondence, topically arranged.

@Bovill, E[dward] W. ENGLISH COUNTRY LIFE, 1780-1830. London: Oxford University Press, 1962.

The enclosure acts, game laws, servants, squires--all aspects of rural social life in the period, gracefully narrated.

Cobban, Alfred. EDMUND BURKE AND THE REVOLT AGAINST THE EIGH-TEENTH CENTURY: A STUDY OF THE POLITICAL AND SOCIAL THINKING OF BURKE, WORDSWORTH, COLERIDGE AND SOUTHEY. London: George Allen and Unwin, 1929.

An influential study by one of the chief analysts of political influences on the Romantics.

Cone, Carl B. THE ENGLISH JACOBINS: REFORMERS IN LATE EIGHTEENTH CENTURY ENGLAND. New York: Charles Scribner's, Sons, 1968.

> A sound, readable account of the Corresponding Societies, treason trials, and related events of the 1790s.

Cunnington, C. Willett, and Phillis Cunnington. HANDBOOK OF ENGLISH COSTUME IN THE NINETEENTH CENTURY. London: Faber and Faber, 1959.

> Though there are many more expensive and more lavishly illustrated books on clothing of the period, this well-organized thick octavo should serve the scholar's (and student's) ordinary needs.

Fetter, Frank Whitson. THE DEVELOPMENT OF BRITISH MONETARY ORTHODOXY, 1797-1876. Cambridge: Harvard University Press, 1965.

> A scholarly account of the controversies over paper money, the gold standard, and the use of the Bank of England to stabilize currency.

Forbes, Duncan. HUME'S PHILOSOPHICAL POLITICS. Cambridge: Cambridge University Press, 1975.

> Traces the political implications of Hume's thought into British politics and political theory.

#Hammond, J[ohn] L., and Barbara Hammond. THE VILLAGE LABOURER, 1760-1832: A STUDY IN THE GOVERNMENT OF ENGLAND BEFORE THE REFORM BILL. London: Longmans, Green, 1911.

> This and the same authors' subsequent studies of the same period, THE TOWN LABOURER (1917) and THE SKILLED LABOURER (1919) are classics of detailed sociological research.

Henriques, Ursula. RELIGIOUS TOLERATION IN ENGLAND, 1787-1833. London: Routledge and Kegan Paul, 1961.

> A study of the political struggles to repeal laws penalizing religious minorities--Roman Catholics, Jews, and dissenting Protestants.

Jaeger, Muriel. BEFORE VICTORIA: CHANGING STANDARDS AND BEHAVIOUR, 1787-1837. [The subtitle appears only on the dust jacket.] London: Chatto and Windus, 1956.

> A perceptive and witty (though not totally scholarly) exploration of the tightening of morals and manners during and after the Regency, concluding with the refusal of Peacock and Lord Melbourne to become "Victorians."

Jerrold, Clare. THE BEAUX AND THE DANDIES: NASH, BRUMMELL, AND D'ORSAY, WITH THEIR COURTS. London: Stanley Paul, ca. 1910.

Entertaining and anecdotal account, with glimpses of Bath and Regency society.

@Kroeber, Karl, ed. BACKGROUNDS TO BRITISH ROMANTIC LITERATURE. San Francisco: Chandler Publishing, 1968.

Contains excerpts from standard books on economic, political, and social history of the period. A convenient supplementary textbook.

*Maccoby, S[imon], ENGLISH RADICALISM, 1786-1832: FROM PAINE TO COBBETT. London: George Allen and Unwin, 1955.

The last to be written of five volumes tracing the English radical tradition from 1762 to 1914, this excellent study features many quotations from obscure and ephemeral sources.

MacLean, Kenneth. AGRARIAN AGE: A BACKGROUND FOR WORDSWORTH. New Haven: Yale University Press, 1950.

Discusses social changes in rural England and their reflection in works by Goldsmith, Crabbe, Blake, Clare, and Wordsworth.

Malcolmson, Robert W. POPULAR RECREATIONS IN ENGLISH SOCIETY, 1700-1850. Cambridge: Cambridge University Press, 1973.

Historical developments in the celebration of holidays and festivals, sports, games, and other pastimes during the course of the industrial revolution (with extensive bibliography).

[Malthus] Bonar, James. MALTHUS AND HIS WORK. 1881, 1924; rpt. New York: A.M. Kelley, 1966.

Long a standard account.

[Malthus] Boner, Harold A. HUNGRY GENERATIONS: THE NINETEENTH-CENTURY CASE AGAINST MALTHUSIANISM. New York: King's Crown Press, 1955.

A Columbia University dissertation, with extensive bibliography.

[Malthus] McCleary, George F. THE MALTHUSIAN POPULATION THEORY. London: Faber and Faber, 1953.

Contains a bibliography of its subject.

Malthus, Thomas Robert. POPULATION: THE FIRST ESSAY. Foreword by Kenneth E. Boulding. Ann Arbor: University of Michigan Press, 1959.

This convenient paperback edition of the 1798 version of AN ESSAY ON THE PRINCIPLE OF POPULATION can be supplemented by the Everyman Library Edition of the much-enlarged second edition of 1803.

_____. THE TRAVEL DIARIES OF THOMAS ROBERT MALTHUS. Ed. Patricia James. Cambridge: Cambridge University Press, 1966.

A vivid introduction to the personality of the man and to his observations on the relationship of population to the food supply in Scandinavia at the end of the eighteenth century.

[Malthus] Smith, Kenneth. THE MALTHUSIAN CONTROVERSY. London: Routledge and Kegan Paul, 1951.

Contains a bibliography.

Marshall, Dorothy. THE ENGLISH POOR IN THE EIGHTEENTH CENTURY: A STUDY IN SOCIAL AND ADMINISTRATIVE HISTORY. London: Routledge and Kegan Paul, 1926.

Analyzes the operations of the Poor Laws, reform of which occupied the attention of PBS, WW, and others.

Mingay, G[ordon] E. ENGLISH LANDED SOCIETY IN THE EIGHTEENTH CENTURY. London: Routledge and Kegan Paul, 1963.

Examines the structure and functions of land-owning families during the beginnings of the industrial revolution. See also F.M.L. Thompson, below.

Moers, Ellen. THE DANDY, BRUMMELL TO BEERBOHM. New York: Viking, 1960.

The account begins with the British Regency society of LB's time but quickly moves to France and to Victorian England.

Poynter, J.R. SOCIETY AND PAUPERISM: ENGLISH IDEAS ON POOR RELIEF, 1795-1834. London: Routledge and Kegan Paul, 1969.

The debates on minimum wages and the early versions of the welfare system, tracing the influence of Bentham and utilitarian thought on the march towards Gradgrind and Bounderby. The volume has an extensive bibliography.

Read, Donald. PETERLOO: THE "MASSACRE" AND ITS BACKGROUND. Manchester, Engl.: Manchester University Press, 1958.

A detailed study of the economic and social background of the area in 1819, as well as of the "massacre" and its aftermath. Contains a map of the scene and a "Select Bibliography."

General and Background Studies

*Ricardo, David. THE PRINCIPLES OF POLITICAL ECONOMY AND TAXATION. Everyman Edition. Introd. F.W. Kolthammer. London: J.M. Dent; New York: E.P. Dutton, 1911.

> This edition is frequently reprinted and provides wide access to the chief work (1817) of the most significant British economic theorist of the age. Ricardo's PRINCIPLES develops the laissez faire principles of Adam Smith in the light of Malthus' population theory.

Rude, George. HANOVERIAN LONDON, 1714-1808. London: Secker and Warburg, 1971.

> Part of the standard History of London series; see also Sheppard, below.

Sheppard, Francis. LONDON 1808-1870: THE INFERNAL WEN. London: Secker and Warburg, 1971.

> Part of the standard History of London series; see also Rude, above.

*Thompson, E[dward] P. THE MAKING OF THE ENGLISH WORKING CLASS. London: Victor Gollancz, 1963.

> A classic of detailed scholarship and passionate writing, from a Marxist perspective.

Thompson, F[rancis] M.L. ENGLISH LANDED SOCIETY IN THE NINETEENTH CENTURY. London: Routledge and Kegan Paul, 1963.

> Continues the study in the period following that covered by Mingay, above.

*Wheatley, Henry B. LONDON, PAST AND PRESENT: ITS HISTORY, ASSO-CIATIONS, AND TRADITIONS. 3 vols. London: John Murray; New York: Scribner and Welford, 1891.

> The most comprehensive aid to the scholar in establishing the significance of allusions to places (neighborhoods, streets, or buildings) in British literature of the nineteenth century. The volumes are arranged in dictionary form.

b. EUROPEAN AND COLONIAL

Clogg, Richard, ed. THE STRUGGLE FOR GREEK INDEPENDENCE: ESSAYS TO MARK THE 150TH ANNIVERSARY OF THE GREEK WAR OF INDEPENDENCE. London: Macmillan, 1973.

> Includes an essay by Robin Fletcher entitled "Byron in Nineteenth-Century Greek Literature," as well as numerous other references to LB. See also Dakin and St. Clair, both cited below.

Includes detailed histories of all earlier firms later absorbed by Barclays, including the firm headed by LB's friend Douglas Kinnaird.

Meteyard, Eliza. THE LIFE OF JOSIAH WEDGWOOD . . ., WITH AN INTRODUCTORY SKETCH OF THE ART OF POTTERY IN ENGLAND. 2 vols. London: Hurst and Blackett, 1865.

A rich (though not totally candid) account of the origins of one of the largest industrial fortunes in England during the period.

Norton, Jane E. GUIDE TO THE NATIONAL AND PROVINCIAL DIRECTORIES OF ENGLAND AND WALES, EXCLUDING LONDON, PUBLISHED BEFORE 1856. London: Royal Historical Society, 1950.

For information on London directories, see Gross, above.

*Robinson, Howard. THE BRITISH POST OFFICE, A HISTORY. Princeton: Princeton University Press, 1948.

A valuable general account; for special problems in the study of Romantic literature, see Cameron and Reiman, SHELLEY AND HIS CIRCLE (cited in Chap. 6.C.3), II, 914-25, and V, 32-34.

4. Printing, Publishing, the Reading Public, and Reviewing Media

*Altick, Richard D. THE ENGLISH COMMON READER: A SOCIAL HISTORY OF THE MASS READING PUBLIC, 1800-1900. Chicago: University of Chicago Press, 1957.

A brilliant analysis of the best sellers and the growth of public literacy during the Romantic and Victorian periods.

#Aspinall, A[rthur]. POLITICS AND THE PRESS, C. 1780-1850. London: Home and Van Thal, 1949.

Tells who paid which British (particularly, London) newspapers to print what political views and traces the growth of the concept of freedom to the press.

Besterman, Theodore, ed. THE PUBLISHING FIRM OF CADELL AND DAVIES: SELECT CORRESPONDENCE AND ACCOUNTS, 1793-1836. London: Oxford University Press, 1938.

A valuable selection from the archives of an important publisher.

Bigmore, E.C., and C.W.H. Wyman. A BIBLIOGRAPHY OF PRINTING, WITH NOTES AND ILLUSTRATIONS. 2 vols. London: Bernard Quaritch, 1884.

Cobban, Alfred. THE SOCIAL INTERPRETATION OF THE FRENCH REVOLU-
TION. Cambridge: Cambridge University Press, 1965.

> A series of lectures by an outstanding student of the French Revolu-
> tion and its influence.

Dakin, Douglas. THE GREEK STRUGGLE FOR INDEPENDENCE, 1821-1833.
Berkeley: University of California Press, 1973.

> Discusses LB's part in the liberation movement; see also Clogg,
> above, and St. Clair, below.

Dowden, Edward, THE FRENCH REVOLUTION AND ENGLISH LITERATURE.
London: Kegan Paul, Trench, Trübner, 1897.

> Dowden (PBS's biographer) also included a briefer essay entitled
> "The French Revolution and Literature" in his STUDIES IN LITERA-
> TURE, 1789-1877 (London, 1902). Dowden's accounts represent
> the older scholarship of generalizations and brief characterization,
> relying little on detail or specificity.

*Lefebvre, Georges. THE FRENCH REVOLUTION. Trans. Elizabeth M. Evan-
son, John H. Stewart, and James Friguglietti. 2 vols. New York: Columbia
University Press, 1962, 1964.

> A general history by one of the world's most renowned scholars in
> the field. Volume 1 covers the Revolution "From Its Origins to
> 1793"; Volume 2, "From 1793 to 1799."

*_____. NAPOLEON. Trans. Henry F. Stockhold and J.E. Anderson. 2
vols. New York: Columbia University Press, 1969.

> A historical account of the Napoleonic era in France from 1799
> through 1815.

Martin, Kingsley. FRENCH LIBERAL THOUGHT IN THE EIGHTEENTH CEN-
TURY: A STUDY OF POLITICAL IDEAS FROM BAYLE TO CONDORCET.
London: Ernest Benn, 1929.

> Long an influential textbook and overview of its subject.

Misra, B[arkey] B[ihari]. THE CENTRAL ADMINISTRATION OF THE EAST IN-
DIA COMPANY, 1773-1834. Manchester, Engl.: Manchester University Press,
1959.

> A more detailed study indebted to the overview by Philips, below.

*Philips, C[yril] H. THE EAST INDIA COMPANY, 1784-1834. Manchester,
Engl.: University of Manchester Press, 1940; corrected reissue, 1961.

A seminal study that has led to a number of more detailed studies of various aspects of its subject, like that of Misra, above.

Pope-Hennessy, James. SINS OF THE FATHERS: A STUDY OF THE ATLANTIC SLAVE TRADERS, 1441-1807. New York: Alfred A. Knopf, 1968.

First published in London in 1967, this study has been superseded by a large number of more recent specialized studies on slavery in various parts of the world.

*Rude, Georges. THE CROWD IN THE FRENCH REVOLUTION. Oxford: Clarendon Press, 1959.

A classic study that corrected earlier generalizations by examining the occupations and background of as many political activists during the period as possible.

* _____. REVOLUTIONARY EUROPE, 1783-1815. New York: Harper and Row, 1964.

An authoritative general survey.

@St. Clair, William. THAT GREECE MIGHT STILL BE FREE: THE PHILHELLENES IN THE WAR OF INDEPENDENCE. London: Oxford University Press, 1972.

The true story behind the myth that involved PBS and LB, among other British writers.

Spencer, Terence J.B. FAIR GREECE! SAD RELIC: LITERARY PHILHELLENISM FROM SHAKESPEARE TO BYRON. London: Weidenfeld and Nicolson, 1954.

Stokes, Eric. THE ENGLISH UTILITARIANS AND INDIA. Oxford: Clarendon Press, 1959.

A specialized study indicative of the infiltration of utilitarian thought into British officialdom during the first half of the century.

Vaughan, Michalina, and Margaret Scotford Archer. SOCIAL CONFLICT AND EDUCATIONAL CHANGE IN ENGLAND AND FRANCE, 1789-1848. Cambridge: Cambridge University Press, 1971.

Seeks to refute or modify the prevailing Marxist and functionalist interpretations of educational change during the industrial revolution and the French Revolution.

3. British Commercial Directories and Histories

Balston, Thomas. WILLIAM BALSTON, PAPER-MAKER: 1759-1849. London: Methuen, 1954.

> A valuable account of a paper manufacturer who began as an assistant to James Whatman and began his own business in 1794.

Chandler, George. FOUR CENTURIES OF BANKING: AS ILLUSTRATED BY THE BANKERS, CUSTOMERS AND STAFF ASSOCIATED WITH THE CONSTITUENT BANKS OF MARTINS BANK LIMITED. London: B.T. Batsford, 1964.

> A detailed account of banking in Liverpool and the North of England. See also Matthews and Tuke on Barclays Bank in London, below.

Coleman, D[onald] C. THE BRITISH PAPER INDUSTRY, 1495-1860: A STUDY IN INDUSTRIAL GROWTH. Oxford: Clarendon Press, 1958.

Copeman, W[illiam] S.C. THE WORSHIPFUL SOCIETY OF APOTHECARIES OF LONDON: A HISTORY, 1617-1967. Oxford: Pergamon, 1968.

> Besides its general historical value, the volume treats JK in a chapter on eminent apothecaries.

Cripps, Ernest C. PLOUGH COURT: THE STORY OF A NOTABLE PHARMA 1715-1927. London: Allen and Hanburys, 1927.

> An illuminating account of a family retail business through the period.

Dickson, P[eter] G.M. THE SUN INSURANCE OFFICE, 1710-1960: THE TORY OF TWO AND A HALF CENTURIES OF BRITISH INSURANCE. Lond Oxford University Press, 1960.

> A detailed, scholarly account.

Gross, C[harles] W.F. THE LONDON DIRECTORIES, 1677-1855. Londo Denis Archer, 1932.

> For information on provincial directories, see Norton, below.

Marillier, H[enry] C. "CHRISTIE'S": 1766-1925. London: Constable,

> An account of the London auction house from its beginnings.

Matthews, P.W., and Anthony W. Tuke. HISTORY OF BARCLAYS BA LIMITED. London: Blades, East, and Blades, 1926.

This valuable resource should be supplemented by bibliographies and reviews of more recent research published in the three major periodicals concerned with the bibliographical analysis of British books: (1) THE LIBRARY, (2) PAPERS OF THE BIBLIOGRAPHICAL SOCIETY OF AMERICA, and (3) STUDIES IN BIBLIOGRAPHY.

Blunden, Edmund. KEATS'S PUBLISHER: A MEMOIR OF JOHN TAYLOR (1781-1864). London: Jonathan Cape, 1936.

A graceful preliminary survey. See also Chilcott, below.

Bourne, H.R. Fox. ENGLISH NEWSPAPERS: CHAPTERS IN THE HISTORY OF JOURNALISM. 2 vols. London, 1887; rpt. New York: Russell and Russell, 1966.

A vigorous, detailed narrative, by a militant freedom-of-the-press advocate, of the history of British newspapers from 1621 on, but concentrating on the first half of the nineteenth century.

#Boyle, Andrew. AN INDEX TO THE ANNUALS (1820-1850). Worcester, Engl.: Andrew Boyle, 1967.

An index to the authors represented in the British annuals during the period indicated. See also Faxon, below.

Chilcott, Tim. A PUBLISHER AND HIS CIRCLE: THE LIFE AND WORK OF JOHN TAYLOR, KEATS'S PUBLISHER. London: Routledge and Kegan Paul, 1972.

Supplements Blunden's earlier study of Taylor.

Clive, John. SCOTCH REVIEWERS: THE EDINBURGH REVIEW, 1802-1815. London: Faber and Faber, 1957.

This useful introduction can be supplemented by books on Constable, Francis Jeffrey, Francis Horner, Henry Brougham, and Sidney Smith.

#Constable, Thomas. ARCHIBALD CONSTABLE AND HIS LITERARY CORRE-SPONDENTS: A MEMORIAL. 3 vols. Edinburgh: Edmonston and Douglas, 1873.

This study, quoting a large number of letters, is a valuable re-source for studying a number of authors in this period (e.g., Campbell, Godwin, James Hogg, and, of course, Scott) as well as the book trade and the EDINBURGH REVIEW.

Cox, Harold, and John E. Chandler. THE HOUSE OF LONGMAN, WITH A RECORD OF THEIR BICENTENARY CELEBRATIONS, 1724-1924. London: Longmans, Green, 1925.

An anniversary gift book, published for private circulation, that sketches the history of one of the great literary publishing firms.

Faxon, Frederick W. LITERARY ANNUALS AND GIFT BOOKS: A BIBLIOG-RAPHY, 1823-1903. Rpt. with supplementary essays by Eleanore Jamieson and Iain Bain. Pinner, Middlesex, Engl.: Private Libraries Association, 1973.

First published in 1912, this, with Boyle's INDEX, above, provides the fullest information on the literary annuals in which a great deal of later (and lesser) Romantic poetry first appeared.

Glaister, Geoffrey Ashall. GLOSSARY OF THE BOOK: TERMS USED IN PAPER-MAKING, PRINTING, BOOKBINDING AND PUBLISHING. London: George Allen and Unwin, 1960.

This extremely valuable reference work gives short articles on his-torically important printers and publishers, as well as illustrated descriptions of techniques used in book production (both modern and historical) and definitions of technical terms. For home use on the latter subject, I highly recommend John Carter's ABC FOR BOOK COLLECTORS (5th ed., New York: Alfred A. Knopf, 1977).

Growoll, A., and Wilberforce Eames. THREE CENTURIES OF ENGLISH BOOK-TRADE BIBLIOGRAPHY. London: Holland Press, 1964.

An essay, with a bibliography of the union lists of publications by English booksellers and publishers.

Handover, P[hyllis] M. PRINTING IN LONDON FROM 1476 TO MODERN TIMES: COMPETITIVE PRACTICE AND TECHNICAL INVENTION IN THE TRADE OF BOOK AND BIBLE PRINTING, PERIODICAL PRODUCTION, JOB-BING, ETC. Cambridge: Harvard University Press, 1960.

A series of lectures giving an overview of its subject.

*Hayden, John O. THE ROMANTIC REVIEWERS, 1802-1824. Chicago: Uni-versity of Chicago Press, 1968 [1969].

Contains pedestrian (but accurate) surveys of the major reviewing periodicals and of the treatment accorded by them to various groups of Romantic writers, followed by a valuable bibliographical appen-dix of periodicals and reviews. Most of the reviews are now avail-able in Reiman's ROMANTIC REVIEWED, below, and/or in the various volumes of the Critical Heritage series published by Rout-ledge and Kegan Paul.

Howe, Ellic. THE LONDON COMPOSITOR: DOCUMENTS RELATING TO WAGES, WORKING CONDITIONS AND CUSTOMS OF THE LONDON PRINT-ING TRADE, 1785-1900. London: The Bibliographical Society, 1947.

A basic tool in the study of the printers of the period.

#Labarre, E.J. DICTIONARY AND ENCYCLOPEDIA OF PAPER AND PAPER-MAKING, WITH EQUIVALENTS OF THE TECHNICAL TERMS IN FRENCH, GERMAN, DUTCH, ITALIAN, SPANISH, AND SWEDISH. 2nd ed., rev. and enl. Amsterdam: Swets and Zeitlinger, 1952.

A marvelous reference took, with extensive bibliography to its date of revision. There are also various specialized books on papermills and watermarks, though most of them concentrate their coverage on the sixteenth, seventeenth, and eighteenth centuries.

Madden, Lionel, and Diana Dixon. THE NINETEENTH-CENTURY PERIODICAL PRESS IN BRITAIN: A BIBLIOGRAPHY OF MODERN STUDIES, 1901-1971. New York: Garland, 1976.

Includes references under people involved with periodicals, as well as under the titles of individual periodicals. This listing supplements W.S. Ward's various works, below, by covering particularly the newspapers of the Romantic period.

Maxted, Ian. THE LONDON BOOK TRADES, 1775-1800: A PRELIMINARY CHECKLIST OF MEMBERS. Folkstone, Kent, Engl.: Dawson, 1977.

In extending Todd's work, below, backwards in time, Marxted gives valuable additional information (and bibliographical references) on printers, booksellers, etc. who carry over into the Romantic period.

Merriam, Harold G. EDWARD MOXON, PUBLISHER OF POETS. New York: Columbia University Press, 1939.

The story of a publisher who, though beginning in 1830, became the publisher of Lamb, STC, JK, PBS, Hunt, Campbell, and WW, as well as later poets (Browning and Tennyson) and lesser figures (Hartley Coleridge, Talfourd, and Patmore).

Mumby, Frank Arthur. PUBLISHING AND BOOKSELLING: A HISTORY FROM THE EARLIEST TIMES TO THE PRESENT DAY. Bibliog. by W.H. Peet. New York: R.R. Bowker, 1931.

An anecdotal account of the book trade from classical times through the 1920s. Chapters 11-13 (pp. 237-321) cover the late eighteenth and the early nineteenth centuries.

#Nangle, Benjamin Christie. THE MONTHLY REVIEW, SECOND SERIES, 1790-1815: INDEXES OF CONTRIBUTORS AND ARTICLES. Oxford: Clarendon Press, 1955.

Also contains brief biographical sketches of leading contributors.

Oliphant, Margaret, and Mrs. Gerald Porter. ANNALS OF A PUBLISHING HOUSE: WILLIAM BLACKWOOD AND HIS SONS, THEIR MAGAZINE AND FRIENDS. 3 vols. Edinburgh: William Blackwood, 1897-98.

> These official annals, begun by Mrs. Oliphant and completed after her death by William Blackwood and his sister Mrs. Porter, contain a valuable array of documents and correspondence.

*Reiman, Donald H., ed. THE ROMANTICS REVIEWED: CONTEMPORARY RE-VIEWS OF BRITISH ROMANTIC WRITERS. 9 vols. New York: Garland, 1972.

> Organized in three parts: Part A, THE LAKE POETS (i.e., WW, STC, Southey, and Lamb), 2 volumes.; Part B, BYRON AND REGENCY SOCIETY POETS (i.e., Rogers, Campbell, and Moore), 5 volumes; Part C, SHELLEY, KEATS, AND LONDON RADICAL WRITERS (i.e., Godwin, Leigh Hunt, Hazlitt, Mary Shelley), 2 volumes. An index to the nine volumes appears at the end of Part C, Volume 2. The series attempts to include all reviews of the poetry of WW, STC, LB, PBS, and JK, from 1793 through 1824, with representative reviews of their prose, of the work of other writers, and of later publications, and an introduction to each periodical.

#Shine, Hill, and Helen Chadwick Shine. THE QUARTERLY REVIEW UNDER GIFFORD: IDENTIFICATION OF CONTRIBUTORS, 1809-1824. Chapel Hill: University of North Carolina Press, 1949.

> Identifies the authors of the anonymous articles, using information from memoirs, MSS at John Murray's, and other documents, but sometimes the evidence is contradictory or incomplete.

#Smiles, Samuel. A PUBLISHER AND HIS FRIENDS: MEMOIR AND CORRE-SPONDENCE OF THE LATE JOHN MURRAY, WITH AN ACCOUNT OF THE ORIGIN AND PROGRESS OF THE HOUSE, 1768-1843. 2 vols. London: John Murray, 1891.

> An invaluable resource for studying the period and the publishing industry, as well as for specific information on LB, Moore, and others.

#Strout, Alan Lang. A BIBLIOGRAPHY OF ARTICLES IN BLACKWOOD'S MAG-AZINE, 1817-1825. Lubbock: Library of Texas Technical College, 1959.

> This valuable study has been supplemented by Brian M. Murray's two articles entitled "Unidentified or Disputed Articles in BLACK-WOOD'S MAGAZINE" in STUDIES IN SCOTTICH LITERATURE, 4 (1967), 144-54, and 9 (1971-72), 107-16.

*Timperley, C[harles] H. A DICTIONARY OF PRINTERS AND PRINTING. London: H. Johnson, 1839; rpt. in 1842 as THE ENCYCLOPEDIA OF LITERARY AND TYPOGRAPHICAL ANECDOTE.

Contains much useful information on the printers with whom the Romantics and their publishers dealt; also gives a running account of the struggle for freedom of the press in Britain.

#Todd, William B. A DIRECTORY OF PRINTERS AND OTHERS IN ALLIED TRADES: LONDON AND VICINITY, 1800-1840. London: Printing Historical Society, 1972.

An indispensible resource for anyone studying the relationship between authors and their printers and publishers in this period.

#Ward, William S. BRITISH PERIODICALS AND NEWSPAPERS, 1789-1832: A BIBLIOGRAPHY OF SECONDARY SOURCES. Lexington: University of Kentucky Press, [1972].

Studies are arranged by periodical, by names of editors and contributors, and by place of publication. There is also an index to the authors of the secondary studies.

_____. INDEX AND FINDING LIST OF SERIALS PUBLISHED IN THE BRITISH ISLES, 1789-1832. Lexington: University of Kentucky Press, 1953.

A basic source giving the name(s), the place and the dates of publication of each British literary periodical that was published (however briefly) during the period.

_____. LITERARY REVIEWS IN BRITISH PERIODICALS, 1798-1826: A BIBLIOGRAPHY, WITH A SUPPLEMENTARY LIST OF GENERAL (NON-REVIEW) ARTICLES ON LITERARY SUBJECTS. 3 vols. New York: Garland, 1972, 1977.

In addition to locating reviews, this bibliography provides the fullest list of literary publications of many minor authors, and the dates of the weekly and monthly reviews often provide the easiest access to the month or week in which the major and minor publications actually appeared. Ward is now working on a similar list for the period 1789-97.

B. INTELLECTUAL AND ARTISTIC BACKGROUND

1. Philosophy and Judeo-Christian Thought

Drummond, William. ACADEMICAL QUESTIONS. London: W. Bulmer, 1805.

Besides being the most important single philosophical influence on PBS, this book epitomizes the skeptical wing of the British empirical school of philosophy.

*Edwards, Paul, ed. THE ENCYCLOPEDIA OF PHILOSOPHY. 8 vols. New York: Macmillan, 1967.

> Like all such general reference works, this one is uneven, but the historical surveys of such topics as Skepticism, Empiricism, and Egoism and Altruism supplement articles on individual philosophers and technical terms. Each article has a bibliography proportioned to its length.

Fairchild, Hoxie Neale. RELIGIOUS TRENDS IN ENGLISH POETRY. Vol. 3: ROMANTIC FAITH: 1780-1830. New York: Columbia University Press, 1948.

> Fairchild, an orthodox Episcopalian to whom Romanticism was a heretical disease, is nevertheless strong on facts and analysis of religious implications. He includes chapters on Burns, Blake, WW, STC, PBS, LB, and JK.

Gill, Frederick C. THE ROMANTIC MOVEMENT AND METHODISM: A STUDY OF ENGLISH ROMANTICISM AND THE EVANGELICAL REVIVAL. London: The Epworth Press (E.C. Barton), 1937.

> Includes a bibliography of its subject.

Le Mahieu, D.L. THE MIND OF WILLIAM PALEY: A PHILOSOPHER AND HIS AGE. Lincoln: University of Nebraska Press, 1976.

> An exposition of the most influential orthodox theologian and moral philosopher in England during the late eighteenth and early nineteenth centuries.

Piper, H[erbert] W. THE ACTIVE UNIVERSE: PANTHEISM AND THE CONCEPT OF IMAGINATION IN THE ENGLISH ROMANTIC POET. London: Athlone [University of London] Press, 1962.

> This "study of 'Romantic Pantheism' and its part in the development of the Romantic theory of the Imagination" moves from the earlier radical thought of Priestley and Erasmus Darwin through the early works of WW and STC.

Reardon, Bernard M.G. RELIGIOUS THOUGHT IN THE NINETEENTH CENTURY, ILLUSTRATED FROM WRITERS OF THE PERIOD. Cambridge: Cambridge University Press, 1966.

> Includes a general introduction, followed by selections from Schleiermacher, Hegel, Feuerbach, D.F. Strauss, Lotze, Ritsch, Harnack, Kierkegaard, Lamennais, Comte, Sabatier, Solovyov, STC, Maurice, Newman, Mansel, J.S. Mill, Jowett, Arnold, Holland, John and Edward Caird, F.H. Bradley, Emerson, Royce, and William James, with biographical and bibliographical introductions.

Roston, Murray. PROPHET AND POET: THE BIBLE AND THE GROWTH OF ROMANTICISM. Evanston, Ill.: Northwestern University Press, 1965.

> A useful (though rather superficial) survey of the impact of eigh-teenth-century attitudes toward biblical language and rhetoric and the use of the same techniques in "Ossian" and the Romantics.

#Shaffer, Elinor S. "KUBLA KHAN" AND "THE FALL OF JERUSALEM": THE MYTHOLOGICAL SCHOOL IN BIBLICAL CRITICISM AND SECULAR LITERA-TURE, 1770-1880. Cambridge: Cambridge University Press, 1975.

> Beginning with a discussion of STC's unwritten epic "The Fall of Jerusalem," Shaffer provides the most learned discussion now avail-able of the growth of the higher criticism and liberal theology in British literary thought from STC through Browning and George Eliot. See also McFarland, in Chapter 4.D.1 of this guide.

@Trawick, Leonard M., ed. BACKGROUNDS OF ROMANTICISM: ENGLISH PHILOSOPHICAL PROSE OF THE EIGHTEENTH CENTURY. Bloomington: Indiana University Press, 1967.

> A useful selection of important passages from the influential works of William Law, George Berkeley, David Hartley, Adam Smith, William Duff, Abraham Tucker, Jacob Bryant, and William God-win, with an introduction, general bibliography, and biographical and bibliographical notes for each author.

*Tuveson, Ernest Lee. THE IMAGINATION AS A MEANS OF GRACE: LOCKE AND THE AESTHETICS OF ROMANTICISM. Berkeley: University of California Press, 1960.

> The impact of the British empirical philosophers on aesthetic theo-ries.

#Wellek, Rene. IMMANUEL KANT IN ENGLAND, 1793-1838. Princeton: Princeton University Press, 1931.

> A classic study so thoroughly researched and executed that it still remains standard for its complex subject.

@Woodhouse, A[rthur] S.P. THE POET AND HIS FAITH: RELIGION AND POETRY IN ENGLAND FROM SPENSER TO ELIOT AND AUDEN. Chicago: University of Chicago Press, 1965.

> An urbane survey by a leading historian of English literature.

2. Mythologies

Anderson, George K. THE LEGEND OF THE WANDERING JEW. Providence, R.I.: Brown University Press, 1965.

A historical study of the legend and literature embodying it, especially important as background to PBS's writings.

Bodkin, Maud. ARCHETYPAL PATTERNS IN POETRY: PSYCHOLOGICAL STUDIES OF THE IMAGINATION. London: Oxford University Press, 1934.

A study first popularized by Hyman in THE ARMED VISION (1948; see C.3, below) that became extremely influential in showing the relevance of Jung's theories of archetypes and the collective unconscious to literary study.

Briggs, K[atharine] M. THE FAIRIES IN ENGLISH TRADITION AND LITERATURE. Chicago: University of Chicago Press, 1967.

Fairies, goblins, imps, changelings, and their ilk in folklore and literature, with dictionary of fairy types and individuals and a substantial bibliography. (The subject treated is "British" rather than English, inasmuch as Celtic folklore predominates.)

*Bush, Douglas. MYTHOLOGY AND THE ROMANTIC TRADITION IN ENGLISH POETRY. Cambridge: Harvard University Press, 1937.

The sequel to Bush's MYTHOLOGY AND THE RENAISSANCE TRADITION IN ENGLISH POETRY (1933), this study covers the eighteenth century, the major and minor English Romantics, the chief Victorian poets and early twentieth century English poetry, as well as some American poets. Bush's lack of sympathy with some Romantics (notably PBS) somewhat vitiates his knowledge of the mythological tradition.

Conway, Moncure Daniel. DEMONOLOGY AND DEVIL-LORE. 2 vols. New York: Henry Holt, 1879.

Though there are more recent studies, these volumes provide a nineteenth-century perspective on the subject.

Feldman, Burton, and Robert D. Richardson. THE RISE OF MODERN MYTHOLOGY, 1680-1860. Bloomington: Indiana University Press, 1972.

Surveys the growth of mythological studies by capsuling the efforts of key writers and movements and printing excerpts from their works, with full bibliography and index.

@Frazer, James George, and Theodor H. Gaster. THE NEW GOLDEN BOUGH: A NEW ABRIDGMENT OF THE CLASSIC WORK. New York: Criterion Books, 1959.

An edited abridgment, correcting a number of Frazer's original theories in the light of subsequent scholarship. Though students of twentieth-century literature should rely on Frazer's original thirteen-volume work (1890--), which directly influenced Modernist writers, this edited abridgment (available in a Mentor paperback edition, 1964), provides the basic theories with more up- to-date evidence and analysis.

@Graves, Robert. GREEK MYTHS. 2 vols. London: Penguin Books, 1955.

Like Edith Hamilton's popular work (below), but Graves is more detailed on the Greek myths, while omitting the Roman material that Hamilton includes.

#Gray, Louis Herbert, and John Arnott MacCulloch, eds. THE MYTHOLOGY OF ALL RACES. 13 vols. New York: Marshall Jones, 1916-32.

Contains sections on the presentation of various ancient gods and mythologies in the visual arts, as well as in their origins and significance. The thirteenth volume is a comprehensive index to the whole, helpful for identifying really obscure mythological allusions, as well as for bringing together various mythological references to (for example) North, North Star, Marriage, Stone, and Thunder.

@Hamilton, Edith. MYTHOLOGY. Boston: Little, Brown, 1940. 2nd ed., 1942.

An accurate and readable retelling of the Greek and Roman myths, suitable for undergraduates to use as a companion to their early study of English poetry employing or alluding to these myths.

Hungerford, Edward B. SHORES OF DARKNESS. New York: Columbia University Press, 1941.

Investigates the syncretic movements in mythological and religious studies in the late eighteenth century and examines the effects of these movements in poems of Blake, JK, PBS, and Goethe.

Kerenyi, C. PROMETHEUS: ARCHETYPAL IMAGE OF HUMAN EXISTENCE, trans. Ralph Manheim. London: Thames and Hudson, 1963.

A work first published in German at Zurich in 1946, this volume presents the mythological and iconographic background, with several plates depicting Promethean art and scenes.

#Lempriere, J[ohn]. A CLASSICAL DICTIONARY; CONTAINING A COPIOUS ACCOUNT OF ALL THE PROPER NAMES MENTIONED IN THE ANCIENT AUTHORS. 11th ed., corrected. London: T. Cadell and W. Davies, 1820.

First published in 1788, this work remained in print in various editions even after Lempriere's death in 1824. JK used an earlier edition as one of his chief sources of Greek mythology.

Manuel, Frank E. THE EIGHTEENTH CENTURY CONFRONTS THE GODS. Cambridge: Harvard University Press, 1959.

> A thorough examination of the revival of interest in pagan gods and mythologies during the Enlightenment and of the reaction against it.

Maurice, Thomas. INDIAN ANTIQUITIES; OR, DISSERTATIONS, RELATIVE TO THE . . . GEOGRAPHICAL DIVISIONS, . . . THEOLOGY, . . . CIVIL LAWS, . . . GOVERNMENT, . . . COMMERCE, AND . . . LITERATURE, OF HINDOSTAN: COMPARED . . . WITH THE RELIGION, LAWS, GOVERN- MENT, AND LITERATURE, OF PERSIA, EGYPT, AND GREECE. 7 vols. London: John White, 1800.

Merivale, Patricia. PAN THE GOAT-GOD: HIS MYTH IN MODERN TIMES. Cambridge: Harvard University Press, 1969.

> Examines the treatment of Pan in literature from the Classical, Medieval, and Renaissance roots through Romantics and Victorians to D.H. Lawrence.

Roberts, J[ohn] M.. THE MYTHOLOGY OF THE SECRET SOCIETIES. New York: Charles Scribner's Sons, 1972.

> Masons, anti-Masons, illuminati, and their ilk before, during, and immediately after the French Revolution.

3. Science, Technology, and Education

Bell, S.P. A BIOGRAPHICAL INDEX OF BRITISH ENGINEERS IN THE 19TH CENTURY. New York: Garland, 1975.

> Brief, alphabetically arranged entries that give only the sources of published information, chiefly from obituaries in nineteenth-century engineering journals.

Bett, W[alter] R. THE INFIRMITIES OF GENIUS. London: Christopher John- son, 1952,

> A popular account by a medical historian of medical and psycho- medical problems (or supposed problems) of great writers, including PBS, JK, and LB.

Brauer, George C., Jr. THE EDUCATION OF A GENTLEMAN: THEORIES OF GENTLEMANLY EDUCATION IN ENGLAND, 1660-1775. New York: Book- man Associates, 1959.

> Contains chapters on the stated goals of education--virtue, public spirit, intellectual acquirements, worldly experience, and good

breeding--as well as on the place of travel and on the debate between advocates of public and private education (with bibliography).

Bullough, Geoffrey. MIRROR OF MINDS: CHANGING PSYCHOLOGICAL
BELIEFS IN ENGLISH POETRY. London: Athlone [University of London] Press,
1962.

Based on the Alexander Lectures at the University of Toronto,
1959-60.

Bush, Douglas. SCIENCE AND ENGLISH POETRY: A HISTORICAL SKETCH,
1590-1950. New York: Oxford University Press, 1950.

These 1949 Patten Lectures at Indiana University contain a chapter
(pp. 79-108) entitled "The Romantic Revolt against Rationalism."

Clarke, M[artin] L. CLASSICAL EDUCATION IN BRITAIN, 1500-1900. Cambridge: Cambridge University Press, 1959.

Chapters 4-8 of this generalized history cover the teaching of the
classics in the schools and the universities immediately before,
during, and after the Romantic period.

Darnton, Robert. MESMERISM AND THE END OF THE ENLIGHTENMENT IN
FRANCE. Cambridge: Harvard University Press, 1968.

Relates the vogue of Franz Anton Mesmer's popular experiments in
hypnotism (which intrigued PBS, among others) to radical movements
in France and on the Continent.

*Ferguson, Eugene S. BIBLIOGRAPHY OF THE HISTORY OF TECHNOLOGY.
Cambridge: Massachusetts Institute of Technology Press, 1968.

Aims to "provide a reasonably comprehensive introduction to primary and secondary sources in the history of technology."

Maniquis, Robert M. "The Puzzling MIMOSA: Sensitivity and Plant Symbols
in Romanticism." SiR, 8 (1969), 129-55.

An important essay suggesting some relationships between the development of the biological sciences and poetic metaphors and
symbols.

Mather, Kirtley F., and Shirley L. Mason, eds. A SOURCE BOOK IN GE-
OLOGY, 1400-1900. Cambridge: Harvard University Press, 1939.

Excerpts of geological and cosmological thought from leading figures, with notes sketching the trends in geological knowledge and
theory.

*Musson, A[lbert] E., and Eric Robinson. SCIENCE AND TECHNOLOGY IN THE INDUSTRIAL REVOLUTION. Toronto: University of Toronto Press, 1969.

> A substantial (500-page), well-indexed introduction to a burgeoning subject.

*Nicolson, Marjorie Hope. THE BREAKING OF THE CIRCLE: STUDIES IN THE EFFECT OF THE "NEW SCIENCE" UPON SEVENTEENTH CENTURY POETRY. Rev. ed. New York: Columbia University Press, 1960.

> Originally a series of lectures, this volume provides a good overview of the change from the Medieval-Renaissance concepts of man and nature to those of the Enlightenment.

_____. MOUNTAIN GLOOM AND MOUNTAIN GLORY: THE DEVELOPMENT OF THE AESTHETICS OF THE INFINITE. Ithaca, N.Y.: Cornell University Press, 1959.

> Expands the ideas in THE BREAKING OF THE CIRCLE (cited above), particularly those on the "aesthetics of the infinite."

_____. NEWTON DEMANDS THE MUSE: NEWTON'S OPTICS AND THE EIGHTEENTH-CENTURY POETS. Princeton: Princeton University Press, 1946.

> An influential study of the impact of science on Enlightenment poetry, with important ramifications for the Romantic poets.

Simon, Brian. STUDIES IN THE HISTORY OF EDUCATION, 1780-1870. London: Lawrence and Wishart, 1960.

> On the impact of reformers, radicals, and the growing power of the middle and working class on the educational system in Britain.

*Singer, C[harles] J[oseph]. A SHORT HISTORY OF SCIENCE TO THE NINETEENTH CENTURY. Oxford: Clarendon Press, 1941.

> Reissued, with new material, as A SHORT HISTORY OF SCIENTIFIC IDEAS TO 1900 (1959).

Snelders, H.A.M. "Romanticism and Naturphilosophie and the Inorganic Natural Sciences, 1797-1840: An Introductory Survey." SiR, 9 (Summer 1970), 193-215.

> Centered on Germany, but with implications for STC and other English thinkers. See also Shaffer (Sec. B.1, above).

Walsh, William. THE USE OF IMAGINATION: EDUCATIONAL THOUGHT AND THE LITERARY MIND. New York: Barnes and Noble, 1960.

> Among the ten chapters on educational perspectives are three directly discussing STC, one on WW, and one on JK.

Whitehead, Alfred North. SCIENCE AND THE MODERN WORLD. New York: Macmillan, 1925.

> A seminal study for the relationship of the ideas of the Romantic poets (among others) to twentieth-century philosophy of science.

4. Architecture and Landscaping

Clark, H.F. THE ENGLISH LANDSCAPE GARDEN. London: Pleiades Books, 1948.

> A brief introductory handbook.

@Clark, Kenneth. LANDSCAPE INTO ART. London: John Murray, 1949.

> Published in America as LANDSCAPE PAINTING (1950), this brief survey with 104 plates is based on Clark's lectures at Oxford.

#Colvin, H[oward] M. A BIOGRAPHICAL DICTIONARY OF ENGLISH ARCHITECTS, 1660-1840. London: John Murray, 1954.

> A standard biographical source.

_____, ed. THE COUNTRY SEAT: STUDIES IN THE HISTORY OF THE BRITISH COUNTRY HOUSE, PRESENTED TO SIR JOHN SUMMERSON. London: Penguin Books, 1970.

Hoskins, W[illiam] G[eorge]. THE MAKING OF THE ENGLISH LANDSCAPE. London: Hodder and Stoughton, 1955.

> Contains eighty-two illustrations and seventeen maps and plans, as well as bibliographies.

Pilcher, Donald. THE REGENCY STYLE, 1800-1830. London: B.T. Batsford, 1947.

> A popular, illustrated account of landscape gardening, architecture, taste, and style in the period indicated.

*Summerson, John [Newenham]. ARCHITECTURE IN BRITAIN 1530-1830. The Pelican History of Art. London: Penguin Books, 1953.

> A handy survey, several times revised.

_____. GEORGIAN LONDON. London: Pleiades Books, 1945.

> Contains both bibliographical footnotes and a select bibliography.

_____. JOHN NASH, ARCHITECT TO KING GEORGE IV. London: George Allen and Unwin, 1935.

> A standard account of the most influential architect of the Regency. This study can be supplemented by Terence Davis' THE ARCHITECTURE OF JOHN NASH (1960), which contains a critical essay on Nash by Summerson.

Turnor, Reginald. NINETEENTH-CENTURY ARCHITECTURE IN BRITAIN. London: B.T. Batsford, 1950.

> Depicts the transition from the classical styles to the Victorian Gothic as a morality play in which the classical is "forward-looking in spirit . . . , a genuine rebirth of humanism, the other looking backward, reactionary, a sort of re-death." The volume has good plates and provocative comments.

Watson, John Richard. PICTURESQUE LANDSCAPE AND ENGLISH ROMANTIC POETRY. London: Hutchinson, 1970.

> Explores the influence of the tradition of Claude Lorraine, Poussin, and Salvator Rosa on the Romantic poets, particularly WW.

5. Painting, Sculpture, and Graphic Arts

a. GENERAL STUDIES

*Boase, T[homas] S.R. ENGLISH ART, 1800-1870. Oxford History of English Art, ed. Boase, Vol. 10. Oxford: Clarendon Press, 1959.

#Bryan, Michael. BRYAN'S DICTIONARY OF PAINTERS AND ENGRAVERS. 4th ed. Rev. and Enl. G.C. Williamson. 5 vols. London: Bell; New York: Macmillan, 1903-05.

> Covers the field from the Italian Renaissance through the period of this guide.

*Burke, Joseph. ENGLISH ART, 1714-1800. Oxford History of English Art, eds. T[homas] S.R. Boase, Vol. 9. Oxford: Clarendon Press, 1975.

Gaunt, William. EVERYMAN'S DICTIONARY OF PICTORIAL ART. 2 vols. London: J.M. Dent, 1962.

> A useful guide by a prolific historian of British painting.

_____. THE RESTLESS CENTURY: PAINTING IN BRITAIN, 1800-1900. London: Phaidon, 1972.

> An illustrated general account.

#George, M. Dorothy. ENGLISH POLITICAL CARICATURE, 1793-1832: A STUDY OF OPINION AND PROPAGANDA. Oxford: Clarendon Press, 1959.

>A study of trends, with ninety-six (black and white) plates. A selection of plates, some in color, from a somewhat longer period can be found in the same author's HOGARTH TO CRUIKSHANK: SOCIAL CHANGE IN GRAPHIC SATIRE (1967).

#Graves, Algernon. A DICTIONARY OF ARTISTS WHO HAVE EXHIBITED WORKS IN THE PRINCIPAL LONDON EXHIBITIONS FROM 1760 TO 1893. 3rd ed., 1901; rpt. Bath: Kingsmead Reprints, 1969.

>A useful resource for locating very obscure painters of the period.

Hardie, Martin. WATER-COLOUR PAINTING IN BRITAIN. Ed. Dudley Snelgrove et al. 3 vols. London: B.T. Batsford, 1966-68.

>The standard history of the art in Britain. Volume 2 is entitled THE ROMANTIC PERIOD.

Larrabee, Stephen A. ENGLISH BARDS AND GRECIAN MARBLES: THE RELATIONSHIP BETWEEN SCULPTURE AND POETRY, ESPECIALLY IN THE ROMANTIC PERIOD. New York: Columbia University Press, 1943.

>An interesting and influential study.

Lipking, Lawrence. THE ORDERING OF THE ARTS IN EIGHTEENTH-CENTURY ENGLAND. Princeton: Princeton University Press, 1970.

>Treats the need for and the concept and achievements of major reference works on painting (by Horace Walpole and Sir Joshua Reynolds), music (by Sir John Hawkins and Charles Burney), and literature (by Thomas Warton and Samuel Johnson).

Lister, Raymond. THE BRITISH MINIATURE. London: I. Pitman and Sons, 1951.

>A survey of miniature portraiture, with sixty-eight plates and a bibliography, by a leading modern miniaturist.

Whitley, William T[homas]. ART IN ENGLAND, 1800-1837. 2 vols. Cambridge: Cambridge University Press, 1928-30.

>The most detailed account of the period, continuing Whitley's study of eighteenth-century artists.

_____. ARTISTS AND THEIR FRIENDS IN ENGLAND, 1700-1799. 2 vols. London: The Medici Society, 1928.

>Detailed, anecdotal account of British artists from "the foundation of Sir Godfrey Kneller's Academy, to the admission of Turner to

the Royal Academy," drawn from MSS, archives, newspapers, and printed books.

b. STUDIES OF INDIVIDUAL ARTISTS

Badt, Durt. JOHN CONSTABLE'S CLOUDS. Trans. Stanley Goldman. London: Routledge and Kegan Paul, 1950.

An important study by a leading German art historian.

Butlin, Martin. THE WATERCOLOURS OF J.M.W. TURNER. London: Barrie and Rockliff, 1962.

See also Rothenstein and Butlin, below.

George, Eric. THE LIFE AND DEATH OF BENJAMIN ROBERT HAYDON HISTORICAL PAINTER, 1786-1846. Oxford: Clarendon Press, 1948; 2nd ed., rev. Dorothy George, 1967.

Gowing, Lawrence. TURNER: IMAGINATION AND REALITY. New York: Museum of Modern Art and Doubleday, 1966.

The catalog of an important exhibition emphasizing Turner's techniques and vision as forerunners of those of later painters.

Haydon, Benjamin Robert. THE DIARY OF BENJAMIN ROBERT HAYDON. Ed. Willard B. Pope. 5 vols. Cambridge: Harvard University Press, 1960.

A scholarly edition useful for insights on the period as well as information on Haydon.

Lister, Raymond. SAMUEL PALMER: A BIOGRAPHY. London: Faber and Faber, 1974.

A pioneering but (according to some early reviewers) unsympathetic and inadequate study of Palmer's life. See also Palmer's LETTERS, below.

Palmer, Samuel. THE LETTERS OF SAMUEL PALMER. Ed. Raymond Lister. 2 vols. Oxford: Clarendon Press, 1974.

This and the biography by Lister, above, provide new resources to study one of the most interesting painters of the period.

Paulson, Ronald. ROWLANDSON: A NEW INTERPRETATION. New York: Oxford University Press, 1972.

Like Paulson's earlier studies of Hogarth and the interrelations of earlier eighteenth-century art and literature, this study of the art of Thomas Rowlandson (1757-1827) probes deeply into the assumptions underlying the techniques and effects Rowlandson produced.

Rothenstein, John, and Martin Butlin. TURNER. New York: George Braziller, 1964.

Dealing with the oil paintings, this volume complements Butlin's study of the watercolors, above.

6. Theater, Music, and Performing Arts

*Arnott, James Fullarton, and John William Robinson. ENGLISH THEATRICAL LITERATURE, 1559-1900: A BIBLIOGRAPHY, INCORPORATING ROBERT W. LOWE'S A BIBLIOGRAPHICAL ACCOUNT OF ENGLISH THEATRICAL LITERATURE (1888). London: Society for Theatre Research, 1970.

The standard bibliography of research materials on the English stage.

*Conolly, L.W., and J.P. Wearing, eds. ENGLISH DRAMA AND THEATRE, 1800-1900. Detroit: Gale Research, 1978.

This Gale Information Guide contains annotated bibliographical and reference entries for the period, as well as dealing with a number of individual authors of the period. A basic reference tool for this period and genre.

Dibdin, Charles. HISTORY AND ILLUSTRATIONS OF THE LONDON THEATRES: COMPRISING AN ACCOUNT OF THE ORIGIN AND PROGRESS OF THE DRAMA IN ENGLAND; WITH HISTORICAL AND DESCRIPTIVE ACCOUNTS OF THE THEATRES ROYAL, COVENT GARDEN, DRURY LANE, HAYMARKET, ENGLISH OPERA HOUSE, AND ROYAL AMPHITHEATRE. London: Privately printed, 1826.

This valuable antiquarian study was published in a large paper quarto format, with seventeen plates, in an edition of only twenty-five copies.

Donohue, Joseph W., Jr. DRAMATIC CHARACTER IN THE ENGLISH RO-MANTIC AGE. Princeton: Princeton University Press, 1970.

Traces the development of dramatic characterizations and acting styles from the Jacobean dramatists through the plays of Goldsmith, Sheridan, and PBS's THE CENCI, with exploration of the studies on Shakespearean character by Lamb, Hazlitt, and others.

Doran, John. "THEIR MAJESTIES SERVANTS": ANNALS OF THE ENGLISH STAGE FROM THOMAS BETTERTON TO EDMUND KEAN. Ed. and rev. Robert W. Lowe. 3 vols. London: J.C. Nimmo, 1888.

Fletcher, Richard M. ENGLISH ROMANTIC DRAMA, 1795-1843. New York: Exposition Press, 1966.

> An imperfect but useful supplements to Nicoll's earlier treatment of the same general topic.

#Genest, John. SOME ACCOUNT OF THE ENGLISH STAGE FROM THE RESTORATION IN 1660 to 1820. 10 vols. Bath, Engl.: H.E. Carrington, 1832.

Gigliucci, Valeria, ed. CLARA NOVELLO'S REMINISCENCES. Memoir by Arthur D. Coleridge. London: Edward Arnold, 1910.

> The reminiscences of the celebrated soprano (1818-1908) whose father was the friend of Hunt, JK, and Mary Shelley and founder of the great firm of London music publishers. There is also a biography, CLARA NOVELLO, by Averil Mackenzie-Grieve (1955).

*Grove, George. DICTIONARY OF MUSIC AND MUSICIANS. 5th ed. Ed. Eric Blom. 9 vols. London: Macmillan, 1955.

> The standard reference work in its field. A new edition is in preparation.

*Hartnoll. Phyllis. THE OXFORD COMPANION TO THE THEATRE. 3rd ed. London: Oxford University Press, 1967.

> A standard reference source, in dictionary form.

Kelly, Michael. THE REMINISCENCES OF MICHAEL KELLY. London: Henry Colburn, 1826.

> The memoirs of a famous Irish-born tenor (1762-1826) who trained in Italy, created roles for Mozart in Vienna, and was a mainstay as composer and performer in London and Dublin from 1787 through about 1814, both in Italian opera and musical entertainments.

Mayer, David III. HARLEQUIN IN HIS ELEMENT: THE ENGLISH PANTO-MIME, 1806-1836. Cambridge: Harvard University Press, 1969.

> The standard survey of a subject of considerable importance to poetry of the period--particularly that of LB and JK.

Nalbach, Daniel. THE KING'S THEATRE, 1704-1867: LONDON'S FIRST ITALIAN OPERA HOUSE. London: Society for Theatre Research, 1972.

> The final four chapters are directly relevant to the period of the rebuilt theater, 1791-1867.

*Nicoll, Allardyce. A HISTORY OF ENGLISH DRAMA, 1660-1900. Vol. 4: A HISTORY OF EARLY NINETEENTH DRAMA, 1800-1850. 2nd ed. Cambridge: University Press, 1955.

The general historical account in the first part of Volume 4 is sound but rather lifeless. The second part of the volume records the titles, dates of performances, and publication information on hundreds of plays, operas, pantomimes, and other performances during the period, arranged by author and with a large section of anonymous works alphabetized by title.

Piggott, Patrick. THE LIFE AND MUSIC OF JOHN FIELD, 1782-1837, CREATOR OF THE NOCTURNE. Berkeley: University of California Press, 1973.

A good biography of a significant English musician who spent a large part of his career in Russia.

Richards, Kenneth, and Peter Thomson, eds. ESSAYS ON NINETEENTH CENTURY BRITISH THEATRE: THE PROCEEDINGS OF A SYMPOSIUM SPONSORED BY THE MANCHESTER UNIVERSITY DEPARTMENT OF DRAMA. London: Methuen, 1971.

A valuable miscellany, containing an essay entitled "Lord Byron's Historical Tragedies" by William Ruddick (pp. 83-94).

Scholes, Percy A. THE GREAT DR. BURNEY: HIS LIFE, HIS TRAVELS, HIS WORKS, HIS FAMILY AND HIS FRIENDS. 2 vols. London: Oxford University Press, 1948.

The life of Dr. Charles Burney, the musician and musicologist (1726-1814), that also has chapters on the state of music at the end of the eighteenth century.

Sherson, Erroll. LONDON'S LOST THEATRES OF THE NINETEENTH CENTURY, WITH NOTES ON PLAYS AND PLAYERS SEEN THERE. London: John Lane, 1925.

Though many of the theaters discussed are of later vintage, this lively, anecdotal account (with indexes to places, plays, and people) is a good introduction to the nonlicensed theaters like Astley's, which played a version of LB's MAZEPPA with a real horse, and the Olympic, where Milman's FAZIO was produced in 1818.

*Westrup, Jack A., and Frank L. Harrison. THE NEW COLLEGE ENCYCLOPEDIA OF MUSIC. Rev. Conrad Wilson. New York: W.W. Norton, 1976.

Claims to be the "most comprehensive and up-to-date one-volume reference work on music in the English language."

7. Language, Linguistics, and Prosody

Aarsleff, Hans. THE STUDY OF LANGUAGE IN ENGLAND, 1780-1860. Princeton, N.J.: Princeton University Press, 1967.

Horne Tooke, Sir William Jones, and the development of the "new philology."

#Bailey, N[athan]. A NEW UNIVERSAL ETYMOLOGICAL ENGLISH DICTIO-NARY. Rev. and corrected by Joseph Nicol Scott. New ed. London, 1772.

Bailey's dictionary, originally published in 1721 and revised by Scott in 1755, was the great forerunner and rival of Dr. Johnson's DICTIONARY. Both were reprinted repeatedly and both cast light on the diction and meaning of poets of the period.

Berry, Francis. POETRY AND THE PHYSICAL VOICE. London: Oxford University Press, 1962.

Includes a chapter entitled "The Voice of Shelley," as well as a discussion of how the voices of individual poets affect the tone of the poetry they write.

Chafe, Wallace L. MEANING AND THE STRUCTURE OF LANGUAGE. Chicago: University of Chicago Press, 1970.

An important study relating meaning to the new linguistic analyses.

Groom, Bernard. THE DICTION OF POETRY FROM SPENSER TO BRIDGES. Toronto: University of Toronto Press, 1955.

An interesting though somewhat impressionistic study.

Hamer, Enid. THE METRES OF ENGLISH POETRY. London: Methuen, 1930.

A valuable handbook of traditional analysis, often reprinted.

#Johnson, Samuel. A DICTIONARY OF THE ENGLISH LANGUAGE . . . IL-LUSTRATED IN THEIR DIFFERENT SIGNIFICATIONS BY EXAMPLES FROM THE BEST WRITERS. TO WHICH ARE PREFIXED, A HISTORY OF THE LANGUAGE, AND AN ENGLISH GRAMMAR. 2 vols. London: Printed by W. Strahan, for J. and P. Knapton; T. and T. Longman; C. Hitch and L. Hawes; A. Millar; and R. and J. Dodsley, 1755.

This classic work was often reprinted (with revisions).

Lanham, Richard A. A HANDLIST OF RHETORICAL TERMS: A GUIDE FOR STUDENTS OF ENGLISH LITERATURE. Berkeley: University of California Press, 1968.

A brief reference work, in dictionary form, that defines the terminology of the classical (and neoclassical) rhetoricians.

Malof, Joseph. A MANUAL OF ENGLISH METERS. Bloomington: Indiana University Press, 1970.

A solid descriptive analysis of English-language metrics.

Mathews, Mitford McLeod. A SURVEY OF ENGLISH DICTIONARIES. London: Oxford University Press, 1933.

A brief but authoritative overview from the beginnings through the OXFORD ENGLISH DICTIONARY. See also Starnes and Noyes, below.

Mayor, Joseph B. CHAPTERS ON ENGLISH METRE. 2nd, enl. ed. Cambridge: Cambridge University Press, 1901.

In addition to general analysis, the volume contains a chapter entitled "Shelley's Metre."

Miles, Josephine. THE PRIMARY LANGUAGE OF POETRY IN THE 1740's AND 1840's. Berkeley: University of California Press, 1950.

Comparisons, using statistical evidence derived from concordances and the like.

#Murray, Lindley. ENGLISH GRAMMAR: COMPREHENDING THE PRINCIPLES AND RULES OF THE LANGUAGE. 2 vols. 2nd ed., improved. York, Engl.: Printed by Thomas Wilson and Son . . . for Longman, Hurst, Rees, and Orme; and Darton and Harvey, London: for Wilson and Son, and R. and W. Spence, York: and for Constable and Co., Edinburgh, 1809.

This, the most popular and influential grammar of the period, casts enormous light on the correctness and purpose of a number of grammatical "errors" by poets of the period.

*THE OXFORD ENGLISH DICTIONARY. 10 vols. Oxford: Clarendon Press, 1884-1921.

Originally entitled A NEW ENGLISH DICTIONARY UPON ETYMOLOGICAL PRINCIPLES. The best single source of information about various meanings, spellings, and associations of words-- especially as used in the nineteenth century. Reissued, corrected, in 12 volumes, with a supplement in 1933.

This valuable tool, once too expensive for home use, is now available in two (bulky) volumes, reasonably priced, as THE COMPACT EDITION OF THE OXFORD ENGLISH DICTIONARY: COMPLETE TEXT, REPRODUCED MICROGRAPHICALLY (1971).

*Partridge, Eric. A DICTIONARY OF SLANG AND UNCONVENTIONAL ENGLISH. 7th ed. 2 vols. in 1. New York: Macmillan, 1970.

The most important single supplement to the OED, so far· as British English slang and vulgarisms are concerned.

Saintsbury, George. A HISTORY OF ENGLISH PROSODY: FROM THE TWELFTH CENTURY TO THE PRESENT DAY. 3 vols. London, 1908, 2nd. ed., 1923; reprinted New York: Russell and Russell, 1961.

The third volume covers the poets from Blake to Swinburne.

Starnes, De Witt T., and Gertrude E. Noyes. THE ENGLISH DICTIONARY FROM CAWDREY TO JOHNSON: 1604-1755. Chapel Hill: University of North Carolina Press, 1946.

More detailed than Mathews for the century and a half it covers.

#Walker, John. A CRITICAL PRONOUNCING DICTIONARY AND EXPOSITOR OF THE ENGLISH LANGUAGE. London: Printed [for several booksellers in London and Glasgow], 1824.

First published in 1791, this often-reprinted authority gives short definitions and some etymologies, as well as then-current pronunciations; the author also wrote a standard book on elocution and a dictionary of rhymes.

Warrack, Alexander. SCOTS DICTIONARY, SERVING AS A GLOSSARY FOR RAMSAY, FERGUSSON, BURNS, SCOTT, GALT, MINOR POETS. New ed. Edinburgh: University of Edinburgh Press, 1965.

Wright, Joseph. THE ENGLISH DIALECT DICTIONARY. 6 vols. London: Henry Frowde, 1898-1905.

This basic source of British dialect words and usages can be supplemented by specialized works on various regional dialects.

Young, George. AN ENGLISH PROSODY ON INDUCTIVE LINES. Cambridge: Cambridge University Press, 1928.

A sensible analysis, deriving theoretical generalizations from past practice.

C. LITERARY BACKGROUND

1. Reference Works

a. BIBLIOGRAPHIES OF ENGLISH LITERATURE

Besides the books listed below, the student and teacher should be aware of three relevant bibliographies: (1) the annual bibliography published with or as a supplement to PMLA (1922 to date); (2) THE YEAR'S WORK IN ENGLISH STUDIES published by the English Association of London (1919 to date); (3) ANNUAL BIBLIOGRAPHY OF ENGLISH LITERATURE, published by the Modern Humanities Research Association (1920 to date).

*Block, Andrew. THE ENGLISH NOVEL, 1740-1850: A CATALOGUE INCLUDING PROSE ROMANCES, SHORT STORIES, AND TRANSLATIONS OF FOREIGN FICTION. London: Grafton, 1939; 2nd ed., 1961.

The standard enumerative bibliography, listed by authors and titles.

#Hamer, Philip M., ed. A GUIDE TO ARCHIVES AND MANUSCRIPTS IN THE UNITED STATES. New Haven: Yale University Press, 1961.

> Though prepared with a bias toward historical manuscripts and archives, this compilation of the manuscripts and archival holdings of libraries all over the country can guide the patient reader to most of the major literary manuscript collections as well. There is a subject index.

*Howard-Hill, T[revor] H. BIBLIOGRAPHY OF BRITISH LITERARY BIBLIOG-RAPHIES. Oxford: Clarendon Press, 1969.

> Arranged by periods, regions, presses, and forms and by genres, subject, and authors, with a detailed index. An extremely valuable resource.

#McNamee, Lawrence F. DISSERTATIONS IN ENGLISH AND AMERICAN LITERATURE: THESES ACCEPTED BY AMERICAN, BRITISH AND GERMAN UNIVERSITIES, 1865-1964. New York: R.R. Bowker, 1968.

> SUPPLEMENT ONE: 1964-1968 was published in 1969; SUPPLE-MENT TWO: 1969-1973 appeared in 1974. The dissertations are arranged by period and subject and indexed by author.

Metzdorf, Robert F. THE TINKER LIBRARY: A BIBLIOGRAPHICAL CATA-LOGUE OF THE BOOKS AND MANUSCRIPTS COLLECTED BY CHAUNCEY BREWSTER TINKER. New Haven: Yale University Library, 1959.

> An important bibliography of British literary first editions, MSS, and related books, especailly of the eighteenth and nineteenth centuries.

NATIONAL UNION CATALOG OF MANUSCRIPT COLLECTIONS, COMPILED BY THE LIBRARY OF CONGRESS FROM REPORTS PROVIDED BY AMERICAN REPOSITORIES. Washington, D.C.: Library of Congress, 1962-- .

> Every three years or so this miscellaneous listing of the manuscript holdings of participating American libraries includes a cumulative index. Much more useful for literary students will be the INDEX OF ENGLISH LITERARY MANUSCRIPT SOURCES now being prepared by a team of British and American scholars centered at the University of Leeds.

#Peddie, Robert Alexander, and Zuinton Waddington, eds. THE ENGLISH CATA-LOGUE OF BOOKS, . . . GIVING IN ONE ALPHABET, UNDER AUTHOR, TITLE AND SUBJECT, THE SIZE, PRICE, MONTH AND YEAR OF PUBLICA-TION, AND PUBLISHER OF BOOKS ISSUED IN THE UNITED KINGDOM OF GREAT BRITAIN AND IRELAND, 1801-1966.

> For the Romantic period, the years 1801-36 have been usefully reprinted (New York: Kraus Reprint, 1963). As the subtitle indicates, an invaluable source of information about publications (especially in London and Edinburgh) during the period.

*Watson, George, ed. THE NEW CAMBRIDGE BIBLIOGRAPHY OF ENGLISH LITERATURE. 5 vols. Cambridge: Cambridge University Press, 1960-77.

> Volume 3 (1969) covers the period 1800-1900, with Volume 2: 1660-1800 (1971) a useful adjunct. The NCBEL theoretically supersedes the CAMBRIDGE BIBLIOGRAPHY OF ENGLISH LITERA- TURE (CBEL) edited by F.W. Bateson (4 vols., 1941), but Bateson's volumes contain fuller information on some topics and are more intelligently arranged. Volume 5 is the general index.

#Wise, Thomas James. THE ASHLEY LIBRARY: A CATALOGUE OF PRINTED BOOKS, MANUSCRIPTS, AND AUTOGRAPH LETTERS. 11 vols. London: For private circulation, 1922-36.

> One of the basic bibliographies of nineteenth-century literary first editions, this catalogue also contains some forgeries of "rare pub- lications" by Victorian authors. The sections on the Romantics are valuable but not exact in their analysis of the sequence of states and issues of (for example) LB's poems.

b. LITERARY HISTORIES

*Baker, Ernest. THE HISTORY OF THE ENGLISH NOVEL. 10 vols. London: Witherby, 1924-36; rpt. New York: Barnes and Noble, 1967.

> The 1967 reprint updates this standard history by adding as a sup- plement for the twentieth century an eleventh volume written by Lionel Stevenson.

@Baugh, Albert C., ed. A LITERARY HISTORY OF ENGLAND. New York: Appleton-Century-Crofts, 1948; 2nd ed., 1967.

> The standard one-volume resumé of facts on the major British writers with a bibliographical supplement and an excellent index.

Booth, Michael R.; Richard Southern; et al. THE REVELS HISTORY OF DRAMA IN ENGLISH. Vol. 6: 1750-1880. London: Methuen, 1975.

> A good, illustrated general history, with bibliography.

@Craig, Hardin, ed. A HISTORY OF ENGLISH LITERATURE. New York: Oxford University Press, 1950.

> Though this volume lost out in the sales competition with Baugh's rival volume (above), Joseph Warren Beach's section, ENGLISH LITERATURE OF THE NINETEENTH AND EARLY TWENTIETH CEN- TURY (reprinted under that title in paperback in 1962), is generally better than Samuel Chew's comparable section in Baugh's HISTORY.

Daiches, David. A CRITICAL HISTORY OF ENGLISH LITERATURE. New York: Ronald Press, 1960.

> A sensitive general survey.

Dobree, Bonamy, and Norman Davis, eds. THE OXFORD HISTORY OF ENG-
LISH LITERATURE. 12 vols. projected. Oxford: Clarendon Press, 1945--.

> The volumes of this joint American and British enterprise that have
> appeared thus far are of mixed quality: the Renaissance volumes
> of C.S. Lewis and Douglas Bush have received general acclaim,
> whereas Volume 9 on the elder Romantics by W[illiam] L. Renwick
> (ENGLISH LITERATURE, 1789-1815) is an unmitigated failure. Ian
> Jack's Volume 10 (ENGLISH LITERATURE, 1815-1832) has received
> a mixed reception, but is generally useful.

*Elton, Oliver. A SURVEY OF ENGLISH LITERATURE, 1780-1880. 4 vols.
London: Edward Arnold, 1912-20.

> Frequently reprinted, these volumes retain their value, in spite of
> the accumulation of new scholarship, because of Elton's fine taste,
> incisive prose style, and thorough study of a wide range of writers.

@Grierson, Herbert J.C., and J.C. Smith. A CRITICAL HISTORY OF ENG-
LISH POETRY. London: Chatto and Windus, 1944; 2nd ed., 1947.

> The best account, in a single volume, of English poetry from An-
> glo-Saxon times to 1939, this survey replaces W.J. Courthope's
> ponderous six-volume HISTORY OF ENGLISH POETRY (1895-1910).

Legouis, Emile, and Louis Cazamian. A HISTORY OF ENGLISH LITERATURE.
Trans. from the French by Helen Douglas Irvine, W.D. MacInnes, and Louis
Cazamian. London: J.M. Dent, 1926-27; revised eds., 1930; 1933.

> First published in Paris, 1924, this fine history held its own with
> contemporary rivals originating in Britain and the United States.
> Though it is now out of date, it is still more perceptive than por-
> tions of the Cambridge and the Oxford histories.

Ward, A.W., and A.R. Waller, eds. THE CAMBRIDGE HISTORY OF ENG-
LISH LITERATURE. 14 vols. Cambridge: Cambridge University Press, 1907-
16. Vol. 15: INDEX, 1927.

> Once a standard reference work, this history has long been out of
> date. Its tone may be best sampled in George Sampson's one-
> volume updated epitome, THE CONCISE CAMBRIDGE HISTORY
> OF ENGLISH LITERATURE (1941).

*Wilkins, Ernest Hatch. A HISTORY OF ITALIAN LITERATURE. Cambridge:
Harvard University Press, 1954.

> The standard English-language survey of the subject.

c. GENERAL LITERARY REFERENCE WORKS

@Altick, Richard D. THE ART OF LITERARY RESEARCH. New York: W.W. Norton, 1963; rev. ed., 1975.

> A personal, but highly interesting and helpful view of the scholarly profession, in the form of a textbook for graduate students in English. This should be read by all serious students of nineteenth-century English literature. Also recommended: Altick's THE SCHOLAR ADVENTURERS (1950).

@Benet, William Rose, ed. THE READER'S ENCYCLOPEDIA: AN ENCYCLO-PEDIA OF WORLD LITERATURE AND THE ARTS. New York: Thomas Y. Crowell, 1948.

> Indebted to Brewer's READER'S HANDBOOK, below, this useful compilation for American readers will soon be replaced (or supplemented) by a READER'S ENCYCLOPEDIA OF ENGLISH LITERATURE, edited by Edgar Johnson, now in progress.

*Bernhardt, William F., ed. GRANGER'S INDEX TO POETRY. 5th ed. New York: Columbia University Press, 1962.

> First published in 1904, this massive work has become the standard tool for locating (by title or first line, with an author index) poems over the whole range of widely reprinted or anthologized poetry. Since later editions tend to emphasize more recent poetry, the early editions are better for locating minor nineteenth-century poems. The 6th edition by William James Smith is the latest (New York: Columbia University Press, 1973).

#A BIOGRAPHICAL DICTIONARY OF LIVING AUTHORS OF GREAT BRITAIN AND IRELAND. London: Henry Colburn, 1816; rpt. 1966.

> A very useful contemporary source of information for minor writers active in or shortly before 1816.

*Brewer, E[benzer] Cobham. THE READER'S HANDBOOK OF FAMOUS NAMES IN FICTION, ALLUSIONS, REFERENCES, PROVERBS, PLOTS, STORIES, AND POEMS. 2 vols. London: various publishers, various dates; 1899 ed.; rpt. 1966.

> First published in the late nineteenth century, this valuable small reference book has been often revised and reissued. Brewer also compiled A DICTIONARY OF PHRASE AND FABLE (rev. ed. 1970).

*Halkett, Samuel, and John Laing. DICTIONARY OF ANONYMOUS AND PSEUDONYMOUS ENGLISH LITERATURE. Enl. ed. by James Kennedy, W.A. Smith, and A.F. Johnson. 7 vols. Edinburgh: Oliver and Boyd, 1926-34. Supplements, 1956, 1962.

This remains the best source for finding out who really wrote a work published anonymously or with an obvious pseudonym. Contains an index.

@Harvey, Paul, ed. THE OXFORD COMPANION TO ENGLISH LITERATURE. 4th ed. Rev. Dorothy Eagle. Oxford: Clarendon Press, 1967.

Originally published in 1932, this is still a useful one-volume reference work containing brief identifications of authors, works, characters, pseudonyms, and places and terms that figure importantly in English literature.

Kunitz, Stanley J., and Howard Haycraft, eds. BRITISH AUTHORS OF THE NINETEENTH CENTURY. New York: H.W. Wilson, 1936.

Remains one basic source of information on secondary authors.

*OXFORD DICTIONARY OF QUOTATIONS. London: Oxford University Press, 1941; 2nd ed., 1953.

In my opinion, this is by far the most useful quotation reference work for students of English literature--greatly superior to recent editions of BARTLETT'S FAMILIAR QUOTATIONS. See also the OXFORD DICTIONARY OF ENGLISH PROVERBS (3rd ed., 1970).

*Peck, Harry Thurston. HARPER'S DICTIONARY OF CLASSICAL LITERATURE AND ANTIQUITIES. 2 vols. New York: American Book Company, n.d.

The preface to the first edition is dated 1896, the prefatory note to the second edition, 1897. This is the standard American reference work comparable to Smith's CLASSICAL DICTIONARY, below.

*Preminger, Alex, ed. ENCYCLOPEDIA OF POETRY AND POETICS. Princeton: Princeton University Press, 1965.

A comprehensive one-volume reference work with 1,000 articles from brief definitions to historical articles of 20,000 words on subjects ranging from Epic and Epigram through German Poetry, Neoclassical Poetics, Spasmodic School, and Spondaic Verse, to Wit and Zeugma.

#Sandys, John Edwin. A HISTORY OF CLASSICAL SCHOLARSHIP. 3 vols. Cambridge: Cambridge University Press, 1904.

The third volume covers the state of scholarship in the eighteenth and nineteenth centuries, but the second volume also describes and evaluates editions that were used by the Romantics.

Smith, William. A CLASSICAL DICTIONARY OF GREEK AND ROMAN BIOGRAPHY, MYTHOLOGY AND GEOGRAPHY. London: John Murray, 1848; 4th ed., rev. by G.E. Marindin, 1894.

> One of the standard sources of information for the nonclassicist. It is important to note that the older the edition, the closer one approaches to what the Romantics knew.

2. Special Studies of Literary Background

Albrecht, William P. THE SUBLIME PLEASURES OF TRAGEDY: A STUDY OF CRITICAL THEORY FROM DENNIS TO KEATS. Lawrence: University Press of Kansas, 1975.

> An analysis of tragic theory from the Restoration through the Romantics.

Amarasinghe, Upali. DRYDEN AND POPE IN THE EARLY NINETEENTH CENTURY: A STUDY OF CHANGING LITERARY TASTE, 1800-1830. Cambridge: Cambridge University Press, 1962.

> A perceptive study of the topic described.

*Bate, Walter Jackson. THE BURDEN OF THE PAST AND THE ENGLISH POET. Cambridge: Harvard University Press, 1970.

> A seminal study of the idea, dominant in certain nineteenth-century poets like JK, that there was little new left to be done in art.

* _____. FROM CLASSIC TO ROMANTIC: PREMISES OF TASTE IN EIGHTEENTH-CENTURY ENGLAND. Cambridge: Harvard University Press, 1946.

> This influential study concludes with a chapter entitled "The English Romantic Compromise."

#Bloom, Harold. THE ANXIETY OF INFLUENCE: A THEORY OF POETRY. New York: Oxford University Press, 1973.

> This and the volume cited next constitute a very personal theory of literature and criticism posing as historical analysis. Taking over Bate's theory in THE BURDEN OF THE PAST AND THE ENGLISH POET (cited above), Bloom adds Freudian elements and sees the history of all poetry (and criticism) as efforts of "strong" poets (and critics) to create a sense of their own originality by rejecting or distorting the ideas of major predecessors. Though there are elements of truth here, Bloom's theory seems to have as its primary object the elevation of the critic to a status equal that of the poet upon whom he writes; it therefore elucidates his own anxieties as

a critic better than it does the writings of major poets. (See also under Bloom in Sec. C.3 and in Chap. 2, below.)

#_____. A MAP OF MISREADING. New York: Oxford University Press, 1975.

See previous item, and see under Bloom in Section C.3., below.

#Brand, C[harles] P. ITALY AND THE ENGLISH ROMANTICS: THE ITAL-·IANATE FASHION IN EARLY NINETEENTH-CENTURY ENGLAND. Cambridge: Cambridge University Press, 1957.

A survey, with useful bibliography, of the renewal of English interest in Italy during the late eighteenth and early nineteenth centuries.

_____. TORQUATO TASSO: A STUDY OF THE POET AND HIS CONTRIBU-TION TO ENGLISH LITERATURE. Cambridge: Cambridge University Press, 1965.

The fullest study of the impact of Tasso on English poetry--particularly the Romantics.

Brisman, Leslie. MILTON'S POETRY OF CHOICE AND ITS ROMANTIC HEIRS. Ithaca, N.Y.: Cornell University Press, 1973.

Provides a more positive alternative view of Milton's influence upon the Romantics than that propounded by Bate in THE BURDEN OF THE PAST AND THE ENGLISH POET and by Bloom in THE ANXIETY OF INFLUENCE (both above).

Chandler, Alice. A DREAM OF ORDER: THE MEDIEVAL IDEAL IN NINE-TEENTH-CENTURY ENGLISH LITERATURE. Lincoln: University of Nebraska Press, 1970.

Discusses the theme in relation to Scott, Cobbett, WW, STC, Southey, Peacock, and some Victorians.

Edwards, Thomas R. IMAGINATION AND POWER: A STUDY OF POETRY ON PUBLIC THEMES. New York: Oxford University Press, 1971.

The chapter on the Romantics focuses on PBS's "The Mask of Anarchy."

Foerster, Donald M. THE FORTUNES OF EPIC POETRY: A STUDY IN ENG-LISH AND AMERICAN CRITICISM 1750-1950. Washington, D.C.: Catholic University of America Press, 1962.

An overview of an important subject. See also H.T. Swedenberg, THE THEORY OF THE EPIC IN ENGLAND 1650-1800 (Berkeley: University of California Press, 1944).

Friederich, Werner Paul. DANTE'S FAME ABROAD: 1350-1850. Rome: Edizione di Storia e Letteratura, 1950.

> A sketchy (bibliographical) overview of this vast subject.

Goldstein, Lawrence. RUINS AND EMPIRE: THE EVOLUTION OF A THEME IN AUGUSTAN AND ROMANTIC LITERATURE. Pittsburgh: University of Pittsburgh Press, 1977.

> After tracing emblems of loss and change through English literature from Spenser to Goldsmith, Goldstein devotes nearly half his book to examining WW's reaction to and use of the convention.

#Hargreaves-Mawdsley, W.N. THE ENGLISH DELLA CRUSCANS AND THEIR TIME, 1783-1828. The Hague: Martinus Nijhoff, 1967.

> A full historical study of Robert Merry and his circle, with extensive bibliography.

Kuhns, Oscar. DANTE AND THE ENGLISH POETS FROM CHAUCER TO TENNYSON. New York: Henry Holt, 1904.

> A useful but somewhat outdated survey.

Laws, G. Malcolm, Jr. THE BRITISH LITERARY BALLAD: A STUDY IN POETIC IMITATION. Carbondale: Southern Illinois University Press, 1972.

> Traces the development of the form from Percy's RELIQUES (1765) through Barham's INGOLDSBY LEGENDS in the Victorian period, with attention to WW, Scott, Beddoes, and others.

Lindenberger, Herbert. HISTORICAL DRAMA: THE RELATION OF LITERATURE AND REALITY. Chicago: University of Chicago Press, 1975.

> Studies the problems that English, French, and German dramatists and their audiences have encountered in the dramatic presentation of historical reality.

Marshall, Roderick. ITALY IN ENGLISH LITERATURE, 1755-1815: ORIGINS OF THE ROMANTIC INTEREST IN ITALY. New York: Columbia University Press, 1934.

> A substantial Columbia dissertation.

Reynolds, Myra. THE TREATMENT OF NATURE IN ENGLISH POETRY BETWEEN POPE AND WORDSWORTH. Chicago: University of Chicago Press, 1896; rev. 2nd ed., 1909.

Shuster, George N. THE ENGLISH ODE FROM MILTON TO KEATS. New York: Columbia University Press, 1940.

> A standard historical survey.

Smith, Eric. BY MOURNING TONGUES: STUDIES IN ENGLISH ELEGY. Ipswich, Engl.: The Bogdell Press, 1977.

> Chapters center on the major elegies of Milton, Gray, PBS, Arnold, and Tennyson.

Stone, P.W.K. THE ART OF POETRY, 1750–1820: THEORIES OF POETIC COMPOSITION AND STYLE IN THE LATE NEO-CLASSIC AND EARLY ROMANTIC PERIODS. London: Routledge and Kegan Paul, 1967.

*Tave, Stuart M. THE AMIABLE HUMORIST: A STUDY IN THE COMIC THEORY AND CRITICISM OF THE EIGHTEENTH AND EARLY NINETEENTH CENTURIES. Chicago: University of Chicago Press, 1960.

> Starting with the theories of "good nature" and "good humor," Tave traces the ideals of amiable "characters" (e.g., Parson Adams, Uncle Toby) into the Romantics' theories of comedy.

Thayer, Mary Rebecca. THE INFLUENCE OF HORACE ON THE CHIEF ENGLISH POETS OF THE NINETEENTH CENTURY. Cornell Studies in English. New Haven: Yale University Press, 1916.

> The standard study of the topic.

Toliver, Harold E. PASTORAL FORMS AND ATTITUDES. Berkeley: University of California Press, 1971.

> A substantial historical examination of pastoral literature from Sidney and Spenser through Saul Bellow and Frost; chapters 9–11 treat the Romantics, especially WW and JK.

*Toynbee, Paget. DANTE IN ENGLISH LITERATURE: FROM CHAUCER TO CARY. 2 vols. London: Methuen, 1909.

> The most authoritative study of Dante's impact in England through H.C. Cary, the first popular translator. See also Kuhns, above.

Unwin, Rayner. THE RURAL MUSE: STUDIES IN THE PEASANT POETRY OF ENGLAND. London: George Allen and Unwin, 1954.

> Especially useful as background for distinguishing WW's "simplicity" from the tradition of "unlearned" or "peasant" poets from Stephen Duck through Burns, Bloomfield, and Clare.

Voisine, Jacques. J.-J. ROUSSEAU EN ANGLETERRE À L'ÉPOQUE ROMANTIQUE: LES ÉCRITS AUTOBIOGRAPHIQUES ET LA LÉGENDE. Paris: Didier, 1956.

> The most substantial study of a very important topic.

Wasserman, Earl R. ELIZABETHAN POETRY IN THE EIGHTEENTH CENTURY. Urbana: University of Illinois Press, 1947.

> A study of the traditions of Spenserian stanzas and other Elizabethan poetic forms among the lesser as well as the greater poets of the eighteenth century.

_____. "Shakespeare and the English Romantic Movement." In THE PERSISTENCE OF SHAKESPEARE IDOLATRY. Ed. Herbert M. Schueller. Detroit: Wayne State University Press, 1964.

> A brief but perceptive essay in a larger study of the whole tradition of Shakespearean influence (all originally lectures).

Wilner, Eleanor. GATHERING THE WINDS: VISIONARY IMAGINATION AND RADICAL TRANSFORMATION OF SELF AND SOCIETY. Baltimore: Johns Hopkins University Press, 1975.

> Wilner attempts "to discover the structural constants in imagination, especially in response to a breakdown of personal and social order," as well as the imagination's role in "mediating social and personal change," through study of change in preliterate societies, in the poetry of Blake and Yeats, and in the work of Karl Marx.

*Wittreich, Joseph Anthony, Jr. THE ROMANTICS ON MILTON: FORMAL ESSAYS AND CRITICAL ASIDES. Cleveland: Western Reserve University Press, 1970.

> A full range of excerpts from poetry, prose, and letters by major and secondary Romantics illustrating their attitudes toward Milton and his writings.

_____, ed. MILTON AND THE LINE OF VISION. Madison: University of Wisconsin Press, 1975.

> Eight original essays on Milton's relationship to Chaucer (Donald R. Howard), Spenser (Kathleen Williams), Sidney (S.K. Heninger, Jr.), the prophetic tradition in poetry (Wittreich), Blake (Jackie DiSalvo), WW (James Rieger), Percy and Mary Shelley and LB (Stuart Curran), and Wallace Stevens and contemporary American poets (Joan Webber).

3. Literary and Critical Theory

*Auerbach, Erich. MIMESIS: THE REPRESENTATION OF REALITY IN WESTERN LITERATURE. Trans. from the German by Willard Trask. Princeton: Princeton University Press, 1953.

> First published in Berne in 1946, this classic study--probing a single problem from Homer to Virginia Woolf--is an analytical thesis-book with both historical and theoretical dimensions.

Bloom, Harold. KABBALAH AND CRITICISM. New York: Seabury Press, 1975.

This slim study extends and elaborates Bloom's theory, set forth in THE ANXIETY OF INFLUENCE and A MAP OF MISREADING (both in Sec. C.2, above), that sees Luria's study of Kabbalah as the epitome of modern critical theory--a comparison that has been criticized as untrue and inadequate both to Luria and to literary criticism.

*Booth, Wayne C. THE RHETORIC OF FICTION. Chicago: University of Chicago Press, 1961.

This widely heralded study of narrative methods should be read in conjunction with two earlier classic theoretical works on fiction, Percy Lubbock's THE CRAFT OF FICTION (1921) and E.M. Forster's ASPECTS OF THE NOVEL (1927).

Brower, Reuben A., ed. FORMS OF LYRIC: SELECTED PAPERS FROM THE ENGLISH INSTITUTE [1968-69]. New York: Columbia University Press, 1970.

Though historical in arrangement, these essays explore changing theoretical presuppositions in the shorter poetic forms.

Chatman, Seymour, ed. APPROACHES TO POETICS: SELECTED PAPERS FROM THE ENGLISH INSTITUTE [1971-72]. New York: Columbia University Press, 1973.

A relatively accessible introduction to structuralism and its relationship to semiology, in lectures on Jakobson, Barthes, John Austin, "affective stylistics," and the development of a "science" of literature.

#Crane, R[onald] S., ed. CRITICS AND CRITICISM: ANCIENT AND MODERN Chicago: University of Chicago Press, 1952.

The most important single production of the Chicago neo-Aristotelians, including Crane, Elder Olson, W.R. Keast, Richard McKeon, Bernard Weinberg, and Norman Maclean.

*Frye, Northrop. ANATOMY OF CRITICISM: FOUR ESSAYS. Princeton: Princeton University Press, 1957.

Perhaps the most influential work of literary theory published in North America in the past thirty years, Frye's analysis of literary symbols, myths, and genres derives, in large part, from his earlier study of Blake (FEARFUL SYMMETRY) and has, therefore, great relevance for studying Romantic poetry. Frye has worked out aspects, implications, and modifications of his ideas in such later collections of essays and lectures, as FABLES OF IDENTITY (1963) and SECULAR SCRIPTURE (1976).

General and Background Studies

Gardner, Helen. THE BUSINESS OF CRITICISM. Oxford: Clarendon Press; London: Oxford University Press, 1959.

> These six lectures from two separate series, one centering on analysis of the Bible, form a unified argument for "the necessity of an historical approach to works of literature and the twin necessity of recognizing the historical nature of our own approach," as well as a plea "for a certain measure of scepticism." This slim volume is a good antidote for some productions of the more relentless system-builders in France and North America.

*Gilbert, Allan H., ed. LITERARY CRITICISM, PLATO TO DRYDEN. New York: American Book Co., 1940; rpt. Detroit: Wayne State University Press, 1962.

> In the reprint, Gilbert added a list of "Corrigenda" to this classic selection of precisely annotated scholarly texts and translations.

Hartman, Geoffrey H. BEYOND FORMALISM: LITERARY ESSAYS, 1958-1970. New Haven: Yale University Press, 1970.

> In addition to general essays relevant to theories of Romanticism, this significant collection contains specific essays on Blake, WW, "Romanticism and Anti-Self-Consciousness," and "Romantic Poetry and the Genius Loci."

_____. THE FATE OF READING AND OTHER ESSAYS. Chicago: University of Chicago Press, 1975.

> A substantial collection of essays later than those appearing in BEYOND FORMALISM, above.

_____. THE UNMEDIATED VISION: AN INTERPRETATION OF WORDSWORTH, HOPKINS, RILKE, AND VALERY. New Haven: Yale University Press, 1954.

Hirsch, E[ric] D[onald], Jr. THE AIMS OF INTERPRETATION. Chicago: University of Chicago Press, 1976.

> Hirsch, building on the work of Edmund Husserl, attempts in his two theoretical works (see also following entry) to find the grounds for determining the meaning of a literary work in a "valid" or objective way, while allowing for relative or subjective appraisals of that work's significance or value in a context beyond itself.

_____. VALIDITY IN INTERPRETATION. New Haven: Yale University Press, 1967.

> See previous entry.

@Hyman, Stanley Edgar. THE ARMED VISION: A STUDY IN THE METHODS OF MODERN LITERARY CRITICISM. New York: Alfred A. Knopf, 1948; rev. ed., abridged by the author, 1955.

> A tribute to the achievements of Yvor Winters, T.S. Eliot, Van Wyck Brooks, Constance Rourke, Maud Bodkin, Caroline Spurgeon, R.P. Blackmur, William Empson, I.A. Richards, and Kenneth Burke (and, in the first edition, Edmund Wilson and Christopher Caudwell), each seen as exemplifying an approach to literary criticism. For a more probing analysis of some of the same critics and methodologies, see Krieger, below.

#Krieger, Murray. THE NEW APOLOGISTS FOR POETRY. Minneapolis: University of Minnesota Press, 1956.

> A perceptive, stringent critique of the achievements and weaknesses of the New Critics, including Hulme, Eliot, Winters, the Chicago neo-Aristotelians, D.G. James, Richards, Ransom, Tate, Cleanth Brooks, and Robert Penn Warren.

Leavis, F[rank] R. REVALUATION: TRADITION AND DEVELOPMENT IN ENGLISH POETRY. London: Chatto and Windus, 1936.

> The most controversial and influential British critic of the 1930s and 1940s here attempts to revalue English literature on thinly moralistic grounds. Being unable to understand complex poetry, he devalues the Romantics (especially PBS).

*Richards, I[vor] A[rmstrong]. PRINCIPLES OF LITERARY CRITICISM. London: Kegan Paul, Trench, Trübner, 1924; 3rd ed., 1928.

> The most important single work of one of the giants of modern literary theory. Whatever flaws of logic may hinder acceptance of Richards' system are compensated for by his great sensitivity to poetry.

Smith, James Harry, and Edd Winfield Parks, ed. THE GREAT CRITICS: AN ANTHOLOGY OF LITERARY CRITICISM. New York: W.W. Norton, 1932; 2nd ed., 1939; 3rd ed., 1951.

> A standard one-volume anthology of criticism from Plato to Anatole France and George Moore. For a more scholarly anthology of the earlier critics, see Gilbert, above.

@Stallman, Robert Wooster, ed. CRITIQUES AND ESSAYS IN CRITICISM, 1920-1948: REPRESENTING THE ACHIEVEMENT OF MODERN BRITISH AND AMERICAN CRITICS. Foreword by Cleanth Brooks. New York: Ronald Press, 1949.

> The selections in this influential anthology embody the high watermark of the New Critics of all schools analyzed in Krieger's volume, above.

Tillyard, E[ustace] M.W., and C[live] S. Lewis.   THE PERSONAL HERESY: A CONTROVERSY. Oxford: Clarendon Press; London: Oxford University Press, 1939.

> Two of Britain's better scholar-critics debate with great skill and humanity whether, or to what extent, poetry is "the 'expression of personality'" and the reader is "supposed to pursue in reading . . . a certain contact with the poet's soul."

*Wellek, Rene.   A HISTORY OF MODERN CRITICISM: 1750-1950. 5 vols. New Haven: Yale University Press, 1955-65.

> A brilliant study, bringing to bear Wellek's unequaled knowledge of Continental, British, and American criticism in an authoritative historical survey. He is, perhaps, unfair to STC, whom he thinks overrated by those unfamiliar with STC's Continental predecessors.

_____.   THE RISE OF ENGLISH LITERARY HISTORY. Chapel Hill: University of North Carolina Press, 1941.

> Traces the early growth of the idea of literary history and literary theory with an extensive bibliography.

*Wellek, René, and Austin Warren.   THEORY OF LITERATURE. New York: Harcourt Brace, 1949.

> A very influential study embodying and defining the orthodoxy of the generation of the New Criticism and possessing great historical depth as well.

4. Descriptive and Analytic Bibliography and Theory of Editing

@Baird, John D., ed.   EDITING TEXTS OF THE ROMANTIC PERIOD: PAPERS GIVEN AT THE CONFERENCE ON EDITORIAL PROBLEMS, UNIVERSITY OF TORONTO, NOVEMBER 1971. Toronto: Hakkert, 1972.

> Contains lectures on problems in editing WW (by W.J.B. Owen), STC (Kathleen Coburn and George Whalley), PBS (Donald H. Reiman), and Jeremy Bentham (J.H. Burns).

#Bowers, Fredson.   PRINCIPLES OF BIBLIOGRAPHICAL DESCRIPTION. Princeton: Princeton University Press, 1949.

> A landmark in the history of analytic and descriptive bibliography, this work has been attacked, misused, and modified by subsequent bibliographers; they cannot ignore it.

*_____.   TEXTUAL AND LITERARY CRITICISM. The Sanders Lectures in Bibliography, 1957-58. Cambridge: Cambridge University Press, 1959.

A painless introduction to the ideas and practice of this giant among modern bibliographers.

Brack, O[mar] M., Jr., and Warner Barnes, eds. BIBLIOGRAPHY AND TEX-
TUAL CRITICISM: ENGLISH AND AMERICAN LITERATURE, 1700 TO THE
PRESENT. Chicago: University of Chicago Press, 1969.

Reprints significant papers by Bruce Harkness, Walter W. Greg,
Fredson Bowers (2), Vinton A. Dearing, James Thorpe, Todd (4),
Arthur Friedman, John M. Robson, Matthew J. Bruccoli (2), David
Hayman, Russell K. Alspach, and James B. Meriwether. A good
introduction to recent developments in textual criticism.

Dearing, Vinton A. MANUAL OF TEXTUAL ANALYSIS. Berkeley: University of California Press, 1959.

One of the chief theoretical works dealing with the question of
how texts relate to one another and how to identify corruptions in
the text resulting from erroneous changes made during the transmission of a text through various copyings or reprintings.

Erdman, David V., and Ephim G. Fogel, eds. EVIDENCE FOR AUTHORSHIP:
ESSAYS ON PROBLEMS OF ATTRIBUTION, WITH AN ANNOTATED BIBLIOG-
RAPHY OF SELECTED READINGS. Ithaca, N.Y.: Cornell University Press,
1966.

A useful 550-page introduction to an extremely complex subject.

*Gaskell, Philip. A NEW INTRODUCTION TO BIBLIOGRAPHY. Oxford:
Cleaendon Press, 1972.

Designed to replace McKerrow (below) this fine handbook gives
considerably more information on books of the eighteenth, nineteenth, and twentieth centuries than does McKerrow's study.

#Greg, Walter W. THE COLLECTED PAPERS OF SIR WALTER W. GREG. Ed.
J[ames] C. Maxwell. Oxford: Clarendon Press, 1966.

These papers from 1900 to 1956 record the growth of modern scientific bibliography in the work of one of its chief founders.

*McKerrow, Ronald B. AN INTRODUCTION TO BIBLIOGRAPHY FOR LITERARY
STUDENTS. Oxford: Clarendon Press, 1927.

Long the standard text for graduate students, this fine book has
been challenged and its authority modified in work by Greg,
Bowers, Tanselle, Thorpe, and Gaskell.

#Tanselle, G. Thomas. "The Editorial Problem of Final Authorial Intention."
STUDIES IN BIBLIOGRAPHY, 29 (1976), 167-211.

A magisterial examination of the important question of how an editor determines which words belong in the text of a critical edition. One of many authoritative essays by Tanselle published in bibliographical journals (especially STUDIES IN BIBLIOGRAPHY) during the past decade.

*Thorpe, James. PRINCIPLES OF TEXTUAL CRITICISM. San Marino, Calif.: Huntington Library, 1972.

A sane, common sense guide to textual critics and editors that may not be as rigorous or precise as the circumstances and modern bibliographical knowledge warrant.

Chapter 2
THE ROMANTIC MOVEMENT

A. BIBLIOGRAPHIES, STUDIES OF REPUTATION AND INFLUENCE, AND PERIODICALS
1. Bibliographies

Bernbaum, Ernest. GUIDE THROUGH THE ROMANTIC MOVEMENT. New York: Thomas Nelson, 1930; rev. ed., 1949.

> This old standby guide and bibliography is out of date but histori-cally interesting for the state of Romantics studies in the 1930s and 1940s.

CATALOG OF BOOKS AND MANUSCRIPTS AT THE KEATS-SHELLEY MEMORIAL HOUSE IN ROME. Boston: G.K. Hall, 1959.

> Photocopies the catalog cards of the 7,500 books and numerous manuscripts in the Memorial House.

*Elkins, A.C., Jr., and L.J. Forstner, eds. THE ROMANTIC MOVEMENT BIBLIOGRAPHY, 1936-1970: A MASTER CUMULATION FROM "ELH," "PHILOGICAL QUARTERLY" AND "ENGLISH LANGUAGE NOTES." 7 vols. Ann Arbor, Mich.: The Pierian Press, in association with R.R. Bowker, 1973.

> Besides collecting the first thirty-five years of the annual bibliog-raphy entitled "The Romantic Movement," which originally appeared in ELH (1937-49) and PQ (1950-64) and continues in ELN (1965 to date), this compilation provides indexes to all thirty-five years.

*Green, David Bonnell, and Edwin Graves Wilson, eds. KEATS, SHELLEY, BYRON, HUNT AND THEIR CIRCLES, A BIBLIOGRAPHY: JULY 1, 1950-JUNE 30, 1962. Lincoln: University of Nebraska Press, 1964.

> An indexed compilation of the first twelve annual bibliographies in K-SJ. Robert A. Hartley is now compiling and indexing those from volumes 13-25, covering publications through 1974.

*Houtchens, Carolyn W., and Lawrence H. Houtchens, eds. THE ENGLISH ROMANTIC POETS AND ESSAYISTS: A REVIEW OF RESEARCH AND CRITI-CISM. Rev. ed. New York: New York University Press, 1966.

> A companion to the volume edited by Frank Jordan, below, this one covers Blake, Lamb, Hazlitt, Scott, Southey, Campbell, Moore, Landor, Hunt, De Quincey, and Carlyle.

*Jordan, Frank, Jr., ed. THE ENGLISH ROMANTIC POETS: A REVIEW OF RESEARCH AND CRITICISM. 3rd rev. ed. New York: Modern Language Association, 1972.

> Updates and replaces the second, revised edition (1956) edited by Thomas M. Raysor. The six chapters cover "The Romantic Move-ment" (Jordan), WW (Ford Swetnam, Jr.), STC (René Wellek, Max F. Schulz), LB (Ernest J. Lovell, Jr.), PBS (Donald H. Rei-man), and JK (David Perkins).

Munby, A.N.L., ed. SALE CATALOGUES OF LIBRARIES OF EMINENT PER-SONS. London: Mansell, with Sothey Parke-Bernet, 1971-- .

> Volume 1 contains (among others) catalogs of the libraries of Robert Bloomfield, Hazlitt, Peacock, Scott, and LB (2); Volume 2 includes Lady Blessington, Rogers, and Hayley; Volume 9 (1974) includes sale catalogs of the libraries of WW, Southey, Moore, Barton, and Haydon. Other volumes will follow.

"Recent Studies in Nineteenth-Century English Literature." In STUDIES IN ENGLISH LITERATURE, 1961-- .

> In the fourth issue of each year, this quarterly includes a review-essay by a leading nineteenth-century specialist of all important books published on the Romantics and Victorians during the pre-vious year. Though varying in emphasis (and quality), these ap-praisals have the advantage of rating studies comparatively and of commenting on recent trends in various scholarly areas.

*"The Romantic Movement: A Selective and Critical Bibliography." In ELH: A JOURNAL OF ENGLISH LITERARY HISTORY, 1937-49; in PHILOLOGICAL QUARTERLY, 1950-64; and in a supplement to ENGLISH LANGUAGE NOTES, 1965-- .

2. Studies of Reputation and Influence

*Bornstein, George. TRANSFORMATIONS OF ROMANTICISM IN YEATS, ELIOT, AND STEVENS. Chicago: University of Chicago Press, 1976.

> The best study thus far of the importance of the Romantics for three key Modernist poets. See also Bornstein's YEATS AND SHELLEY (1970).

_____, ed. ROMANTIC AND MODERN: REVALUATIONS OF LITERARY TRADITION. Pittsburgh: University of Pittsburgh Press, 1976.

Includes essays on the impact of the Romantics upon the Modernists by Stuart M. Sperry, Walter H. Evert, Michael Goldman, Richard Haven, Bornstein, A. Walton Litz, Herbert N. Schneidau, Hugh Witemeyer, Glenn O'Malley, James A.W. Heffernan, E.D.H. Johnson, Joseph Blotner, and John D. Margolis.

*Gottfried, Leon. MATTHEW ARNOLD AND THE ROMANTICS. Lincoln: University of Nebraska Press, 1963.

The best of three studies with similar titles and focus (the others written by William A. Jamison, 1958, and D.G. James, 1961).

Kermode, Frank. ROMANTIC IMAGE. London: Routledge and Kegan Paul, 1957.

In spite of its title, this important study concerns itself primarily with Yeats and fin de siècle Romanticism, but it also relates the Romantic tradition to Modernist poetic theory and refutes Eliot's theory of a "dissociation of sensibility" during the eighteenth and nineteenth centuries.

Praz, Mario. THE ROMANTIC AGONY. Trans. from the Italian by Angus Davidson. London: Oxford University Press, 1933; 2nd ed., 1950.

Pursues the theme of sado-masochism from a few (generally minor) poems by the major English and German Romantics through de Sade and later nineteenth-century figures in England, Germany, Italy, France, and America in such writers and artists as Baudelaire, D'Annunzio, Swinburne, Wilde, and Delacroix.

3. Periodicals Specializing in the Romantics

As the scholar knows and the student who glances over any bibliography of current publications on the Romantics will observe, there are hundreds of periodicals around the world that from time to time publish articles, notes, and reviews on the British Romantic writers. The following periodicals, however, devote their entire attention to writers (not necessarily all poets) of this period and ought to be known and used by scholars, teachers, and serious students of the period.

THE BYRON JOURNAL. London: The Byron Society, 1973-- .

This annual publishes lectures, short critical articles, book reviews on LB and his circle, and news of the activities of Byron Societies around the world. Members of the Byron Society of America also receive a newsletter with short articles and reports on the activities of its members.

CHARLES LAMB BULLETIN. (Formerly CHARLES LAMB SOCIETY BULLETIN).
London: The Charles Lamb Society, 1935-- .

> This quarterly publishes chiefly lectures, notes, and news items,
> many containing references to WW and STC, as well as Southey,
> Lloyd, Dyer, and other minor literary friends of Lamb.

*KEATS-SHELLEY JOURNAL. New York: Keats-Shelley Association of America,
1951-- .

> This annual includes major critical articles, shorter notes, and re-
> views on JK, PBS, LB, Hunt, Hazlitt, and their circles, as well
> as an annual comprehensive bibliography and notes on events of
> interest to the membership.

KEATS-SHELLEY MEMORIAL BULLETIN. London: Keats-Shelley Memorial
Association, 1910, 1913, 1950-- .

> An annual distributed to members of the Keats-Shelley Association
> of America, as well as to direct subscribers, this slim volume con-
> tains short articles and notes, as well as news of the Memorial
> Association.

MILTON AND THE ROMANTICS. Statesboro: Georgia Southern College,
1975-- .

> A slim annual publication containing short articles and reviews on
> the English Romantics' use of and reaction to Milton's life and
> works.

*STUDIES IN ROMANTICISM. Boston: Boston University, Autumn 1961-- .

> A quarterly containing articles, notes, and reviews on such sub-
> jects as the music, art, science, religion, philosophy, and eco-
> nomics of the period, as well as on European and American Roman-
> tic literature.

*THE WORDSWORTH CIRCLE. Philadelphia: Temple University, 1970-- .

> A quarterly that publishes lectures, short articles, notes, and (in
> the summer issue) reviews of books on all the Romantics. There
> are often special issues devoted to a single writer (e.g. Landor,
> Southey, Austen) or topic (WW's EXCURSION, periodicals during
> the Romantic period); there are also checklists of scholarship on
> WW and STC and of the holdings of various research libraries of
> rare books by and about them and their circles.

B. ANTHOLOGIES OF ENGLISH ROMANTIC POETRY

Grigson, Geoffrey, ed. THE ROMANTICS: AN ANTHOLOGY OF ENGLISH PROSE AND POETRY. Cleveland: World Publishing, 1962.

> Juxtaposes bits and fragments of poetry and prose by major and minor British and American writers to illustrate the development of various themes within the Romantic period; useless as a text and misleading for general readers but interesting for the advanced student and teacher.

Heath, William, ed. MAJOR BRITISH POETS OF THE ROMANTIC PERIOD. New York: Macmillan, 1973.

> Generous selections from Blake, WW, STC, LB, PBS, nnd JK, with sparse but often perceptive annotation, a brief "General Bibliography," and indexes of titles and first lines.

Marshall, William H., ed. THE MAJOR ENGLISH ROMANTIC POETS: AN ANTHOLOGY. New York: Washington Square Press, 1963.

> Includes only poems by STC, WW, LB, PBS, and JK, without notes but with a general introduction and a selective bibliography on each poet, and indexes of titles and authors and of first lines.

Reed, Albert Granberry, ed. THE ROMANTIC PERIOD. New York: Charles Scribner's Sons, 1929; 1957.

> Selections from the (chiefly lyric) poetry of Cowper, Crabbe, Burns, Blake, WW, STC, Southey, Scott, Campbell, Moore, LB, PBS, JK, Landor, Hood, and Hunt, as well as prose by WW, STC, Lamb, Hazlitt, and De Quincey, with (outdated) introduction and notes and indexes.

Ridenour, George M. ROMANTIC POETRY. Englewood Cliffs, N.J.: Prentice-Hall, 1973.

> Includes only poetry of the Regency--selections from Scott, Landor, LB, PBS, Keats, and Clare (but none from Blake, WW, or STC), with a good introduction.

White, R[eginald] J., ed. POLITICAL TRACTS OF WORDSWORTH, COLERIDGE AND SHELLEY. Cambridge: Cambridge University Press, 1953.

> A convenient, though not textually authoritative, edition with introduction and index.

C. STUDIES OF ENGLISH ROMANTIC WRITERS

Ball, Patricia M. THE CENTRAL SELF: A STUDY IN ROMANTIC AND
VICTORIAN IMAGINATION. London: Athlone [University of London] Press,
1968.

> Explores the Romantics' search for imaginative self-understanding
> through the contrasting modes of the "egotistical" and the "chame-
> leon"--treating WW, STC, LB, PBS, and JK, before moving on to
> the Victorian criterion of "sincerity" and analysis of Tennyson,
> Arnold, and Browning.

#Beaty, Frederick L. LIGHT FROM HEAVEN: LOVE IN BRITISH ROMANTIC
LITERATURE. DeKalb: Northern Illinois University Press, 1971.

> The most comprehensive study of its subject, this volume examines
> various types of love as treated by Burns, Blake, Scott, WW, STC,
> LB, PBS, and JK (under thematic rather than chronological head-
> ings).

Benziger, James. IMAGES OF ETERNITY: STUDIES IN THE POETRY OF RE-
LIGIOUS VISION FROM WORDSWORTH TO T.S. ELIOT. Carbondale:
Southern Illinois University Press, 1962.

> Contains sane discussions of the major Romantics from the angle of
> their individual religious orientations.

Blackstone, Bernard. THE LOST TRAVELLERS: A ROMANTIC THEME WITH
VARIATIONS. London: Longmans, 1962.

> A stimulating analysis of the "strangers and pilgrims" theme in
> Blake, WW, STC, LB, PBS, and (less fully) in JK.

*Bloom, Harold. THE VISIONARY COMPANY: A READING OF ENGLISH
ROMANTIC POETRY. New York: Doubleday, 1961; rev. ed., Ithaca, N.Y.:
Cornell University Press, 1971.

> Bloom's most useful book on the Romantics, containing much intel-
> ligent discussion of individual poems.

Bostetter, Edward E. THE ROMANTIC VENTRILOQUISTS: WORDSWORTH,
COLERIDGE, KEATS, SHELLEY, BYRON. Seattle: University of Washington
Press, 1963.

> One of the last of the "new humanist" critics of the Romantics,
> Bostetter finds large flaws in the lives, thought, and works of WW,
> STC, PBS, and JK. Only LB's skepticism meets his tests for ma-
> turity and widsom.

Bowra, C. Maurice. THE ROMANTIC IMAGINATION. Cambridge: Harvard University Press, 1949; London: Oxford University Press, 1950.

After an opening lecture entitled "The Romantic Imagination," Bowra includes lectures on Blake's SONGS OF INNOCENCE AND EXPERIENCE, "The Ancient Mariner," "Ode on Intimations of Immortality," PROMETHEUS UNBOUND, "Ode on a Grecian Urn," DON JUAN, and works by Poe, D.G. Rossetti, Swinburne, and Christina Rossetti, before concluding with "The Romantic Achievement," in which Bowra--a classical scholar and comparatist--attempts to locate the English Romantics within Western cultural development.

Brinton, Crane C. THE POLITICAL IDEAS OF THE ENGLISH ROMANTICS. London: Oxford University Press, 1926.

Once influential, this study is distorted by the author's hostility to the Romantics' liberalism.

Chayes, Irene H. "Rhetoric as Drama: An Approach to the Romantic Ode." PMLA, 79 (1964), 67-79.

An important article illustrating the mode of the Romantic poem through excellent readings of "Dejection," "West Wind," and "Nightingale," and more general allusions to other Romantic odes.

Enscoe, Gerald. EROS AND THE ROMANTICS: SEXUAL LOVE AS A THEME IN COLERIDGE, SHELLEY AND KEATS. The Hague, Netherlands: Mouton, 1967.

Oversimplified insofar as its larger subject is concerned, this dissertation contains intelligent readings of several poems by the three poets.

Evans, Bertrand. GOTHIC DRAMA FROM WALPOLE TO SHELLEY. Berkeley: University of California Press, 1947.

After the nine chapters treating the Gothic revival in England through the work of "Monk" Lewis, Evans in the last three chapters discusses "Gothic Acting Drama, 1801-1816" (plays by Sotheby, G.C. Carr, Tobin, and Maturin), "Joanna Baillie and Gothic Drama," and "Gothic Survival in Literary Drama" (plays by WW, STC, Scott, PBS, and LB).

Foakes, R[eginald] A. THE ROMANTIC ASSERTION: A STUDY IN THE LANGUAGE OF NINETEENTH CENTURY POETRY. New Haven: Yale University Press, 1958.

A rather thin study of the way several English poets, including WW, JK, and PBS, use assertive language as a rhetorical device.

Frye, Northrop. A STUDY OF ENGLISH ROMANTICISM. Studies in Language and Literature. New York: Random House, 1968.

>Includes a discussion of Romanticism as a change "in the language of poetic mythology" and includes critical analysis of such poems as PROMETHEUS UNBOUND, ENDYMION, and Beddoes' DEATH'S JEST-BOOK.

*Gerard, Albert S. ENGLISH ROMANTIC POETRY: ETHOS, STRUCTURE, AND SYMBOL IN COLERIDGE, WORDSWORTH, SHELLEY, AND KEATS. Berkeley: University of California Press, 1968.

>This study, a development from Gerard's earlier book in French (L'IDÉE ROMANTIQUE DE LA POESIE EN ANGLETERRE, 1955), is a mature and intelligent analysis of major poems of WW, STC, PBS, and JK.

Harris, R[onald] W. ROMANTICISM AND THE SOCIAL ORDER 1780-1830. London: Blanford Press, 1969.

>A historian's view of English literary figures, with chapters on Godwin, Blake, WW, STC, Scott, Southey, PBS, JK, and LB, each keyed to one of the sociointellectual issues of the age.

Herford C[harles] H. THE AGE OF WORDSWORTH. London: G. Bell and Sons, 1897; 3rd rev. ed., 1899.

>Though somewhat dated, this sensible handbook to the period has never really been replaced by a modern study that provides basic information on the poets and the period in concise, readable form.

Hough, Graham. THE ROMANTIC POETS. London: Hutchinson, 1953.

>A brief critical introduction, containing chapters on Gray, WW and STC, LB, PBS, and JK.

James, D[avid] G[wilym]. THE ROMANTIC COMEDY: AN ESSAY ON ENGLISH ROMANTICISM. London: Oxford University Press, 1948.

>The Romantic poets are condescendingly used to promote James's pet theory that poetry or the imagination should never be allowed to usurp the role of religion.

Knight, G. Wilson. THE STARLIT DOME: STUDIES IN THE POETRY OF VISION. London: Oxford University Press, 1941.

>Contains imaginative explorations of the symbolism of WW, STC, PBS, and JK.

#Kroeber, Karl. ROMANTIC NARRATIVE ART. Madison: University of Wisconsin Press, 1960.

> Treats the beginnings of English Romantic narrative poetry from the ballad tradition (including Chatterton) through tales, WW's PRELUDE and LB's and Scott's narratives.

*Langbaum, Robert. THE POETRY OF EXPERIENCE: THE DRAMATIC MONOLOGUE IN MODERN LITERARY TRADITION. New York: Random House, 1957.

> This seminal study, though centering on Browning and Tennyson, includes important discussions of the development of the dramatic monologue among the English Romantics, including discussions of poems by each of the major poets.

Prickett, Stephen. ROMANTICISM AND RELIGION: THE TRADITION OF COLERIDGE AND WORDSWORTH IN THE VICTORIAN CHURCH. Cambridge: Cambridge University Press, 1976.

Rodway, Allan. THE ROMANTIC CONFLICT. London: Chatto and Windus, 1963.

> A general survey of English Romanticism, treating the social and historical background and such "pre-Romantics" as Smart, Chatterton, and Cowper, as well as Blake, WW, STC, PBS, LB, and JK. Rodway fails to understand or appreciate the greatest poems by the major poets (particularly PBS).

Roppen, Georg, and Richard Sommer. STRANGERS AND PILGRIMS: AN ESSAY ON THE METAPHOR OF JOURNEY. Oslo: Norwegian Universities Press, 1964.

> Like Blackstone's study, above, this volume traces the imagery and symbolism of the pilgrimage or quest through a series of poems by WW, STC, LB, and Victorians through Yeats.

*Swingle, L[arry] J. "On Reading Romantic Poetry." PMLA, 86 (1971), 974-81.

> An important essay, for teachers and students alike, arguing convincingly that Romantic poetry asks questions to unsettle the reader and leads him to doubt accepted dogmas and to consult his own experience, rather than providing pat answers from a new dogma.

_____. "Romantic Unity and English Romantic Poetry." JEGP, 74 (1975), 361-74.

> An important essay that qualifies a number of M.H. Abrams' assertions in NATURAL SUPERNATURALISM (see Sec. 2.D, below).

Vogler, Thomas A. PRELUDES TO VISION: THE EPIC VENTURE IN BLAKE, WORDSWORTH, KEATS, AND HART CRANE. Berkeley: University of California Press, 1971.

> Seeing the epic subject of the Romantic and Modernist poet as the search for a heroic subject, Vogler examines THE FOUR ZOAS, THE PRELUDE, the HYPERION poems, and THE BRIDGE as examples of modern epics.

Wasserman, Earl R. "The English Romantics: The Grounds of Knowledge." SiR, 4 (1964), 17–34.

> An important brief survey of the epistemological dilemma faced by the Romantics, and the individual solutions of WW, STC, PBS, and JK.

Weiskel, Thomas. THE ROMANTIC SUBLIME: STUDIES IN THE STRUCTURE AND PSYCHOLOGY OF TRANSCENDENCE. Baltimore: Johns Hopkins University Press, 1976.

> A significant exploration (from a viewpoint at once sympathetic to the Romantics' experience and skeptical of their interpretations of it) of the theory and practice of the sublime in Kant and Burke, Collins, Blake, WW, PBS, JK, and Wallace Stevens.

#Wilkie, Brian. ROMANTIC POETS AND EPIC TRADITION. Madison: University of Wisconsin Press, 1965.

> A significant study of attempts to transform and revitalize the epic through close analysis of specific poems by Southey, Landor, WW, PBS, JK, and LB.

*Woodring, Carl. POLITICS IN ENGLISH ROMANTIC POETRY. Cambridge: Harvard University Press, 1970.

> A major study, providing (with Woodring's earlier study of POLITICS IN THE POETRY OF COLERIDGE, see Chap. 4.D.2) the best total analysis of the impact of political theories and events on the major and minor English poetry of the period.

Wormhoudt, Arthur. THE DEMON LOVER: A PSYCHOANALYTICAL APPROACH TO LITERATURE. New York: Exposition Press, 1949.

> Explicates in reductive Freudian terms poems by STC, WW, JK, PBS, and LB. According to the Foreword by Edmund Bergler, M.D., the reader "is not asked to believe in every detail" but "to judge for himself how unconscious reactions of poets, as expressed in their poems, . . . acquire a very specific meaning if viewed in the light of modern psychiatry."

D. ROMANTICISM AS AN INTERNATIONAL PHENOMENON

*Abrams, M[eyer] H. THE MIRROR AND THE LAMP: ROMANTIC THEORY AND THE CRITICAL TRADITION. New York: Oxford University Press, 1953.

> A classic study that not only traces the change in critical terminol-
> ogy from a metaphor "comparing the mind to a reflector of exter-
> nal objects" to one which compared the mind "to a radiant pro-
> jector which makes a contribution to the objects its perceives,"
> but also forces other scholars to take seriously such metaphorical
> language and to plumb its implications. This book is so well or-
> ganized and clearly written that it can be used as a model for ad-
> vanced students on how to think and write on almost any topic.

* _____. NATURAL SUPERNATURALISM: TRADITION AND REVOLUTION IN ROMANTIC LITERATURE. New York: W.W. Norton, 1971.

> A learned and perceptive analysis of how English and Continental.
> Romantics transformed traditional religious values and symbols into
> a humanistic substitute for theism that persists to our own time.
> See also Swingle, Sec. 2.C, above.

Babinski, Hubert F. THE MAZEPPA LEGEND IN EUROPEAN ROMANTICISM. New York: Columbia University Press, 1974.

> Shows the wide use made by European writers and artists of the
> story behind LB's poem.

Beach, Joseph Warren. THE CONCEPT OF NATURE IN NINETEENTH-CEN-TURY ENGLISH POETRY. New York: Macmillan, 1936, 2nd ed. New York: Pageant Book Co., 1956.

> After an introduction and seven substantial chapters devoted pri-
> marily to the concept of "nature" in WW and PBS, Beach broadens
> his study to Goethe, Carlyle, STC, Emerson, Whitman, Arnold,
> Tennyson, Browning, and later Victorians.

Boas, George. "The Romantic Self: An Historical Sketch." SiR, 4 (1964), 1-16.

> Sketches the concept of unique individuality from its (limited) be-
> ginning in Hellenic times, through the Hellenistic biographers,
> Christian, Stoic, and Neoplatonic introspective writers, through
> Montaigne to Rousseau and the Romantics, and down to the present.

Eichner, Hans, ed. "ROMANTIC" AND ITS COGNATES: THE EUROPEAN HISTORY OF A WORD. Toronto: University of Toronto Press, 1972.

> The article entitled "England: Romantic--Romanticism" is by
> George Whalley; other essays treat the development of the word

before 1790, its currency in Germany, France, Italy, Spain, Scandinavia, and Russia, and "Trends of Recent Research on West European Romanticism."

Fass, Barbara. LA BELLE DAME SANS MERCI AND THE AESTHETICS OF RO-MANTICISM. Detroit: Wayne State University Press, 1974.

Examines JK's poem, adapting the legend of the fairy mistress in the light of such continental motifs as those of the Lorelei and the Venusberg, through the works of nineteenth- and early twentieth-century writers from Mérimée through Yeats and Mann.

*Frye, Northrop, ed. ROMANTICISM RECONSIDERED: SELECTED PAPERS FROM THE ENGLISH INSTITUTE. New York: Columbia University Press, 1963.

Four important examinations of the theory and practice of Romanticism by Frye, Abrams, Trilling, and Wellek.

Furst, Lilian R. ROMANTICISM IN PERSPECTIVE: A COMPARATIVE STUDY OF ASPECTS OF THE ROMANTIC MOVEMENTS IN ENGLAND, FRANCE, AND GERMANY. London: Macmillan, 1969.

Examines the Romantic movement in the three countries, in search of "family likenesses" and individual differences.

Hayter, Alethea. OPIUM AND THE ROMANTIC IMAGINATION. London: Faber and Faber, 1968.

Includes chapters on STC and JK (as well as De Quincey, Poe, Crabbe, Baudelaire, et al.) and treats Scott briefly in a chapter entitled "Some Writers Who Took Opium Occasionally."

Hirsch, E[ric] D[onald], Jr. WORDSWORTH AND SCHELLING: A TYPOLOG-ICAL STUDY OF ROMANTICISM. New Haven: Yale University Press, 1960.

Studies the thought of the young WW and Schelling (who did not know each other's work) for similarities to show the existence of a European Romanticism deriving from the intellectual situation shared by all writers of the age.

Jones, Howard Mumford. REVOLUTION AND ROMANTICISM. Cambridge: Harvard University Press, 1974.

A generalized survey by one of the old master teachers of English and American Romanticism.

Kaplan, Fred. MIRACLES OF RARE DEVICE: THE POET'S SENSE OF SELF IN NINETEENTH-CENTURY POETRY. Detroit: Wayne State University Press, 1972.

#Kroeber, Karl. THE ARTIFICE OF REALITY: POETIC STYLE IN WORDSWORTH FOSCOLO, KEATS, AND LEOPARDI. Madison: University of Wisconsin Press, 1964.

> Studies the similarities between WW and JK and two Italian Romantics to demonstrate the breadth of the Romantic movement in Europe. See also G.L. Bickersteth, LEOPARDI AND WORDSWORTH (1927).

Massey, Irving, "The Romantic Movement: Phrase or Fact?" DALHOUSIE REVIEW, 44 (1955), 396-412.

> Argues systematically that the evidence for a "Romantic movement" in European literature just doesn't exist, or (if it does) adds nothing to our understanding of individual poems.

*Peckham, Morse. BEYOND THE TRAGIC VISION: THE QUEST FOR IDENTITY IN THE NINETEENTH CENTURY. New York: George Braziller, 1962.

> A learned, wide-ranging, and stimulating study (including discussions of musicians, painters, philosophers, and scientists as well as poets and novelists) that attempts to trace the development of modern thought from the intellectual quests of the nineteenth-century's greatest creative minds.

_____. "On Romanticism: Introduction." SiR, 9 (1970), 217-24.

> Introduces a special issue of SiR entitled "The Concept of Romanticism," containing lecture-essays by Bloom, Hartman (on Romanticism in France), Richard P. Adams (on American Romanticism), Barry S. Brook (on Romantic music), F.X. Shea, S.J. ("Religion and the Romantic Movement"), and Kroeber (against apocalyptic theories of Romanticism).

*_____. "Toward a Theory of Romanticism: II. Reconsiderations." SiR, 1 (1961), 1-8.

> One of the most important recent theories of Romanticism in a brief, clear form that every student can and should read; Peckham has expanded and illustrated his thesis in BEYOND THE TRAGIC VISION, above. This essay and other relevant papers are reprinted in Peckham's THE TRIUMPH OF ROMANTICISM: COLLECTED ESSAYS (Columbia: University of South Carolina Press, 1970).

Randall, John Herman, Jr. "Romantic Reinterpretations of Religion." SiR, 2 (1963), 189-212.

> Arguing that "the original thinkers among the religious Idealists were all Germans," because "the hold of religious orthodoxy had been broken first in Germany," Randall traces three schools of German expositors: (1) Hegel and his followers, who saw religion

as a means to <u>knowledge</u> through symbols; (2) Herder, Schleier-
macher, and their followers, who saw religion as "a form of art
and <u>aesthetic experience</u>"; (3) exponents of religion as a <u>moral
action,</u> beginning with ideas of Kant and Fichte and culminating
in the thought of Ritschl. See also Fritz Marti's "Schelling on
God and Man," SiR, 3 (1964), 65-76.

Rogers, Stephen J., Jr. CLASSICAL GREECE IN THE POETRY OF CHENIER,
SHELLEY, AND LEOPARDI. Notre Dame, Ind.: University of Notre Dame
Press, 1974.

A study of Hellenic influences on the lyric poetry of three diverse
Romantics, with a useful bibliography of related studies.

Sabin, Margery. ENGLISH ROMANTICISM AND THE FRENCH TRADITION.
Cambridge: Harvard University Press, 1976.

Schenk, H[ans] G. THE MIND OF THE EUROPEAN ROMANTICS: AN ESSAY
IN CULTURAL HISTORY. Pref. by Isaiah Berlin. London: Constable, 1966.

One of the most far-reaching books in English, including not only
Beethoven, LB, Delacroix, and others, but also Atterbom, Baader,
Lermontov, Mickiewicz, Oehlenschlager, Pugin, and Wergeland.

Sutherland, Donald. ON, ROMANTICISM. New York: New York University
Press, 1971.

A witty and provocative exploration of the nature of art and literature described as Romantic, Classic, and Baroque. PBS figures
importantly as the epitome of the Romantic poet.

Thorslev, Peter L., Jr. "The Romantic Mind Is Its Own Place." COMPARA-
TIVE LITERATURE, 15 (1963), 250-68.

The revival of the Renaissance tradition of the Satanic villain-hero
and the influence of Satan's speeches in PARADISE LOST (I. 250-
59, and IV. 73-75) on the conception of the isolated hero in
works by Schiller, Goethe, Blake, PBS, and LB.

*Wellek, Rene. "The Concept of 'Romanticism' in Literary History." COM-
PARATIVE LITERATURE, 1 (1949), 1-23, 147-72.

A learned and most important answer to Lovejoy's contention in
"On the Discrimination of Romanticisms" (PMLA, 1924) that "Romantic" and "Romanticism" are purely subjective terms in literary
history.

_____. "German and English Romanticism: A Confrontation." SiR, 4 (1964),
35-56.

A learned and informative sketch of interactions between the principal writers and an analysis of the differences between the two romanticisms; reprinted in Wellek's CONFRONTATIONS (1965).

E. MISCELLANEOUS ESSAYS TREATING TWO OR MORE ENGLISH ROMANTIC POETS

1. Biographical Emphasis

@Cameron, Kenneth Neill, ed. ROMANTIC REBELS: ESSAYS ON SHELLEY AND HIS CIRCLE. Cambridge: Harvard University Press, 1973.

Reprints most of the substantial essays from volumes 1-4 of SHELLEY AND HIS CIRCLE, edited by Cameron (Chap. 6.C.3). These include essays by Cameron on PBS, Godwin, Hunt, the death of Harriet Shelley, the elopement of PBS's sister, and the provenance of PBS MSS; by David V. Erdman on LB (2); by Eleanor L. Nicholes on Wollstonecraft and on Peacock; by Sylva Norman on Mary Shelley; and by F. L. Jones on the Shelley-Hogg correspondence of 1815.

Elwin, Malcolm. THE FIRST ROMANTICS. London: Macdonald, 1947.

A joint biography of WW and STC through 1802, with a full topical index.

Erdman, David V. "Coleridge, Wordsworth, and the Wedgwood Fund." BNYPL, 60 (1956), 425-43, 487-507.

An important study of the relations of Godwin, WW, and STC with Josiah Wedgwood, who was acting as philanthropist.

Morley, Edith J., ed. BLAKE, COLERIDGE, WORDSWORTH, LAMB, ETC., BEING SELECTIONS FROM THE REMAINS OF HENRY CRABB ROBINSON. Manchester, Engl.: The University Press, 1922.

Serious students of the period should also know the larger selections from Crabb Robinson's famous diaries, edited by Thomas Sadler (3 vols., 1869) and Edith J. Morley (3 vols., 1938).

2. Critical Emphasis

Balslev, Thora. KEATS AND WORDSWORTH: A COMPARATIVE STUDY. Copenhagen: Munksgaard, 1962.

Detailed analysis of JK's responses to WW's poetry, with a record of "echoes" and good analysis of the two poets ideas of myth.

Echeruo, J.C. "Shelley on Wordsworth." ENGLISH STUDIES IN AFRICA, 11 (1968), 117-45.

The most comprehensive study of PBS's reaction to WW.

Fogle, Richard Harter. THE IMAGERY OF KEATS AND SHELLEY: A COMPARATIVE STUDY. Chapel Hill: University of North Carolina Press, 1949.

Besides the comparison indicated by the title, Fogle includes a defense of the Romantic poets against the attacks of the New Critics. The book, important in its day, now seems somewhat dated by the changed attitude that it helped initiate towards the Romantics.

Krieger, Murray. THE CLASSIC VISION: THE RETREAT FROM EXTREMITY IN MODERN LITERATURE. Baltimore: Johns Hopkins University Press, 1971.

Includes an important chapter on WW (pp. 149-96).

Perkins, David. THE QUEST FOR PERMANENCE: THE SYMBOLISM OF WORDSWORTH, SHELLEY, AND KEATS. Cambridge: Harvard University Press, 1959.

Contains nine chapters, three on each poet. Perkins lucidly explores a number of issues raised by other critics (particularly Bate, Bush, and Wasserman) during the 1950s.

3. General Collections

*Abrams, M[eyer] H., ed. ENGLISH ROMANTIC POETS: MODERN ESSAYS IN CRITICISM. New York: Oxford University Press, 1960; 2nd ed., 1975.

In the original edition, this collection contained twenty-five essays; general studies by A.O. Lovejoy, W.K. Wimsatt, and Abrams; on Blake by Frye, Gleckner, and Bloom; on WW by Willey, Carlos Baker, Charles Williams, and Trilling; on STC by George McLean Harper, G. Wilson Knight, and House; on LB by Eliot, Ronald Bottrall, and Lovell; on PBS by C.S. Lewis, Leavis, Pottle, and Donald Davie; and on JK by Bush, Bate, Brooks, Wasserman, and Fogle. The second edition reprints fourteen additional essays, but drops several earlier ones.

Chapman, John A. PAPERS ON SHELLEY, WORDSWORTH, AND OTHERS. London: Oxford University Press, 1929.

The first three (of twelve) miscellaneous essays treat "Shelley and Francis Thompson," WW, and STC.

#Eliot, T[homas] S[tearns]. THE USE OF POETRY AND THE USE OF CRITI-
CISM. Cambridge: Harvard University Press, 1933.

> Contains, among other lectures, famous and influential critiques
> of "Wordsworth and Coleridge" and "Shelley and Keats."

Elledge, W. Paul, and Richard L. Hoffman, eds. ROMANTIC AND VICTOR-
IAN: STUDIES IN MEMORY OF WILLIAM H. MARSHALL. Rutherford, N.J.:
Fairleigh Dickinson University Press, 1971.

> Fifteen (of nineteen) essays concern the Romantics, major and/or
> minor, written by a cross-section of noted Romanticists, including
> Peckham, Thorslev, Woodring, Fogle, McGann, and Stillinger.

Fogle, Richard Harter. THE PERMANENT PLEASURE: ESSAYS ON CLASSICS
OF ROMANTICISM. Athens: University of Georgia Press, 1974.

> Reprints fifteen essays, published from 1948 through 1970, on Brit-
> ish and American Romantics.

Gleckner, Robert F., and Gerald E. Enscoe, eds. ROMANTICISM: POINTS
OF VIEW. Englewood Cliffs, N.J.: Prentice-Hall, 1962; 2nd ed., much
rev. 1970.

> The first edition reprints twenty-two essays or excerpts from books--
> from Pater (1889) and Babbitt to Foakes and Wasserman (1959)--
> giving different definitions and judgments of Romanticism. The
> second edition drops eight of the original selections and adds seven
> new ones.

Griggs, Earl Leslie, ed. WORDSWORTH AND COLERIDGE: STUDIES IN
HONOR OF GEORGE MCLEAN HARPER. Princeton: Princeton University
Press, 1939.

> Thirteen essays by major scholars, in addition to an appreciation
> of Harper and a bibliography of his publications.

*Hilles, Frederick W., and Harold Bloom, eds. FROM SENSIBILITY TO RO-
MANTICISM: ESSAYS PRESENTED TO FREDERICK A. POTTLE. New York:
Oxford University Press, 1965.

> The first twelve essays in this excellent miscellany concern them-
> selves chiefly with eighteenth-century poetry--Pope (3), Johnson
> (2), Collins, Gray (3), and Burns--as well as two more general
> essays on "Local Attachment and Cosmopolitanism" and Scottish
> vernacular poetry. The last fourteen essays, beginning with Mar-
> tin Price's "The Picturesque Moment," move into the Romantic
> age--including studies of Blake (by Hollander, Hagstrum, and
> Erdman), WW (by Charles Ryskamp, Cleanth Brooks, and Hartman),
> STC (Coburn and Boulger), LB (Ridenour and Hirsch), PBS (Wasser-
> man), and JK (Bloom)--and conclude with Abrams' extremely im-

portant essay, "Structure and Style in the Greater Romantic Lyric."
Several of these essays have since been reprinted elsewhere, but
this remains a significant collection.

Jefferson, D.W., ed. THE MORALITY OF ART: ESSAYS PRESENTED TO G.
WILSON KNIGHT BY HIS COLLEAGUES AND FRIENDS. London: Routledge
and Kegan Paul, 1969.

Includes four essays on the Romantics by Patricia Ball (STC),
Douglas Grant (LB), John Jones (JK), and G.M. Matthews (PBS).

Knight, G[eorge] Wilson. NEGLECTED POWERS: ESSAYS ON NINETEENTH
AND TWENTIETH CENTURY LITERATURE. London: Routledge and Kegan Paul,
1971.

A collection of recent lectures and essays on various topics.

Kumar, Shiv K., ed. BRITISH ROMANTIC POETS: RECENT REVALUATIONS.
New York: New York University Press, 1966.

Reprints essays and sections of books (chiefly from the 1950s). The
collection includes reprints of general essays by Peckham and Foakes;
Bush, Raysor, Edwin Morgan, and Stallknecht on WW; L.G. Salinger, E.E. Stoll, and House on STC; Wilfred Dowden, Rutherford,
and Bowra on LB; R.H. Fogle, Carlos Baker, and Stewart C. Wilcox on PBS; and Cleanth Brooks and Sperry on JK. There are also
original essays on JK by Blackstone and Kumar.

Logan, James V., John E. Jordan, and Northrop Frye, eds. SOME BRITISH
ROMANTICS: A COLLECTION OF ESSAYS. Columbus: Ohio State University Press, 1966.

Includes general essays by Karl Kroeber on "Trends in Minor Ro-
mantic Narrative Poetry" (treating Crabbe, Southey, Landor, Hunt,
Peacock, Beddoes, Praed, and Hood) and William S. Ward on
"Periodical Literature," as well as essays by Frye on Blake, Jack
on Hunt and Clare, Grant on De Quincey, Coburn on Hazlitt,
Tillotson on Lamb, Mercier on Landor, and John Henry Raleigh on
Scott's fiction.

Orel, Harold. ENGLISH ROMANTIC POETS AND THE ENLIGHTENMENT:
NINE ESSAYS ON A LITERARY RELATIONSHIP. Studies on Voltaire and the
Enlightenment, ed. Theodore Besterman, Vol. 103. Banbury, Engl.: Voltaire
Foundation, 1973.

Explores the impact of Enlightenment ideas on eight English poets:
Burns, Blake, STC, WW, Scott, LB, JK, and PBS.

Orel, Harold and George J. Worth, eds. THE NINETEENTH-CENTURY
WRITER AND HIS AUDIENCE: SELECTED PROBLEMS IN THEORY, FORM,
AND CONTENT. Lawrence: University of Kansas Press, 1969.

> Includes essays by W.P. Albrecht on Hazlitt and JK and by Orel
> on LB, Thomas Talfourd, and Browning.

Peckham, Morse. THE TRIUMPH OF ROMANTICISM: COLLECTED ESSAYS.
Columbia: University of South Carolina Press, 1970.

> Collects many of Peckham's important essays on the theory of Ro-
> manticism and individual writers.

#Reiman, Donald H., Michael C. Jaye, and Betty T. Bennett, eds. THE EVI-
DENCE OF THE IMAGINATION: STUDIES OF INTERACTIONS BETWEEN LIFE
AND ART IN ENGLISH ROMANTIC LITERATURE. New York: New York Uni-
versity Press, 1978.

> A significant collection of sixteen original essays on Blake, WW
> (6), Lamb, Wollstonecraft, PBS (2), LB, JK, Peacock, Mary Shel-
> ley, and Claire Clairmont's niece. The essays are by the editors
> and by Eileen Sanzo, Erdman, Woodring, Paul Magnuson, Irene
> Tayler, Joyce Hemlow, Marcelle Thiébaux, G.M. Matthews, John
> Lavelle, Marchand, Aileen Ward, William Walling, and Marion
> K. Stocking.

Riese, Teut Andreas, and Dieter Riesner, eds. VERSDICHTUNG DER ENG-
LISCHEN ROMANTIK: INTERPRETATIONEN. Berlin: Erich Schmidt, 1968.

> Significant studies, in German or English, of specific poems by
> Chatterton, Burns, Blake (2), WW (4), STC (3), Scott's lyrics,
> LB, PBS (4), JK (4), and Landor.

Ryals, Clyde de L., ed. NINETEENTH-CENTURY LITERARY PERSPECTIVES:
ESSAYS IN HONOR OF LIONEL STEVENSON. Durham, N.C.: Duke University Press, 1974.

> In addition to substantial material on the Victorians, this volume
> includes essays by John Clubbe on LB, U.C. Knoepflmacher on
> STC, Fogle on JK, and Martin J. Svaglic on PBS.

Sherwood, Margaret. UNDERCURRENTS OF INFLUENCE IN ENGLISH RO-
MANTIC POETRY. Cambridge: Harvard University Press, 1934.

> Includes essays on WW (2), JK, and Browning (2).

Thorburn, David, and Geoffrey Hartman, eds. ROMANTICISM: VISTAS,
INSTANCES, CONTINUITIES. Ithaca, N.Y.: Cornell University Press, 1973.

Reprints essays by Wimsatt, Hartman, Brombert, de Man, Pottle, Bloom, and Peter Brooks, in addition to new essays by Michael Cooke, Roger Shattuck, Cleanth Brooks, and Thorburn.

Thorlby, Anthony, ed. THE ROMANTIC MOVEMENT. London: Longmans, 1967.

Strings together twenty-six excerpts from various twentieth-century theorists of Romanticism with stimulating editorial comment, and then adds selected "Documents" representative of such varied thinkers as Rousseau, Burke, Manzoni, and Kierkegaard.

Thorpe, Clarence D[eWitt]; Carlos Baker; and Bennett Weaver, eds. THE MAJOR ENGLISH ROMANTIC POETS: A SYMPOSIUM IN REAPPRAISAL. Carbondale: Southern Illinois University Press, 1957.

Includes twenty original essays: general studies by Elizabeth Nitchie, R.H. Fogle, and Fairchild; Josephine Miles, Stallknecht, and Darbishire on WW; McLuhan, D.G. James, and Coburn on STC; Lovell, Pratt, and Marchand on LB; R.D. Havens, Baker, S.C. Wilcox, and Read on PBS; and Bate, Bush, Cleanth Brooks, and J.M. Murry on JK.

Chapter 3

WILLIAM WORDSWORTH (1770-1850)

Besides the general bibliographies of English literature and of the Romantic poets or the Romantic movement, see the chapter on STC, below, for several items that also include materials on WW.

A. CONCORDANCES, BIBLIOGRAPHIES, AND STUDIES OF REPUTATION AND INFLUENCE

1. Concordances

*Cooper, Lane, ed. A CONCORDANCE TO THE POEMS OF WILLIAM WORDS-WORTH. London: Smith, Elder, 1911.

> Based on Hutchinson's Oxford text of 1907 (see Hutchinson in Sec. B.1, below).

2. Bibliographies

Broughton, Leslie N., ed. THE WORDSWORTH COLLECTION FORMED BY CYNTHIA MORGAN ST. JOHN. Ithaca, N.Y.: Cornell University Press, 1931.

> For other portions of Cornell's great Wordsworth collection, see subsequent entries under Broughton and Healey.

_____ THE WORDSWORTH COLLECTION . . .: A SUPPLEMENT TO THE CATALOGUE. Ithaca, N.Y.: Cornell University Press, 1942.

Gordan, John D. WILLIAM WORDSWORTH, 1770-1850. AN EXHIBITION. New York: New York Public Library, 1950.

> Books and MSS in the Berg Collection, New York Public Library.

*Healey, George Harris. THE CORNELL WORDSWORTH COLLECTION. A CATALOGUE OF BOOKS AND MANUSCRIPTS PRESENTED TO THE UNIVERSITY BY MR. VICTOR EMANUEL CORNELL, 1919. Ithaca, N.Y.: Cornell University Press, 1957.

> This volume--together with THE INDIANA WORDSWORTH COLLECTION (below), Metzdorf's TINKER LIBRARY, and Wise's ASHLEY LIBRARY catalogues (both cited in Chap. 1.C.1.a)--provides all necessary data on the early editions of Wordsworth's works and contemporary Wordsworthiana.

*Henley, Elton F., and David H. Stam. WORDSWORTHIAN CRITICISM 1945-1964. Rev. ed. New York: New York Public Library, 1965.

> Corrects and updates a similar title (same authors and publisher) of 1960. For related books, see Logan and Stam, below.

THE INDIANA WORDSWORTH COLLECTION: A BRIEF ACCOUNT OF THE COLLECTION, TOGETHER WITH A CATALOGUE OF THE EXHIBIT HELD IN THE LILLY LIBRARY ON THE OCCASION OF THE BICENTENARY OF WORDSWORTH'S BIRTH. Bloomington, Ind.: The Lilly Library, 1970.

> The introductory essay on "The Collection" is signed R[ussell] N[oyes].

*Logan, James V. WORDSWORTHIAN CRITICISM: A GUIDE AND BIBLIOGRAPHY. Columbus: Ohio State University Press, 1961.

> A second printing of a work first published in 1947, this volume covers studies through 1944. For later materials, see under Henley and Stam in this section.

Patton, C.H., ed. THE AMHERST WORDSWORTH COLLECTION. Amherst, Mass.: Amherst College, 1936.

> Describes Patton's collection which, along with those at Cornell and Indiana, is one of the best in the United States.

*Stam, David H. WORDSWORTHIAN CRITICISM 1964-1973, INCLUDING ADDITIONS TO WORDSWORTHIAN CRITICISM 1945-1964. New York: New York Public Library and Readex Books, 1974.

> Supplements books listed above under Henley and Logan.

#White, W.H., ed. A DESCRIPTION OF THE WORDSWORTH AND COLERIDGE MANUSCRIPTS IN THE POSSESSION OF MR. T. NORTON LONGMAN. London: Longmans, 1897.

> These important MSS are now preserved at Yale University Library.

Wise, Thomas J[ames]. TWO LAKE POETS: A CATALOGUE OF PRINTED BOOKS, MANUSCRIPTS AND AUTOGRAPH LETTERS BY WILLIAM WORDS-WORTH AND SAMUEL TAYLOR COLERIDGE. London: Privately printed, 1927.

> A selection from Wise's Ashley Library (see Chap 1.C.1.a).

NOTE: See also Section B.4, Textual Studies, below.

3. Studies of Reputation and Influence

Newton, Annabel. WORDSWORTH IN EARLY AMERICAN CRITICISM. Chi-·cago: University of Chicago Press, 1928.

> A pioneering study often supplemented—for example, by Leon Howard in MLN, 48 (1933), and Lewis Leary, MLN, 58 (1943).

*Peek, Mary Katherine. WORDSWORTH IN ENGLAND: STUDIES IN THE HISTORY OF HIS FAME. Bryn Mawr, Pa.: Privately printed, 1943.

> WW's reputation in England from 1793 through the 1920s (with bibliography).

B. EDITIONS

Inasmuch as all the works included in this section are editions or republications of poetry or prose by William Wordsworth, his name will not appear unless it is included in the title or unless the works of one or more other writers also appear in the same volume (in which case each author's name will be included as part of the title).

1. Collected Poetry and Collected Prose

*de Selincourt, Ernest, and Helen Darbishire, eds. THE POETICAL WORKS OF WILLIAM WORDSWORTH. 5 vols. Oxford: Clarendon Press, 1940-49, Rev. 2nd eds. and 2nd impressions (beginning with vol. 2), 1952-- .

> These five volumes, and the de Selincourt-Darbishire edition of THE PRELUDE (see Sec. 3, Individual Titles, below) have con-stituted the standard edition of WW's poetry since the 1940s and will remain the standard insofar as the Cornell Wordsworth (see Parrish, below) does not republish WW's final versions. Still in print, this edition must be in every library that supports study of the Romantic poets.

Dowden, Edward, ed. THE POETICAL WORKS OF WILLIAM WORDSWORTH. 7 vols. London: George Bell and Sons, 1892.

> Valuable introduction, notes, and selected variant readings. The poems are given in WW's arrangement by categories.

George, A[ndrew] J., ed. THE COMPLETE POETICAL WORKS OF WILLIAM WORDSWORTH. Cambridge Edition. Boston: Houghton Mifflin, 1904.

> Arranged in chronological order; outdated by subsequent textual scholarship.

Grosart, A[lexander] B., ed. PROSE WORKS OF WILLIAM WORDSWORTH. 3 vols. London: Edward Moxon, 1876.

> This edition of Grosart and that of Knight (below)--though incomplete and flawed--remained standard texts of WW's prose until the edition of Owen and Smyser (below) was published.

*Hutchinson, Thomas, ed. POETICAL WORKS. New ed., rev. Ernest de Selincourt. Oxford Standard Authors Edition. London: Oxford University Press, 1950.

> Originally published in 1895, this is still the best one-volume collected edition. It lacks notes and the print is too small to make it suitable as a university textbook, however.

Knight, William, ed. THE POETICAL WORKS OF WILLIAM WORDSWORTH. 8 vols. London: Macmillan, 1896.

> Based on Knight's edition of 1882-86. The poems are arranged in chronological order.

_____. PROSE WORKS OF WILLIAM WORDSWORTH. 2 vols. London: Macmillan, 1896.

> Along with Grosart's text (above), this title was a useful stopgap until the publication of the edition by Owen and Smyser, cited below.

Morley, John, ed. THE COMPLETE POETICAL WORKS OF WILLIAM WORDSWORTH. London: Macmillan, 1888.

> The text, based on Moxon's 1857 edition, is supplemented by the first publication of THE RECLUSE (issued separately by Macmillan the same year). The poems are arranged in chronological order.

*Owen, W[arwick] J.B., and Jane Worthington Smyser, eds. THE PROSE WORKS OF WILLIAM WORDSWORTH. 3 vols. Oxford: Clarendon Press, 1974.

This sterling edition, with accurate texts and copious annotation, supersedes those of Grosart and Knight (both cited above), which will remain on the shelves of scholars only because of the costliness of the new edition.

#Parrish, Stephen [Maxfield], gen. ed. THE CORNELL WORDSWORTH. Ithaca, N.Y.: Cornell University Press, 1975--.

For the first two of twenty or more projected volumes in this edition, see Gill and Parrish (Sec. B.3, Individual Titles, below).

THE POETICAL WORKS OF WILLIAM WORDSWORTH. 6 vols. London: Edward Moxon, 1849-50.

Contains WW's final approved text of his poems, excluding THE RECLUSE, and some thirty minor poems published earlier or remaining in MS.

2. Selected Poetry and Prose

a. GENERAL EDITIONS

Arnold, Matthew, ed. POEMS OF WORDSWORTH. London: Macmillan, 1879.

A selection historically influential largely because of its famous Introduction.

Hartman, Geoffrey H., ed. THE SELECTED POETRY AND PROSE OF WORDSWORTH. Signet Classic Poetry Series. New York: New American Library, 1970.

With an introduction but little annotation.

Peacock, Markham L., Jr., ed. THE CRITICAL OPINIONS OF WILLIAM WORDSWORTH. Baltimore: Johns Hopkins University Press, 1950.

A well-indexed compilation of WW's formal and informal comments on (1) literary and aesthetic problems, (2) other authors and their writings, (3) his own works.

Zall, Paul M., ed. LITERARY CRITICISM OF WILLIAM WORDSWORTH. Regents Critics Series. Lincoln: University of Nebraska Press, 1969.

A full collection of the critical prose.

b. TEACHING EDITIONS

Baker, Carlos, ed. WILLIAM WORDSWORTH'S THE PRELUDE, WITH A SELEC-
TION FROM THE SHORTER POEMS, THE SONNETS, THE RECLUSE AND THE
EXCURSION, AND THREE ESSAYS ON THE ART OF POETRY. Rinehart Edi-
tion. New York: Holt, Rinehart and Winston, 1948; rev. and enl., 1954.

> An inexpensive text outdated by later research and by Stillinger's
> Riverside Edition (see below).

*Stillinger, Jack, ed. WILLIAM WORDSWORTH: SELECTED POEMS AND
PREFACES. Riverside Edition. Boston: Houghton Mifflin, 1965.

> Well-edited selection, with authoritative texts and excellent fac-
> tual notes.

Van Doren, Mark, ed. WILLIAM WORDSWORTH: SELECTED POETRY. Modern Library Edition. New York: Random House, 1950.

> Contains a generous selection of poetry, the Preface to LYRICAL
> BALLADS (with its appendix), and an Introduction by Van Doren,
> but no notes. As a textbook it is inferior to both Baker's and
> Stillinger's editions (cited above).

3. Individual Titles

Comparetti, Alice P., ed. THE WHITE DOE OF RYLSTONE. Ithaca, N.Y.:
Cornell University Press, 1940.

> Based on the 1850 text, with variant readings, notes, and a se-
> lection of critical comment.

*Darbishire, Helen, ed. WORDSWORTH'S POEMS IN TWO VOLUMES, 1807.
Oxford: Clarendon Press, 1914; second edition, 1952.

> Contains a useful introduction and notes.

*de Selincourt, Ernest, ed. THE PRELUDE OR GROWTH OF A POET'S MIND,
EDITED FROM THE MANUSCRIPTS WITH INTRODUCTION, TEXTUAL AND
CRITICAL NOTES. Oxford: Clarendon Press, 1926; second edition, rev.
Helen Darbishire, 1959.

> A landmark in Wordsworthian scholarship, this volume, in which
> the 1805 and 1850 texts of THE PRELUDE are printed on facing
> pages, provided accessible evidence and stimulated wide interest
> in the development of Wordsworth's thought between those dates
> and in the MSS that documented such changes. All later study
> and publication of the "two-book PRELUDE" and so forth derive
> from this (now much corrected and revised) seminal edition.

@ _____ . THE PRELUDE: OR, GROWTH OF A POET'S MIND (TEXT OF 1805). London: Oxford University Press, 1933; rev. impression by Helen Darbishire, 1960; 2nd ed. corrected by Stephen Gill, 1970.

A separate (corrected) publication of the 1805 text published along with the 1850 text in the previous item.

_____ . WORDSWORTH'S GUIDE TO THE LAKES. London: Humphrey Milford, 1926.

The text is that of the fifth edition (1835).

Dicey, A.V., ed. WORDSWORTH'S TRACT ON THE CONVENTION OF CINTRA. London: Humphrey Milford, 1915.

Long the standard separate edition of this important pamphlet.

#Gill, Stephen, ed. THE SALISBURY PLAIN POEMS OF WILLIAM WORDS-WORTH: SALISBURY PLAIN, OR A NIGHT ON SALISBURY PLAIN; ADVENTURES ON SALISBURY PLAIN (INCLUDING THE FEMALE VAGRANT); GUILT AND SORROW; OR, INCIDENTS UPON SALISBURY PLAIN. The Cornell Wordsworth, Vol. 1. Ithaca, N.Y.: Cornell University Press, 1975.

The first of a projected twenty or so volumes of The Cornell Wordsworth (see Parrish, under Sec. B.1, Collected Poetry, above), a wholly new edition of WW's poetry with facsimiles of the MSS of various dates, as well as the versions WW ultimately published.

Littledale, H[arold], ed. WORDSWORTH AND COLERIDGE, LYRICAL BALLADS, 1798. London: Oxford University Press, 1911.

Reprinted frequently, this volume reproduces the poems in their original texts and order.

Maxwell, J[ames] C[outts], ed. THE PRELUDE: A PARALLEL TEXT. Harmondsworth, Engl.: Penguin Books, 1971.

A careful reworking from the MSS of the 1805 and 1850 texts on facing pages, with useful notes.

Merchant, W.M., ed. A GUIDE THROUGH THE DISTRICT OF THE LAKES . . ., WITH ILLUSTRATIONS BY JOHN PIPER. London: Rupert Hart-Davis. 1951.

The text is that of the 1835 "fifth edition."

*Owen, W[arwick] J[ack] B., ed. WORDSWORTH AND COLERIDGE: LYRICAL BALLADS, 1798. London: Oxford University Press, 1967.

Includes a long introduction and notes and commentary on the poems.

#_____. WORDSWORTH'S PREFACE TO LYRICAL BALLADS. Copenhagen: Rosenkilde and Bagger, 1957.

> The standard separate edition of the Preface, with full collations, notes, and detailed commentary.

#Parrish, Stephen [Maxfield], ed. THE PRELUDE, 1798-1799. The Cornell Wordsworth, Vol. 2. Ithaca, N.Y.: Cornell University Press, 1977.

> Presents the earliest MSS of THE PRELUDE, both in facsimile and in transcription, with helpful introduction and notes.

Potts, Abbie Findlay, ed. THE ECCLESIASTICAL SONNETS OF WILLIAM WORDSWORTH. A CRITICAL EDITION. New Haven: Yale University Press, 1922.

> Discusses MSS, dates, structure, and literary analogues.

Reynolds, E.E., ed. THE EXCURSION, PRECEDED BY BOOK 1 OF THE RE-CLUSE. London: Macmillan, 1935.

4. Textual Sources and Studies

Jordan, John E. "The Hewing of PETER BELL." SEL, 7 (1967), 559-603.

> A detailed analysis of the transformations of WW's poem through six surviving MSS and published textual variants from 1819 through 1845.

Woof, Robert S. "Wordsworth's Poetry and Stuart's Newspapers: 1797-1803." STUDIES IN BIBLIOGRAPHY, 15 (1962), 149-89.

> An important checklist and analysis of WW's poems printed in the MORNING POST and the COURIER, with discussion of STC's role in revising as well as transmitting them. Woof also reassigns the authorship of a few poems.

C. BIOGRAPHICAL SOURCES AND STUDIES

1. Primary Documents

Field, Barron. MEMOIRS OF WORDSWORTH. Ed. Geoffrey Little. Sydney, Australia: Sydney University Press, 1975.

> Late-published memoir written in 1839 by Field (1786-1846), a friend of Leigh Hunt as well as WW.

Healey, George H. WORDSWORTH'S POCKET NOTEBOOK. Ithaca, N.Y.: Cornell University Press, 1942.

Lists of appointments and scraps of verse jotted during visits to London, Cambridge, and Oxford, 1839-40.

Hutchinson, Sara. THE LETTERS OF SARA HUTCHINSON, FROM 1800 TO 1835. Ed. Kathleen Coburn. Toronto: University of Toronto Press, 1954.

A useful, well edited and indexed source of news about the WW household (and STC).

*Jordan, John E. DE QUINCEY TO WORDSWORTH: A BIOGRAPHY OF A RELATIONSHIP, WITH THE LETTERS OF THOMAS DE QUINCEY TO THE WORDSWORTH FAMILY. Berkeley: University of California Press, 1962.

A valuable resource and analysis for the study of the Wordsworths and De Quincey.

*Reed, Mark L. WORDSWORTH: THE CHRONOLOGY OF THE EARLY YEARS, 1770-1799. Cambridge: Harvard University Press, 1967.

Drawing upon all sources, published and unpublished, available to him, Reed has assembled as nearly as he can a day-by-day, week-by-week, record of WW's life, reading, and writing. See also the sequel, cited below.

* _____. WORDSWORTH: THE CHRONOLOGY OF THE MIDDLE YEARS, 1800-1815. Cambridge: Harvard University Press, 1975.

Continues the valuable work of the previous volume.

Robinson, Crabb. CORRESPONDENCE OF CRABB ROBINSON WITH THE WORDSWORTH CIRCLE. Ed. Edith J. Morley. 2 vols. Oxford: Clarendon Press, 1927.

Wordsworth, Dorothy. JOURNALS OF DOROTHY WORDSWORTH. Ed. Ernest de Selincourt. 2 vols. London: Macmillan, 1941.

This edition replaces an earlier two-volume edition by Knight, but its text of the Grasmere Journal has been superseded by Moorman's text (see Sec. C.2, Biographies, below).

* _____. JOURNALS OF DOROTHY WORDSWORTH. THE ALFOXDEN JOURNAL 1798; THE GRASMERE JOURNALS 1800-1803. Introd. Helen Darbishire. Ed. Mary Moorman. London: Oxford University Press, 1971; corrected 1973, 1974.

This paperback text of the most important journals supersedes earlier editions by Knight, de Selincourt, and Darbishire, all of which omitted some crucial passages in the Grasmere Journals.

#Wordsworth, John. THE LETTERS OF JOHN WORDSWORTH. Ed. Carl H. Ketcham. Ithaca, N.Y.: Cornell University Press, 1969.

> Provides the fullest account of the life and death-by-shipwreck of WW's favorite brother, as well as letters between 1792 and 1805.

#Wordsworth, Mary (née Hutchinson). LETTERS OF MARY WORDSWORTH, 1800-1855. Ed. Mary E. Burton. Oxford: Clarendon Press, 1958.

> Though generally impersonal, these surviving letters add details and facts about daily life in WW's home.

*Wordsworth, William, and Dorothy Wordsworth. THE LETTERS OF WILLIAM AND DOROTHY WORDSWORTH. Ed. Ernest de Selincourt. Part 1: EARLY LETTERS (1787-1805). Oxford: Clarendon Press, 1935; rev. ed. by Chester L. Shaver, 1967 as THE EARLY YEARS, 1787-1805. Part 2: 1806-1820. 2 vols. Oxford: Clarendon Press, 1937; rev. ed. by Mary Moorman and Alan G. Hill, 2 vols., 1969-70, as THE MIDDLE YEARS, 1806-1820. Part 3: 1821-1850. 3 vols. Oxford: Clarendon Press, 1937; rev. ed. by Alan G. Hill, 4 vols., to be published as THE LATER YEARS, 1821-1850.

2. Biographies

#Harper, George McLean. WILLIAM WORDSWORTH: HIS LIFE, WORKS, AND INFLUENCE. 2 vols. New York: Charles Scribner's Sons, 1916.

> For a generation the standard biography, this work still bears comparison with Moorman's (below), though the latter incorporates many recently discovered facts.

*Moorman, Mary. WILLIAM WORDSWORTH: A BIOGRAPHY. Vol. 1: THE EARLY YEARS, 1770-1803. Vol. 2: THE LATER YEARS, 1803-1850. Oxford: Clarendon Press, 1957, 1965.

> The standard biography, written with historical accuracy and fidelity but lacking in appreciation of poetic effects or psychological implications.

Wordsworth, Christopher. MEMOIRS OF WILLIAM WORDSWORTH. 2 vols. London: Edward Moxon, 1851.

> This "official" biography by WW's nephew suppresses or omits almost every facet of the poet's character except his late piety and dignity.

3. Studies of a Period or an Aspect of WW's Life

Beatty, Frederika. WILLIAM WORDSWORTH OF DOVE COTTAGE: A STUDY OF THE POET'S MOST PRODUCTIVE DECADE, JUNE 1797-MAY 1807. New York: Bookman Associates, 1964.

Blanchard, Frances. PORTRAITS OF WORDSWORTH. London: George Allen and Unwin, 1959.

> Reproduces sixty-three of eighty-seven known portraits of WW, with notes on the artist and occasion of each.

*de Selincourt, Ernest. DOROTHY WORDSWORTH. Oxford: Clarendon Press, 1933.

> The standard biography. See also Maclean, below.

Douglas, Wallace W. WORDSWORTH: THE CONSTRUCTION OF A PERSONALITY. Kent, Ohio: Kent State University Press, 1968.

> A psychological study based on the work of Erik Erikson and Melanie Klein.

Fink, Z[era] S. THE EARLY WORDSWORTHIAN MILIEU: A NOTEBOOK OF CHRISTOPHER WORDSWORTH WITH A FEW ENTRIES BY WILLIAM WORDSWORTH. New York: Oxford University Press, 1958.

> Prints, with extensive commentary, a twenty-seven page notebook kept when WW was fourteen and fifteen years old.

Golden, Morris. THE SELF OBSERVED: SWIFT, JOHNSON, WORDSWORTH. Baltimore: Johns Hopkins University Press, 1972.

> An intelligent, readable comparison of the qualities of self-awareness in three dissimilar personalities.

Harper, George McLean. WORDSWORTH'S FRENCH DAUGHTER. Princeton: Princeton: Princeton University Press, 1921.

> The first detailed account of Caroline, WW's daughter by Annette Vallon. See also Legouis, below.

#Heath, William. WORDSWORTH AND COLERIDGE: A STUDY OF THEIR LITERARY RELATIONS IN 1801-1802. Oxford: Clarendon Press, 1970.

> A detailed analysis of the personal interactions, among WW, STC, Dorothy W., Sara C., and Sara and Mary Hutchinson, in the light of their literary consequences.

Jay, Eileen. WORDSWORTH AT COLTHOUSE: AN ACCOUNT OF THE POET'S BOYHOOD YEARS SPENT IN THE REMOTE LAKELAND HAMLET OF COLTHOUSE. Kendal, Engl.: Titus Wilson and Son, 1970.

#Legouis, Emile. THE EARLY LIFE OF WILLIAM WORDSWORTH, 1770-1798. Trans. J.W. Matthews. London: J.M. Dent, 1897; rpt. with additions, 1921, 1932.

Translated from the French first edition (Paris, 1896), this book remains a major study of its chosen area.

_____. WILLIAM WORDSWORTH AND ANNETTE VALLON. London: J.M. Dent, 1922.

Extends the research of Harper into WW's French romance.

Maclean, Catherine M. DOROTHY WORDSWORTH, THE EARLY YEARS. London: Chatto and Windus, 1932.

More "popular" in presentation than de Selincourt's biography of Dorothy, this remains a sensitive attempt to interpret Dorothy's character.

Meyer, George Wilbur. WORDSWORTH'S FORMATIVE YEARS. Ann Arbor: University of Michigan Press, 1943.

Emphasizes the elements of social protest in WW's early poetry, while contrasting the hard reality of WW's early life with the imaginative reconstruction of it in THE PRELUDE.

#Onorato, Richard J. THE CHARACTER OF THE POET: WORDSWORTH IN THE PRELUDE. Princeton: Princeton University Press, 1971.

An important psychoanalytic study of WW, as he reveals himself through his poetry--particularly THE PRELUDE.

Rawnsley, Hardwicke Drummond. REMINISCENCES OF WORDSWORTH AMONG THE PEASANTRY OF WESTMORLAND. Introd. Geoffrey Tillotson. London: Dillon's University Bookshop, 1968.

Reprinted from LAKE COUNTRY SKETCHES (1903).

#Schneider, Ben Ross, Jr. WORDSWORTH'S CAMBRIDGE EDUCATION. Cambridge: Cambridge University Press, 1957.

A detailed account of Cambridge during the 1780s and 1790s centered on the years of WW's residence there, as well as of his reaction to his experience of it.

Sergeant, Howard. THE CUMBERLAND WORDSWORTH. London: Williams and Northgate, 1950.

Centers on the period before WW's marriage and on relations among WW, Dorothy Wordsworth, and STC.

Thompson, T[homas] W. WORDSWORTH'S HAWKSHEAD. Ed. Robert Woof. London: Oxford University Press, 1970.

A close analysis of the site of WW's school years and crucial
vacation times.

Todd, F[rancis] M. POLITICS AND THE POET: A STUDY OF WORDSWORTH.
London: Methuen, 1957.

Traces the course of WW's political thought from his university
days to his later years.

D. CRITICISM

1. General Studies

*Bateson, F[rederick] W. WORDSWORTH: A RE-INTERPRETATION. London:
Longmans, 1954; 2nd ed., 1956.

A major study of aesthetic and personal influence in WW's poetry,
especially the relations of WW's poetry to his feelings for his
sister.

Batho, Edith C. THE LATER WORDSWORTH. Cambridge: Cambridge University Press, 1933.

The first book after the revelations of Harper and Legouis to argue
for essential continuity between WW's early and late poetry.

#Beatty, Arthur. WILLIAM WORDSWORTH: HIS DOCTRINE AND ART IN
THEIR HISTORICAL RELATIONS. Madison: University of Wisconsin Press,
1922.

A landmark study which first called attention to the influence on
WW of David Hartley and the British sensationalist philosophers
and psychologists.

Drabble, Margaret. WORDSWORTH. New York: Arco, 1969.

A brief, sensible, students' introduction to WW's life and poetry.

Garber, Frederick. WORDSWORTH AND THE POETRY OF ENCOUNTER.
Urbana: University of Illinois Press, 1971.

Explores the poetry thematically in terms of WW's "object-con-
sciousness," his difficult epistemological struggle to "know" the
people and objects outside himself, and emphasizes the private
nature of WW's vision.

#Groom, Bernard. THE UNITY OF WORDSWORTH'S POETRY. London: Mac-
millan, 1966.

Emphasizing the organic development of WW's later poetry from the work of 1798-1807, Groom is strong on WW's religious and moral opinions.

*Hartman, Geoffrey H. WORDSWORTH'S POETRY, 1787-1814. New Haven: Yale University Press, 1964.

An important study that has influenced all subsequent interpretations of WW's poetry either directly or through reactions to its complex (and essentially irreducible) argument. Briefly, Hartman sees WW's problem (and the subject of his poetry) as a need both to identify with the lives of common humanity and natural creation and to know himself transcendent and special--an observer of such struggles from a remote height.

Herford, C[harles] H. WORDSWORTH. London: Routledge, 1930.

A brief, sound (if dated) biography and critical analysis, concentrating on the years before 1815.

Jones, James. THE EGOTISTICAL SUBLIME: A HISTORY OF WORDSWORTH'S IMAGINATION. London: Chatto and Windus, 1954.

Traces WW's poetry through three stages--the early poetry of "Solitude and Relationship," a period of indecision, and a later phase of "The Baptised Imagination."

@Noyes, Russell. WILLIAM WORDSWORTH. Twayne's English Authors Series. New York: Twayne, 1971.

A reliable introduction to WW's life and work for the student and general reader.

Purkis, John. A PREFACE TO WORDSWORTH. London: Longmans, 1970.

A student's handbook enhanced by good illustrations.

#Rader, Melvin M. WORDSWORTH: A PHILOSOPHICAL APPROACH. Oxford: Clarendon Press, 1967.

Explores the influence of Plato, the British empirical philosophers, Hartley, and others, in Wordsworth's poetry and subsumes Rader's study entitled PRESIDING IDEAS IN WORDSWORTH'S POETRY (1931).

Read, Herbert. WORDSWORTH. London: Jonathan Cape, 1930.

A series of lectures emphasizing WW's poetic and spiritual collapse as the result of his "betrayal" of Annette Vallon and the French Revolution.

#Salvesen, Christopher. THE LANDSCAPE OF MEMORY: A STUDY OF WORDSWORTH'S POETRY. London: Arnold, 1965.

> A perceptive analysis of the role of memory in WW's poetry through THE WHITE DOE OF RYLSTONE.

Sperry, W[illiam] L. WORDSWORTH'S ANTI-CLIMAX. Cambridge: Harvard University Press, 1935.

> An important study of religion, philosophy, and politics in WW's life and poetry, emphasizing the later falling off of his powers.

*Stallknecht, Newton P. STRANGE SEAS OF THOUGHT: STUDIES IN WIL-LIAM WORDSWORTH'S PHILOSOPHY OF MAN AND NATURE. Durham, N.C.: Duke University Press, 1945; rpt. Bloomington: Indiana University Press, 1958.

> An important study relating WW's early philosophical orientation to Plotinus, Spinoza, Kant, and, especially, Boehme. Stall-knecht regrets WW's retreat from faith in the schöne seele.

Weaver, Bennett. WORDSWORTH: POET OF UNCONQUERABLE MIND, A COLLECTION OF ESSAYS ON WORDSWORTH'S POETRY. Ed. Charles L. Proudfit. Ann Arbor, Mich.: George Wahr, 1965.

> Collects Weaver's seven important essays on WW from the period 1934-40 and the title essay of 1960.

*Woodring, Carl [R]. WORDSWORTH. Riverside Studies in Literature. Boston: Houghton Mifflin, 1963; corrected ed. Cambridge: Harvard University Press, 1968.

> The best introduction for students and nonspecialist teachers, this study also contains mature and original critical observations of value to specialist scholars.

2. Studies of Particular Works, Periods, and Themes

Abercrombie, Lascelles. THE ART OF WORDSWORTH. Ed. Ralph Abercrombie. London: Oxford University Press, 1952.

> Includes five lectures given in 1935 and a chapter on PETER BELL. Besides dealing with matters of structure and diction, Abercrombie traces WW's decline to his inability to live with the solitude that nourished his mystical experiences with nature.

Ashton, Thomas L. "THE THORN: Wordsworth's Insensitive Plant." HUNT-INGTON LIBRARY QUARTERLY, 35 (1972), 171-87.

Explicates the unity between the narrating sea-captain's superstitious nature and the story of Martha Ray herself.

Averill, James H. "Suffering and Calm in Wordsworth's Early Poetry." PMLA, 91 (1976), 223-34.

Using WW's early poems like "The Ruined Cottage," Averill explores the significance of the contrasts between tales of human suffering and scenes of natural calm and beauty and relates these contrasts to a theory of catharsis.

Bauer, N. Stephen. "Early Burlesques and Parodies of Wordsworth." JEGP, 74 (1975), 553-69.

A checklist, with descriptive introduction, of forty-five British parodies and burlesques, 1801-36.

Brantley, Richard E. WORDSWORTH'S "NATURAL METHODISM." New Haven: Yale University Press, 1975.

Arguing that Evangelical Protestant modes of thought and diction are the most essential features of WW's poetry, Brantley first traces the Wesleyan influence on WW and briefly examines THE PRELUDE, THE EXCURSION, and some shorter poems.

Broughton, Leslie N. THE THEOCRITEAN ELEMENT IN THE WORKS OF WILLIAM WORDSWORTH. Halle, Germany: Max Niemeyer, 1920.

Relates WW to the classical pastoral tradition.

#Burton, Mary E. THE ONE WORDSWORTH. Chapel Hill: University of North Carolina Press, 1942.

Examines closely the textual changes between the 1805-06 and the 1850 versions of THE PRELUDE and concludes that the older WW was a better man, as well as "a vastly better poet than his younger self" (p. 227). Such a conclusion casts suspicion on the methodology employed.

#Chard, Leslie F., II. DISSENTING REPUBLICAN: WORDSWORTH'S EARLY LIFE AND THOUGHT IN THEIR POLITICAL CONTEXT. The Hague: Mouton, 1972.

Explores WW's biography and political thought of the 1790s in connection with the traditions of the English Dissenters and especially the circle of Joseph Johnson the publisher.

Clarke, C[olin] C. ROMANTIC PARADOX: AN ESSAY ON THE POETRY OF WORDSWORTH. London: Routledge and Kegan Paul, 1962.

A brief exploration, through WW's diction, of the way he perceived the world around him.

Coe, Charles N. WORDSWORTH AND THE LITERATURE OF TRAVEL. New York: Bookman Associates, 1953.

Studies WW's reading and use of travel books, and adds useful lists of those reflected in WW's poetry.

#Curtis, Jared R. WORDSWORTH'S EXPERIMENTS WITH TRADITION. THE LYRIC POEMS OF 1802, WITH TEXTS OF THE POEMS BASED ON EARLY MANUSCRIPTS. Ithaca, N.Y.: Cornell University Press, 1971.

A perceptive examination of WW's struggles of 1802, as shown in the various versions of the great poems written then.

Danby, John F. THE SIMPLE WORDSWORTH: STUDIES IN THE POEMS 1797-1807. London: Routledge and Kegan Paul, 1960.

A brief and rather thin study that gives more than ordinary attention to THE WHITE DOE OF RYLSTONE.

@Darbishire, Helen. THE POET WORDSWORTH. Oxford: Clarendon Press, 1950.

A slim, learned volume derived from the Clark Lectures (1949) on the poetry of 1798-1808 (including THE PRELUDE).

de Selincourt, Ernest. THE EARLY WORDSWORTH. English Association, Presidential Address. Oxford: Oxford University Press, 1936.

A valuable brief summary of a period by one of the most knowledgeable WW scholars.

Dings, John Garetson. THE MIND IN ITS PLACE: WORDSWORTH, "MICHAEL," AND THE POETRY OF 1800. Salzburg: University of Salzburg Studies in English, 1973.

Intelligent but unsustained examination of WW and his poems of 1800, including especially "Home at Grasmere."

Durrant, Geoffrey. WILLIAM WORDSWORTH. Cambridge: Cambridge University Press, 1969.

Treats, at a level designed for British secondary schools, poems written by WW between 1798 and 1805.

_____. WORDSWORTH AND THE GREAT SYSTEM: A STUDY OF WORDSWORTH'S POETIC UNIVERSE. Cambridge: Cambridge University Press, 1970.

Examines WW's interest in Newtonian science and its appearances in his poetry.

Eggenschwiler, David. "Wordsworth's DISCORDIA DISCORS." SiR, 8 (1969), 78-94.

A study of "shifting perspectives" in WW's poetry, centering on "Resolution and Independence" and the Immortality Ode.

Fausset, Hugh l'Anson. THE LOST LEADER: A STUDY OF WORDSWORTH. London: Jonathan Cape, 1933.

Fausset's study of WW's early years leads him to conclude (contra Batho, in Sec. D.1, above) that WW's desertion of Annette Vallon and of revolutionary France did split his career.

#Ferry, David. THE LIMITS OF MORTALITY: AN ESSAY ON WORDSWORTH'S MAJOR POEMS. Middletown, Conn.: Wesleyan University Press, 1959.

An influential, if controversial, study suggesting that WW preferred nature to human beings because he could not cope with the fact of death.

Gates, Barbara. "Wordsworth's Symbolic White Doe: 'The Power of History in the Mind.'" CRITICISM, 17 (1975), 234-45.

Greenbie, Marjorie L. Barstow. WORDSWORTH'S THEORY OF POETIC DIC-TION: A STUDY OF THE HISTORICAL AND PERSONAL BACKGROUND OF THE LYRICAL BALLADS. New Haven: Yale University Press, 1917.

Examines WW's theory and practice in relation to older theories and to STC's impact on WW's thinking.

#Grob, Alan. THE PHILOSOPHIC MIND: A STUDY OF WORDSWORTH'S POETRY AND THOUGHT, 1797-1805. Columbus: Ohio State University Press, 1973.

An important study emphasizing the empirical elements of WW's thought and their ramifications in his early poetry.

#Havens, Raymond D. THE MIND OF A POET: A STUDY OF WORDSWORTH'S THOUGHT WITH PARTICULAR REFERENCE TO THE PRELUDE. Baltimore: Johns Hopkins University Press, 1941.

This title is sometimes bound in two volumes. The first section (or volume) is an important study of WW's thought, while the second part (or volume) provides a section-by-section, line-by-line commentary on THE PRELUDE. Though valuable on some passages, the study is weakened by Havens' failure to discern the relevance of other details to the poem's overall design.

#Heffernan, James A.W. WORDSWORTH'S THEORY OF POETRY: THE TRANS-
FORMING IMAGINATION. Ithaca, N.Y.: Cornell University Press, 1969.

A substantial treatment of WW's poetics, concentrating on the
change in emphasis after 1800 from "feeling" to "imagination."

Hill, Alan G. "New Light on THE EXCURSION." ARIEL, 5 (1974), 37-47.

Points out important structural parallels between WW's poem and
the dialogue OCTAVIUS by Minucius Felix, an early Christian
apologist whose book was in WW's library.

Huxley, Aldous L. "Wordsworth in the Tropics." YALE REVIEW, 18 (1929),
672-83. Rpt. in Huxley's DO WHAT YOU WILL (New York, 1930).

Huxley asserts that WW failed to comprehend the dangerous and
ruthless aspects of nature that he might have learned in the tropics. The essay epitomizes the kind of attack that the Romantics
encountered when their personal philosophies, derived from individual experiences, had been elevated by their admirers into rules
for all human conduct.

#Jacobus, Mary. TRADITION AND EXPERIMENT IN WORDSWORTH'S LYRICAL
BALLADS (1798). Oxford: Clarendon Press, 1976.

A substantial study of the past traditions embodied in LYRICAL
BALLADS and of the original departures in WW's early poems.

Johnson, Lee M. WORDSWORTH AND THE SONNET. Anglistica, No. 29.
Copenhagen: Rosenkilde and Bagger, 1973.

The most detailed study of its subject, marred by an inadequate
perspective on the history of the sonnet in the eighteenth century
and inadequate on WW's sonnets written before 1802.

#Johnston, Kenneth R. "'Home at Grasmere': Reclusive Song." SiR, 14 (1975),
1-28.

Excellent analysis (and argument with earlier critics) by a leading
younger Wordsworthian.

*Jordan, John E. WHY THE LYRICAL BALLADS? Berkeley: University of
California Press, 1976.

An important exploration of the context and creation of the landmark publication.

* _____. "Wordsworth's Humor." PMLA, 73 (1958), 81-93.

The best available study of WW's early humor and the change to
sobriety that marked his later development.

King, Alec. WORDSWORTH AND THE ARTIST'S VISION: AN ESSAY IN INTERPRETATION. London: Athlone [University of London] Press, 1966.

> A hortatory appreciation of WW's modern relevance.

#Kroeber, Karl. ROMANTIC LANDSCAPE VISION: CONSTABLE AND WORDSWORTH. Madison: University of Wisconsin Press, 1975.

> An imaginative, pioneering comparison of the shared vision of artists working in dissimilar mediums.

Lacey, Norman. WORDSWORTH'S VIEW OF NATURE AND ITS ETHICAL CONSEQUENCES. Cambridge: Cambridge University Press, 1948.

> Argues that WW failed to value properly his own mystical experience of nature, partly because he overvalued Dorothy's less reflective attitude.

#Lindenberger, Herbert. ON WORDSWORTH'S PRELUDE. Princeton: Princeton University Press, 1963.

> An important volume containing a series of essays that approach THE PRELUDE from various angles and cohere into a rounded treatment.

Lyon, Judson Stanley. THE EXCURSION: A STUDY. New Haven: Yale University Press, 1950.

> The history of the poem's composition, its source, analogues, style, meaning, and reputation.

McConnell, Frank D. THE CONFESSIONAL IMAGINATION: A READING OF WORDSWORTH'S PRELUDE. Baltimore: Johns Hopkins University Press, 1974.

> Places THE PRELUDE in the tradition of philosophic literature evolving from St. Augustine's CONFESSIONS.

McFarland, Thomas. "Creative Fantasy and Matter-of-Fact Reality in Wordsworth's Poetry." JEGP, 75 (1976), 1-24.

> Explores WW's dedication to facts and to literalness in three directions, showing how (1) WW's rejection of "pure imagination" occasionally weakens his poetry, (2) an urge toward fantasy was often held in creative tension with the urge to fact, (3) WW sometimes is able to treat reality "under the conditions of fantasy."

Marsh, Florence G. WORDSWORTH'S IMAGERY: A STUDY IN POETIC VISION. New Haven: Yale University Press, 1952.

Explores imagery in general as well as WW's images of light and
darkness, people, sounds, water, and architecture, and WW's own
ideas of imagery.

#Miles, Josephine. WORDSWORTH AND THE VOCABULARY OF EMOTION.
Berkeley: University of California Press, 1942.

Based on quantitative analysis of WW's use of various emotionally
charged words, this study relates changes in WW's critical reputation to fashions in the acceptance of such a vocabulary.

Morken, Joel. "Structure and Meaning in THE PRELUDE, Book V." PMLA,
87 (1972), 246-54.

WW's reaction against contemporary educational theorists.

Murray, Roger N. WORDSWORTH'S STYLE: FIGURES AND THEMES IN THE
LYRICAL BALLADS OF 1800. Lincoln: University of Nebraska Press, 1967.

Detailed analysis of such topics as word-repetition, transitive and
intransitive verbs, synecdoche, and metaphor in the 1800 volume.

Noyes, Russell. WORDSWORTH AND THE ART OF LANDSCAPE. Bloomington: Indiana University Press, 1968.

Provides (illustrated) historical surveys of landscape painting, landscape gardening, and the tradition of scenic or picturesque tourism
before concluding with a chapter devoted to landscapes in WW's
poetry.

Ogden, John T. "The Power of Distance in Wordsworth's PRELUDE." PMLA,
88 (1973), 246-59.

WW's use of physical distance (complementing his use of memory
of the past) to achieve philosophical detachment or, by moving to
a close-up, to break the detachment and achieve humane sympathy.

_____. "The Structure of Imaginative Experience in Wordsworth's PRELUDE."
WC, 6 (1975), 290-98.

A significant exploration of four stages in the process by which
WW's mind interacts with the external world.

Owen, W[arwick] J[ack] B. WORDSWORTH AS CRITIC. Toronto: University
of Toronto Press, 1969.

The fullest and most balanced account of Wordsworth's critical
theory.

#Parrish, Stephen Maxfield. THE ART OF THE LYRICAL BALLADS. Cambridge: Harvard University Press, 1973.

> Integrates Parrish's important studies of WW and STC from 1957 through 1970, and is, along with the books by Jordan and Jacobus (above), one of the three best specialized books on the poems published in LYRICAL BALLADS.

Perkins, David. WORDSWORTH AND THE POETRY OF SINCERITY. Cambridge: Harvard University Press, 1964.

> Argues that WW failed to communicate with a broader audience because he was unable to reconcile the demands of "sincerity" and the rhetorical techniques of "art."

Potts, Abbie Findlay. THE ELEGIAC MODE: POETIC FORM IN WORDSWORTH AND OTHER ELEGISTS. Ithaca, N.Y.: Cornell University Press, 1967.

> Studies PETER BELL, the Lucy poems, THE PRELUDE, and THE EXCURSION in the light of a tradition stretching from the ancients to Dylan Thomas.

* _____. WORDSWORTH'S PRELUDE: A STUDY OF ITS LITERARY FORM. Ithaca, N.Y.: Cornell University Press, 1953.

> The best single study of literary influences and echoes in THE PRELUDE.

Pulos, C[ristos] E. "The Unity of Wordsworth's Immortality Ode." SiR, 13 (1974), 179-88.

> Argues for the unity of the poem by analyzing WW's use of the imagery of "light" and "visionary gleam."

Ramsey, Jonathan. "Seeing and Perceiving in Wordsworth's AN EVENING WALK." MLQ, 36 (1975), 272-92.

> The psychology and epistemology of WW's early poems related to his maturing perspective.

Reed, Mark L. "Wordsworth, Coleridge, and the Plan of the LYRICAL BALLADS." UNIVERSITY OF TORONTO QUARTERLY, 34 (1965), 238-53.

> Argues that STC's retrospective talk of a joint enterprise was not accurate and that WW was chiefly responsible for both the poems and the theory behind LYRICAL BALLADS.

Ruoff, Gene W. "Religious Implications of Wordsworth's Imagination." SiR, 12 (1973), 670-92.

Arguing that recent commentaries have treated WW's theory of the imagination as incoherent or timid because they have judged him by standards applicable to STC or Blake, Ruoff examines WW's theory of the imagination in terms of "modern phenomenological enquiries into . . . mystical experience and language." He finds that WW respected the imagination as a limited, fallible tool, not as a means of apprehending transcendental truths.

#Scoggins, James. IMAGINATION AND FANCY: COMPLEMENTARY MODES IN THE POETRY OF WORDSWORTH. Lincoln: University of Nebraska Press, 1966.

A detailed study of WW's changing use of the terms and his changing principles of classifying his poems.

Shackford, Martha H[ale]. WORDSWORTH'S INTEREST IN PAINTERS AND PICTURES. Wellesley, Mass.: Wellesley Press, 1945.

Includes a valuable chronological list (now incomplete because of newly published letters) of WW's mentions of painters.

*Sheats, Paul D. THE MAKING OF WORDSWORTH'S POETRY, 1785–1798. Cambridge: Harvard University Press, 1973.

An important study of WW's early poetry; reviewers have generally described it as the best yet published.

#[Smyser], Jane Worthington. WORDSWORTH'S READING OF ROMAN PROSE. New Haven: Yale University Press, 1946.

An important examination of Roman stoic thought in WW's life and art.

Storch, R[udolph] F. "Wordsworth and Constable." SiR, 5 (1966), 121–38.

Relates WW and the painter through their central concern with motion and calm. For the development of related ideas, see Kroeber, ROMANTIC LANDSCAPE VISION: CONSTABLE AND WORDSWORTH, above.

Thomas, Gordon Kent. WORDSWORTH'S DIRGE AND PROMISE: NAPOLEON, WELLINGTON, AND THE CONVENTION OF CINTRA. Lincoln: University of Nebraska Press, 1971.

Examines WW's tract on the Convention of Cintra in connection with his supposedly growing conservatism and finds no sudden change in his thought.

Trilling, Lionel. "The Immortality Ode." In his THE LIBERAL IMAGINATION. New York: Viking, 1950. Pp. 123-43.

> An important and influential reading.

Welsford, Enid. SALISBURY PLAIN: A STUDY IN THE DEVELOPMENT OF WORDSWORTH'S MIND AND ART. Oxford: Blackwell, 1966.

> Examines in detail the poems growing out of WW's wanderings near Stonehenge in 1793.

Wesling, Donald. WORDSWORTH AND THE ADEQUACY OF LANDSCAPE. New York: Barnes and Noble, 1970.

> A brief study that traces WW's increasing humanization of his land-scapes, adding first philosophical meditation and then human narratives.

Wiener, David. "Wordsworth, Books, and the Growth of a Poet's Mind." JEGP, 74 (1975), 209-20.

> Attempts to place the discussion of books in THE PRELUDE, V, within the context of WW's thought.

Wilkie, Brian. "Wordsworth and the Tradition of the Avant-Garde." JEGP, 72 (1973), 194-222.

> A wide-ranging, stimulating essay that places WW in (or at the head of) the tradition of valuing novelty and originality for (among other things) its own sake.

#Wlecke, Albert O. WORDSWORTH AND THE SUBLIME. Berkeley: University of California Press, 1973.

> A phenomenological approach to WW's conception of the sublime.

#Wordsworth, Jonathan. THE MUSIC OF HUMANITY: A CRITICAL STUDY OF WORDSWORTH'S RUINED COTTAGE, INCORPORATING TEXTS FROM A MANUSCRIPT OF 1799-1800. London: Nelson, 1969.

> Reedits in its original form one of WW's best early poems and comments on its implications.

Wordsworth, Jonathan, and Stephen Gill. "The Two-Part PRELUDE OF 1798-99." JEGP, 72 (1973), 503-25.

> A detailed discussion of the earliest "complete" version of THE PRELUDE recoverable from WW's MSS; the text has since published in the third edition of the NORTON ANTHOLOGY OF ENGLISH LITERATURE, ed. M.H. Abrams et al.

3. Collections of Miscellaneous Essays

@Abrams, M[eyer] H[oward], ed. WORDSWORTH: A COLLECTION OF CRITI-
CAL ESSAYS. Englewood Cliffs, N.J.: Prentice-Hall, 1972.

> Reprints portions of books by John Jones, Cleanth Brooks, Ferry,
> Perkins, Danby, Bloom, Hartman, Jonathan Wordsworth, and
> Abrams himself, as well as articles by Trilling, Mayo, Parrish,
> de Man, and Neil H. Hertz.

Clutterbuck, Nesta, ed. WILLIAM WORDSWORTH 1770-1970: ESSAYS OF
GENERAL INTEREST ON WORDSWORTH AND HIS TIME. Grasmere, Engl.:
Trustees of Dove Cottage, 1970.

> Twelve brief essays and poems in forty-five pages.

@Davis, Jack, ed. DISCUSSIONS OF WILLIAM WORDSWORTH. Boston: D.C.
Heath, 1964.

> Reprints comments on WW's poetry by thirteen critics: Coleridge,
> Arnold, A.C. Bradley, Willey, Abrams, Leavis, Davie, Read,
> Norman Maclean, Paul Goodman, Trilling, Hartman, and John
> Jones.

de Selincourt, Ernest. WORDSWORTHIAN AND OTHER STUDIES. Oxford:
Clarendon Press, 1947.

Dunklin, Gilbert T., ed. WORDSWORTH: CENTENARY STUDIES. Princeton:
Princeton University Press, 1951.

> The positive essays--by Pottle, Griggs, John Crowe Ransom, B.
> Ifor Evans, Lionel Trilling, and Sperry--are, perhaps, less interest-
> ing today than Douglas Bush's egregious "minority report" attack-
> ing WW because he wasn't a Christian humanist like Milton.

Garrod, H[eathcote] W. WORDSWORTH: LECTURES AND ESSAYS. 2nd ed.
Oxford: Clarendon Press, 1927.

> Miscellaneous essays, once influential but now rather dull to any
> but beginning students.

Jones, Alun R., and William Tydeman, eds. WORDSWORTH, LYRICAL BAL-
LADS: A CASEBOOK. London: Macmillan, 1972.

> Includes texts of the poems and commentary by WW, STC, Southey,
> Burney, John Wilson, and Arnold, as well as seven twentieth-cen-
> tury essays or parts of books.

McMaster, Graham, ed. WILLIAM WORDSWORTH: A CRITICAL ANTHOLOGY. Penguin Critical Anthologies. Harmondsworth, Engl.: Penguin Books, 1972.

> Reprints excerpts from ten twentieth-century essays and books by Lyon, Donald Davie, Bateson, John Jones, Mayo, W.W. Robson, Ferry, Jonathan Bishop, Hartman, Jonathan Wordsworth, and Christopher Ricks.

Montgomery, Marion. THE REFLECTIVE JOURNEY TOWARD ORDER. Athens: University of Georgia Press, 1973.

> A series of essays chiefly on WW's poetry, seeing it as a bridge between Dante and twentieth-century writers.

#Thomson, A.W., ed. WORDSWORTH'S MIND AND ART: ESSAYS. Edinburgh: Oliver and Boyd, 1969.

> Besides reprints of papers or portions of books by William Minto, Roger Sharrock, Bostetter, D.G. James, and E.A. Horsman, there are five original essays by Donald Davie, Owen, Anthony Conran, Thomson, and Bernard Blackstone.

*Wordsworth, Jonathan, ed. BICENTENARY WORDSWORTH STUDIES IN MEMORY OF JOHN ALBAN FINCH. Ithaca, N.Y.: Cornell University Press, 1970.

> An important collection, reprinting one article by Finch and publishing original essays and studies by Finch (2), Parrish, Woof, Ford T. Swetnam, Jr., Moorman, Gill, Abrams, Jacobus, Basil Willey, Reed, David Pirie (on STC), Jordan, Carol Landon, Healey, Robert Osborn, Beth Darlington, and Jonathan Wordsworth.

Chapter 4
SAMUEL TAYLOR COLERIDGE (1772-1834)

Because the creative lives of STC and WW were so closely intertwined, many titles in the previous chapter are useful to the study of STC, just as a number here are relevant to WW. The reader must glance over the titles in both chapters in order to determine which may be relevant to his particular area of study.

A. CONCORDANCES, BIBLIOGRAPHIES, AND STUDIES OF REPUTATION AND INFLUENCE
1. Concordances

*Logan, Sister Eugenia, ed. A CONCORDANCE TO THE POETRY OF SAMUEL TAYLOR COLERIDGE. Saint Mary-of-the-Woods, Ind.: [Privately printed], 1940.

> Based on the text of the E.H. Coleridge edition (Oxford University Press, 1912.)

2. Bibliographies

*Haven, Richard, Josephine Haven, and Marianne Adams. SAMUEL TAYLOR COLERIDGE: AN ANNOTATED BIBLIOGRAPHY OF CRITICISM AND SCHOLARSHIP. Vol. 1: 1793-1899. Boston: G.K. Hall, 1976.

> This detailed listing of secondary sources is excellent in every way. A second volume, continuing the listing from 1900, is being prepared by Walter B. Crawford and Edward V. Lauterbach.

*Jackson, J.R. de J., ed. COLERIDGE: THE CRITICAL HERITAGE. London: Routledge and Kegan Paul, 1970.

> This excellent selection of contemporary comment on Coleridge's works from 1794 through 1834 supplements THE ROMANTICS REVIEWED, especially on the prose works.

3. Studies of Reputation and Influence

Duffy, John, ed. COLERIDGE'S AMERICAN DISCIPLES: THE SELECTED COR-
RESPONDENCE OF JAMES MARSH. Amherst: University of Massachusetts
Press, 1973.

> Marsh (d. 1842) was the first of STC's American enthusiasts (bring-
> ing out the first American editions of AIDS TO REFLECTION,
> 1829, THE FRIEND, 1831, etc.); about fifty of his letters and
> fifty more by such American contemporaries as Richard Henry Dana,
> Joseph Torrey, and George Ticknor illustrate the early influence
> of STC's thinking on American intellectuals, chiefly those in New
> England.

Reardon, Bernard M.G. FROM COLERIDGE TO GORE: A CENTURY OF
RELIGIOUS THOUGHT IN BRITAIN. London: Longmans, 1971.

> Along with books by Elinor S. Shaffer (see Chap. 1.B.1) and
> Charles Richard Sanders (below), this volume places STC within
> the context of developments in biblical scholarship and liberal
> theology in eighteenth- and nineteenth-century Europe.

Sanders, Charles Richard. COLERIDGE AND THE BROAD CHURCH MOVE-
MENT. Durham, N.C.: Duke University Press, 1942.

> In addition to its ostensible subject--STC's influence on the younger
> generation--this book stood for twenty-five or thirty years as the
> clearest account of STC's religious beliefs.

B. EDITIONS

1. Collected Editions

*Ashe, T[homas], ed. COLERIDGE'S WORKS. Bohn's Standard Library. 8
vols. London: George Bell, 1883-85.

> A revision, with considerable additions, of the edition originally
> published by Henry Bohn in 1858.

*Coburn, Kathleen, gen. ed.; Bart Winer, assoc. ed. THE COLLECTED WORKS
OF SAMUEL TAYLOR COLERIDGE. Bollingen [Foundation] Series 75. Princeton: Princeton University Press; London: Routledge and Kegan Paul, 1969-- .

> This elaborate, ambitious undertaking has gone (and is now going)
> through many transformations; there have been two or three changes
> in the editor(s) assigned to some individual titles. The most prom-
> inent STC scholars in Canada, the United States, and Great
> Britain are associated with the edition. As of mid-1978, the plan

and production of the Bolligen-Princeton edition stands as follows:

1. LECTURES 1795: ON POLITICS AND RELIGION, ed. Lewis Patton and Peter Mann (published 1971).

2. THE WATCHMAN, ed. Lewis Patton (published 1970).

3. ESSAYS ON HIS TIMES, ed. David V. Erdman (3 vols., published 1978).

4. THE FRIEND, ed. Barbara E. Rooke (2 vols., published 1969).

5. LECTURES 1808-1819: ON LITERATURE, ed. Reginald A. Foakes (forthcoming).

6. LAY SERMONS, ed. F.J. White (published 1972).

7. BIOGRAPHIA LITERARIA, ed. W.J. Bate (forthcoming).

8. LECTURES 1818-1819: ON THE HISTORY OF PHILOSOPHY, ed. Thomas McFarland (forthcoming).

9. AIDS TO REFLECTION, ed. J[ohn] B. Beer (forthcoming).

10. ON THE CONSTITUTION OF CHURCH AND STATE, ed. John Colmer (published 1976).

11. SHORTER WORKS AND FRAGMENTS, ed. E.E. Bostetter, Heather J. Jackson, and J.R. de J. Jackson (forthcoming).

12. MARGINALIA, ed. George Whalley, with the assistance of Raimonda Modiano et al. (the first of these four or five vols. is now in press).

13. LOGIC, ed. J.R. de J. Jackson (in press).

14. TABLE TALK, ed. Carl Woodring (forthcoming).

15. OPUS MAXIMUM, ed. Thomas McFarland (forthcoming).

16. POETICAL WORKS, ed. George Whalley (forthcoming).

17. GENERAL INDEX

Shedd, W[illiam] G.T., ed. COMPLETE WORKS OF SAMUEL TAYLOR COLE-RIDGE. 7 vols. New York: Harper and Brothers, 1853.

> Far from "complete' and accurate, this edition and that of Ashe (above) must be consulted for texts of individual titles until the Bollingen--Princeton COLLECTED WORKS (see Coburn, above) has been fully published.

2. Collected Poetry

*Campbell, James Dykes, ed. THE POETICAL WORKS OF SAMUEL TAYLOR COLERIDGE. London: Macmillan, 1893.

Based on STC's edition of 1829 (the last to receive his personal attention), this edition features Campbell's excellent biographical introduction, as well as STC's own topical arrangement of the poems.

*Coleridge, Ernest Hartley, ed. THE POETICAL WORKS OF SAMUEL TAYLOR COLERIDGE. 2 vols. Oxford: Clarendon Press, 1912.

Still in print, this edition is more nearly complete than Campbell's and features a chronological arrangement of the poems. The same text, sans part of its apparatus, is available in the Oxford Standard Authors Edition.

3. Selected Poetry and Prose

a. GENERAL EDITIONS

#Brinkley, Roberta Florence, ed. COLERIDGE ON THE SEVENTEENTH CENTURY. Durham, N.C.: Duke University Press, 1955.

Collects everything that STC wrote on the literature, religion, science, and philosophy of the seventeenth century and its writers.

@Coburn, Kathleen, ed. INQUIRING SPIRIT: A COLERIDGE READER. London: Routledge and Kegan Paul, 1951.

An illuminating selection, short excerpts from STC's prose works and notebooks, arranged in ten categories (e.g., Language, Literary Criticism, Science, Religion).

b. TEACHING EDITIONS

Beer, John, ed. SAMUEL TAYLOR COLERIDGE: POEMS, SELECTED AND EDITED WITH A NEW INTRODUCTION. Everyman's Library. London: J.M. Dent; New York: E.P. Dutton, 1974.

Colmer, John, ed. COLERIDGE: SELECTED POEMS. New Oxford English Series. London: Oxford University Press, 1965.

Annotated selections include the "conversation poems," the imaginative masterpieces, and a few early political poems.

Empson, William, and David Pirie, eds. COLERIDGE'S VERSE: A SELECTION. New York: Schocken Books, 1973.

Contains a few poems not in most selections, a lengthy Introduction (lecture) by Empson, and textual commentary and critical notes by Pirie.

Garrod, H[eathcote] W., ed. COLERIDGE: POETRY & PROSE, WITH ESSAYS BY HAZLITT, JEFFREY, DE QUINCEY, CARLYLE & OTHERS. Oxford: Clarendon Press, 1925.

> Contains the usual poems (inadequately annotated) and about twenty-five pages of prose. Out of date for student use.

Potter, Stephen, ed. COLERIDGE: POETRY & PROSE. London: Nonesuch Press, 1933.

> A generous selection of poetry, letters, and prose, with a hundred pages of notes, all in print so small that only the very keen-eyed can read it comfortably.

@Richards, I[vor] A., ed. THE PORTABLE COLERIDGE. New York: Viking, 1950.

> A generous selection of poetry, letters, and prose, with an excellent introduction and a chronology, but no informational notes.

*Schneider, Elisabeth, ed. SAMUEL TAYLOR COLERIDGE: SELECTED POETRY AND PROSE. Rinehart Edition. New York: Holt, Rinehart and Winston, 1951; 2nd ed., enl., 1971.

> The selections, the notes, and the (comparative) price of this edition make it a suitable undergraduate textbook.

Stauffer, Donald, ed. SELECTED POETRY AND PROSE OF COLERIDGE. Modern Library Edition. New York: Random House, 1951.

> Though containing a large selection of prose, this edition (which lacks both letters and informational notes) is inferior to Richards' PORTABLE COLERIDGE or Schneider's Rinehart Edition (both cited above) for both the student and the general reader.

4. Individual Titles

#Coburn, Kathleen, ed. THE PHILOSOPHICAL LECTURES OF SAMUEL TAYLOR COLERIDGE, HITHERTO UNPUBLISHED. New York: Philosophical Library, 1949.

> The first printing of some important lectures that helped scholars begin a reappraisal of STC's philosophy and techniques as a lecturer.

#Foakes, R[eginald] A., ed. COLERIDGE ON SHAKESPEARE: THE TEXT OF THE LECTURES OF 1811-12. London: Routledge and Kegan Paul, 1971.

> Goes a long way toward replacing Thomas M. Raysor's valuable COLERIDGE'S SHAKESPEAREAN CRITICISM (1930; Everyman Library, 1960).

Gardner, Martin, ed. THE ANNOTATED ANCIENT MARINER. New York: Bramhall House, 1965.

> Contains notes and information culled from earlier editions and commentaries, as well as the 1798 and 1834 texts of the poem.

@Gettmann, Royal A., ed. THE RIME OF THE ANCIENT MARINER: A HAND-BOOK. San Francisco: Wadsworth, 1961.

> A very useful classroom edition, containing (on facing pages) the texts of 1798 and 1834, with useful critical selections and teaching aids.

*Shawcross, J[ohn], ed. BIOGRAPHIA LITERARIA BY S.T. COLERIDGE . . . WITH HIS AESTHETICAL ESSAYS. 2 vols. London: Oxford University Press, 1907.

> This standard edition is dated and will be rendered obsolete when the appropriate volumes of the new Bolligen-Princeton edition appear (see Coburn, in Sec. B.1, Collected Editions, above).

*Watson, George, ed. BIOGRAPHIA LITERARIA, OR BIOGRAPHICAL SKETCHES OF MY LITERARY LIFE AND OPINIONS. London: J.M. Dent, 1956; corrected ed., 1965.

> Currently the best teaching edition of the BIOGRAPHIA, with excellent (if sparse) annotation.

5. Textual Sources and Studies

#Erdman, David V. "Lost Poem Found: The Cooperative Pursuit and Recapture of an Escaped Coleridge 'Sonnet' of 72 Lines." BNYPL, 65 (1961), 249-68.

> Describes how to locate a poem published ephemerally and incorrectly described by its author.

Johnson, Mary Lynn. "How Rare Is a 'Unique Annotated Copy' of Coleridge's SIBYLLINE LEAVES? A Partial Answer, with a Variant of 'Lines on Donne.'" BNYPL, 78 (1975), 451-81.

> Describes eighteen annotated copies, transcribing the most interesting of STC's marginalia, and reconstructs the printing history of the book.

#Whalley, George. "Coleridge's Poetical Canon: Selection and Arrangement." REVIEW OF ENGLISH LITERATURE, 7 (1966), 9-24.

> Argues for the inclusion of some ephemeral poems later rejected by STC from his collected poetry.

C. BIOGRAPHICAL SOURCES AND STUDIES

Besides the items listed here, the reader will find meaningful contemporary comments and information on STC's life in the letters of his friends (e.g., Lamb, Southey, and WW); in Lamb's essays, particularly "Christ's Hospital Five and Twenty Years Ago" and "The Two Races of Men" (both 1820); in Hazlitt's WORKS, especially "My First Acquaintance with Poets" (1823) and THE SPIRIT OF THE AGE (1825); in the essays of De Quincey; and in the biographies and letters of most literary men of the period.

1. Primary Documents

Allsop, Thomas. LETTERS, CONVERSATIONS, AND RECOLLECTIONS OF S.T. COLERIDGE. 2 vols. London: Edward Moxon, 1836; 3rd ed., 1864.

> Written by a political liberal and religious freethinker who was a friend and disciple of STC from about 1818 onwards, this volume is a useful corrective to the more conservative pictures by STC's family and more orthodox later friends.

*Armour, Richard W., and Raymond F. Howes. COLERIDGE THE TALKER: A SERIES OF CONTEMPORARY DESCRIPTIONS AND COMMENTS. Ithaca, N.Y.: Cornell University Press, 1940; new ed., with addenda, New York, 1969.

> Over a hundred descriptions by STC's contemporaries of his spell-binding conversations.

Carlyle, Thomas. LIFE OF JOHN STERLING. London: Chapman and Hall, 1851.

> Important for its (satirical) picture of STC's influence on Sterling, F.D. Maurice, and the other younger leaders of the Broad Church movement.

Coleridge, Henry Nelson. SPECIMENS OF THE TABLE-TALK OF THE LATE SAMUEL TAYLOR COLERIDGE. 2 vols. London: John Murray, 1835.

> Though H.N. Coleridge revised and shaped his records of his uncle's conversations in strange ways only now being untangled by Carl Woodring, this edition was an important influence on STC's reputation.

*Coleridge, Samuel Taylor. COLLECTED LETTERS. Ed. Earl Leslie Griggs. 6 vols. Oxford: Clarendon Press, 1956-71.

> The usefulness of this, the only attempt at a complete edition, is limited by inadequate annotation and inferior indexes.

* _____. THE NOTEBOOKS. Ed. Kathleen Coburn. Bollingen [Foundation] Series L. New York: Pantheon Books, 1957-- .

> Each of the three "volumes" published to date consists of two separate parts, the first containing the texts of entries (arranged chronologically) from Coleridge's notebooks and the second part containing notes, keyed to the numbers of the notebook entries.

#Cottle, Joseph. REMINISCENCES OF SAMUEL TAYLOR COLERIDGE AND ROBERT SOUTHEY. London: Houlston and Stoneman, 1847.

> Important account by the early Bristol friend and publisher of STC, WW, and Southey.

#Gillman, James. LIFE OF SAMUEL TAYLOR COLERIDGE. IN TWO VOLUMES. London: Pickering, 1838.

> Only the first volume was published, and--inasmuch as it covers the period before Gillman knew STC--its value lies chiefly in its inclusion of some letters and notes by STC.

Pollin, Burton R., and Redmond Burke. "John Thelwall's Marginalia in a Copy of Coleridge's BIOGRAPHIA LITERARIA." BNYPL, 74 (1970), 73-94.

> A running comment on STC's life and theories by an early radical friend.

#Sanford, Mrs. Henry. THOMAS POOLE AND HIS FRIENDS. 2 vols. London: Macmillan, 1888.

> Poole's cousin provides a full account of his friendship with STC, including much of their correspondence.

Stuart, Daniel. "Anecdotes of the Poet Coleridge." GENTLEMAN'S MAGAZINE, n.s. 9 (1838), 485-92, 577-90; n.s. 10 (1938), 23-27, 124-28.

> Stuart, editor of the MORNING POST, defends his dealings with STC against "misrepresentations" by STC and by Henry Nelson Coleridge.

2. Biographies

*Bate, Walter Jackson. COLERIDGE. Masters of World Literature Series. New York: Macmillan, 1968.

> This concise but authoritative critical biography is probably the best starting point for the student and nonspecialist teacher of STC.

*Campbell, James Dykes. SAMUEL TAYLOR COLERIDGE: A NARRATIVE OF EVENTS OF HIS LIFE. London: Macmillan, 1894.

> This model short biography originated as the biographical introduction to Campbell's edition of STC's POETICAL WORKS (1893).

Carpenter, Maurice. THE INDIFFERENT HORSEMAN: THE DIVINE COMEDY OF SAMUEL TAYLOR COLERIDGE. London: Elek Books, 1954.

#Chambers, E[dmund] K. SAMUEL TAYLOR COLERIDGE: A BIOGRAPHICAL STUDY. Oxford: Clarendon Press, 1938.

> Fatally marred by Chambers' acknowledged lack of sympathy for his subject.

Charpentier, John. COLERIDGE, THE SUBLIME SOMNAMBULIST. Trans. M.V. Nugent. New York: Dodd, Mead, 1929.

> A fictionalized popular narration of STC's career.

Fausset, Hugh l'Anson. SAMUEL TAYLOR COLERIDGE. London: Jonathan Cape, 1926.

> A popularized life devoted chiefly to the years before 1820.

#Fruman, Norman. COLERIDGE: THE DAMAGED ARCHANGEL. New York: George Braziller, 1971.

> A massive, carefully wrought, and fully documented biography shaped into a moralistic attack on STC and STC scholars. Important to the teacher and scholar as a source book on the questions about STC that require answers: some answers appear in the books of Woodring and Colmer (both in Sec. D.2), others in those of McFarland and Barfield (both in Sec. D.1).

*Willey, Basil. SAMUEL TAYLOR COLERIDGE. London: Chatto and Windus; New York: W.W. Norton, 1972.

> A sympathetic, knowledgeable biography that gives more attention than is customary to STC's late period at Highgate and accounts for much in STC's life and in the development of his ideas as aspects of his pilgrimage toward Christian orthodoxy.

3. Studies of a Period or an Aspect of STC's Life

*Coburn, Kathleen. THE SELF CONSCIOUS IMAGINATION: A STUDY OF THE COLERIDGE NOTEBOOKS. London: Oxford University Press, 1974.

> These three Riddell Memorial Lectures are entitled "The Self Conscious Self," "The Self and Others, and Some Principles of Education," and "The Self and the Natural and Spiritual Worlds."

Samuel Taylor Coleridge

Cornwell, John. COLERIDGE: POET AND REVOLUTIONARY, 1772-1804. London: Allen Lane, 1973.

> A substantial, well-informed account of STC's early development.

*Erdman, David V. "Coleridge and the 'Review Business.'" WC, 6 (1975), 3-50.

> The torso of an important uncompleted book on STC's ambivalence about periodical reviews--both reviews of his works and his reviews of others.

_____. "Coleridge in Lilliput: The Quality of Parliamentary Reporting in 1800." SPEECH MONOGRAPHS, 27 (1960), 33-62.

> Detailed account of STC's brief stint as parliamentary reporter for the MORNING POST, with analysis of the lack of agreement among (and accuracy of) the parliamentary reports of the day.

_____. "Coleridge on Coleridge: The Context (and Text) of His Review of 'Mr. Coleridge's Second Lay Sermon.'" SiR, 1 (1961), 47-64.

> How--and why--STC came to review his own publication in the COURIER, with a text of his (very favorable) review.

_____. "Coleridge, Wordsworth, and the Wedgwood Fund." BNYPL, 60 (1956), 425-43, 487-507.

> Important both on STC's financial and personal relations with the Wedgwood brothers and on his and WW's ideas on education and child rearing.

_____. "Immoral Acts of a Library Cormorant: The Extent of Coleridge's Contributions to the CRITICAL REVIEW." BNYPL, 63 (1959), 433-54, 515-30, 575-87.

> A detailed analysis of STC's reviewing in one periodical, with attributions of new reviews.

@Hanson, Lawrence. LIFE OF SAMUEL TAYLOR COLERIDGE: THE EARLY YEARS. London: Oxford University Press, 1939.

> A perceptive examination of Coleridge's intellectual development-- as well as the facts of his life--to 1800.

@Hayter, Althea. A VOYAGE IN VAIN: COLERIDGE'S JOURNEY TO MALTA IN 1804. London: Faber and Faber, 1973.

> A well-written account of STC's personal tragedy, but lacking a sense of the social and political context in which STC spent his Mediterranean sojourn.

#Lawrence, Berta. COLERIDGE AND WORDSWORTH IN SOMERSET. Newton Abbot, Devon, Engl.: David and Charles; New York: Barnes and Noble, 1970.

> Centers on Coleridge, Thomas Poole, and John Chester, as well as local topography. Contains twenty-three valuable illustrations.

@Lefebure, Molly. SAMUEL TAYLOR COLERIDGE: A BONDAGE OF OPIUM. London: Victor Gollancz, 1974.

> Despite the sensational title, this is a sane, readable popular account of STC's life through 1816.

#McFarland, Thomas. "Coleridge's Plagiarisms Once More: A Review Essay." YALE REVIEW, 63 (1974), 252-86.

> A detailed critique of Fruman's COLERIDGE: THE DAMAGED ARCHANGEL (Sec. C.2); centering on the plagiarism issue.

____. "The Symbiosis of Coleridge and Wordsworth." SiR, 11 (1972), 263-303.

> The fullest discussion of the interrelations between the two men.

@Potter, Stephen. COLERIDGE AND S.T.C. 1935; rpt. New York: Russell and Russell, 1965.

> An illuminating study of the interrelations between "personality" ("Coleridge"--"the continuously evolving, experiencing, truly living person") and "the fixed character back into which each successive metamorphosis tends to relapse" ("S.T.C.").

#Schneider, Elisabeth. COLERIDGE, OPIUM, AND KUBLA KHAN. Chicago: University of Chicago Press, 1953.

> An important study of the probable place of drugs in the workings of STC's imagination.

#Sultana, Donald E. SAMUEL TAYLOR COLERIDGE IN MALTA AND ITALY. Oxford: Basil Blackwell, 1969.

> Valuable for its detailed analysis of the locales and local traditions STC encountered in Malta, but perhaps too dogmatic in the claims for some of its original discoveries.

#Whalley, George. COLERIDGE AND SARA HUTCHINSON AND THE ASRA POEMS. Toronto: University of Toronto Press, 1955.

> An excellent examination of STC's doomed love for Sara Hutchinson and its reflection in his poetry, with transcription of Sara's copy book containing poems by STC.

D. CRITICISM

1. General Studies

Adair, Patricia M. THE WAKING DREAM: A STUDY OF COLERIDGE'S POETRY. London: Arnold, 1967.

> Largely biographical and psychological in orientation, this study is weakest on "The Ancient Mariner," strongest on "Kubla Khan."

*Barfield, Owen. WHAT COLERIDGE THOUGHT. London: Oxford University Press, 1971.

> The most thorough exploration of the concept of polarity in STC's thought, written in the spirit of a direct analysis of STC's ideas without undue reference to the traditions out of which they developed, an approach that occasionally leads to oversimplification.

Beer, John B. COLERIDGE THE VISIONARY. London: Chatto and Windus, 1959.

> Brings STC's thought from the entire corpus of his writings to bear on the great poems.

Grant, Allan. A PREFACE TO COLERIDGE. London: Longmans, 1972.

> Useful data, illustrations, and maps surround texts of major poems and pedestrian critical commentary. A serviceable background aid for students.

@House, Humphry. COLERIDGE: THE CLARK LECTURES, 1951-52. London: Rupert Hart-Davis, 1953.

> Contains brief but sensitive and important explorations of basic problems in the study of STC, as well as readings of selected poems.

*Lowes, John Livingstone. THE ROAD TO XANADU: A STUDY IN THE WAYS OF THE IMAGINATION. Boston: Houghton Mifflin, 1927.

> A landmark in scholarship, vastly influential in study of the Romantics for at least a quarter of a century. Lowes pursued the imagery of "Kubla Khan" and "The Rime of the Ancient Mariner" through a not-so-short course in the books STC read.

*McFarland, Thomas. COLERIDGE AND THE PANTHEIST TRADITION. Oxford: Clarendon Press, 1969.

> The most important single exposition of the unity (within a dialectical diversity) of STC's thought, as well as the most spirited de-

fense of STC's use of German writers. McFarland places STC's ideas within the larger tradition of thought going back to Spinoza (and ultimately to Plato) to show that the questions he dealt with were more fundamental than the language in which he framed his attempted answers.

@Radley, Virginia L. SAMUEL TAYLOR COLERIDGE. Twayne's English Author Series. New York: Twayne, 1966.

Aside from a disastrous chapter on the Romantic tradition and a tendency to impose Coleridge's own critical categories too rigidly upon his poems, this introduction for students and general readers fulfills its function competently.

*Schulz, Max F. THE POETIC VOICES OF COLERIDGE: A STUDY OF HIS DESIRE FOR SPONTANEITY AND PASSION FOR ORDER. Detroit: Wayne State University Press, 1963.

This valuable study of all STC's poetry categorizes eight different "poetic voices" in STC's output and attempts both to relate the methods of each to one another and to evaluate STC's success in working with their various forms.

Walsh, William. COLERIDGE: THE WORK AND THE RELEVANCE. London: Chatto and Windus, 1967.

A general study that emphasizes the "realist" in STC, seeking to derive from STC's various writings an anti-Romantic Leavisite position on social issues.

*Watson, George. COLERIDGE THE POET. London: Routledge and Kegan Paul, 1966.

A clear, vigorous defense and elucidation of STC's poetic achievement.

2. Studies of Particular Works, Periods, and Themes

#Appleyard, J[oseph] A. COLERIDGE'S PHILOSOPHY OF LITERATURE: THE DEVELOPMENT OF A CONCEPT OF POETRY, 1791-1819. Cambridge: Harvard University Press, 1965.

An excellent account of the development of STC's ideas on literature.

Badawi, M.M. COLERIDGE: CRITIC OF SHAKESPEARE. Cambridge: Cambridge University Press, 1973.

Shows that STC brought many ideas into British Shakespearean criticism that had not been there in the eighteenth century, as well as fresh critical vocabulary.

Baker, James Volant. THE SACRED RIVER: COLERIDGE'S THEORY OF IMAGINATION. Baton Rouge: Louisiana State University Press, 1957.

> An exploration of the roles of "conscious" and "unconscious" activity in STC's theory of the imagination that naively overemphasizes STC's originality (even among British thinkers) in his interest in the subconscious.

#Barth, J. Robert, S.J. COLERIDGE AND CHRISTIAN DOCTRINE. Cambridge: Harvard University Press, 1969.

> Concentrating on the years 1815-34, Barth explicates STC's thought in the light of traditional Christian doctrine and its twentieth-century developments.

_____. "Symbol as Sacrament in Coleridge's Thought." SiR, 11 (1972), 320-31.

> Explores the centrality of STC's conception of "symbol," relating it to his religious orientation.

Berkoben, Lawrence D. "CHRISTABEL: A Variety of Evil Experience." MLQ, 25 (1964), 400-11.

> A clear presentation of most of the ambiguities and problems in CHRISTABEL, providing an excellent introduction to discussion of the poem.

_____. COLERIDGE'S DECLINE AS A POET. The Hague, Netherlands: Mouton, 1975.

#Bonjour, Adrien. COLERIDGE'S "HYMN BEFORE SUNRISE": A STUDY OF FACTS AND PROBLEMS CONNECTED WITH THE POEM. Lausanne, Switzerland: Imprimerie La Concorde, 1942.

> The most detailed discussion of the poem, STC's own account of its composition, and the Friederike Brun poem on which it was based. See also A.P. Rossiter (TIMES LITERARY SUPPLEMENT, 28 September and 25 October 1951) and Lawrence D. Berkoben (ELN, 1966).

Boulger, James D. COLERIDGE AS RELIGIOUS THINKER. New Haven: Yale University Press, 1961.

> Explores the relationship of STC's thought to the British theological tradition.

_____. "Coleridge on Imagination Revisited." WC, 4 (1973), 13-24.

Examines STC's theory of imagination in BIOGRAPHIA, chapter 13, in the context of the Aristotelian tradition.

#Calleo, David P. COLERIDGE AND THE IDEA OF THE MODERN STATE. New Haven: Yale University Press, 1966.

Emphasizes STC's theory of the state and his idea of the British Constitution. Less useful than Colmer's COLERIDGE, CRITIC OF SOCIETY, below, in relating STC's theory to the practical political situation of his day.

Chandler, Alice. "Structure and Symbolism in 'The Rime of the Ancient Mariner.'" MLQ, 26 (1965), 401-13.

Chayes, Irene H. "A Coleridgean Reading of 'The Ancient Mariner.'" SiR, 4 (1965), 81-103.

An important essay. Using STC's later additions and references to the poem's theme as significant authorial commentary, Chayes examines the implications of the gloss and (especially) the Latin epigraph from Burnet, the narrative viewpoint, and sections of the BIOGRAPHIA LITERARIA and AIDS TO REFLECTION that relate to the poem. Her reading suggests that the Mariner's adventures represent the course of those who pursue delusions beyond the bounds of orthodoxy.

_____. "'Kubla Khan' and the Creative Process." SiR, 6 (1966), 1-21.

Examines STC's later prefatory note for clues to his "covert critical commentary" on the poem, filling in the situation of the poet and the relationships of the three stanzas to one author.

Colmer, John. "Coleridge and the Life of Hope." SiR, 11 (1972), 332-41.

Explores the centrality of the idea of hope--including political hopes--to STC's thought.

_____. COLERIDGE, CRITIC OF SOCIETY. Oxford: Clarendon Press, 1959.

Intelligently probes the relationships between STC's self-imposed political mission and his potential audience(s), through analysis of current social and political conditions and ideological movements. Especially valuable with regard to STC's early prose, therein complementing Woodring's study of political implications in the poetry (below, this section).

Deschamps, Paul. LA FORMATION DE LA PENSÉE DE COLERIDGE (1722-1804). Paris: Didier, 1964.

A thorough and sound synthesis of scholarship on the thought and writings of STC through 1804.

Ebbatson, J.R. "Coleridge's Mariner and the Rights of Man." SiR, 11 (1972), 171-206.

An attempt, building on Empson (below), to correct recent Christian, Freudian, Jungian, and existential readings by placing STC's poem in the context of his (and the age's) political ideas.

Empson, William. "The Ancient Mariner." CRITICAL QUARTERLY, 6 (1964), 289-319.

Argues that the true subject of STC's poem is belated British guilt about maritime expansion and the exploitation of primitive peoples.

Fairbanks, A. Harris. "The Form of Coleridge's Dejection Ode." PMLA, 90 (1975), 874-84.

Distinguishes "Dejection" from STC's blank verse conversation poems and discusses STC's innovations in the form of the ode (see also Chayes, Chap. 2.C.).

Fields, Beverly. REALITY'S DARK DREAM: DEJECTION IN COLERIDGE. Kent, Ohio: Kent State University Press, 1967.

A Freudian study of the early life and poetry through "Dejection: An Ode" (1802).

Fogel, Daniel Mark. "A Compositional History of the BIOGRAPHIA LITERARIA." STUDIES IN BIBLIOGRAPHY, 30 (1977), 219-34.

This important account (drawing on unpublished correspondence by STC's friends, publisher, and printer) provides the most detailed chronology for the development of STC's chief work of literary theory and criticism.

Fogle, Richard Harter. THE IDEA OF COLERIDGE'S CRITICISM. Berkeley: University of California Press, 1962.

Attempts to systematize STC's critical theory and then shows how STC applies it in his criticism of Wordsworth and Shakespeare.

#Harding, John Anthony. COLERIDGE AND THE IDEA OF LOVE: ASPECTS OF RELATIONSHIP IN COLERIDGE'S THOUGHT AND WRITING. Cambridge: Cambridge University Press, 1975.

An earnest, substantial effort to take up the challenge of Fruman and to "show where [Coleridge's] true originality lay" by exploring the subject of "relationship" in all aspects of STC's thought, including his political philosophy.

*Haven, Richard. PATTERNS OF CONSCIOUSNESS: AN ESSAY ON COLE-RIDGE. Amherst: University of Massachusetts Press, 1969.

> An important study that attempts to relate the ideas in STC's poetry and prose fairly directly to his own experiences.

Heninger, S[imeon] K., Jr. "A Jungian Reading of 'Kubla Khan.'" JOURNAL OF AESTHETICS AND ART CRITICISM, 18 (1960), 358-67.

> A significant reading of the poem in terms of its archetypal images of integration and disintegration of personality, with a suggestion as to why STC insisted that the poem is unfinished.

#Jackson, J.R. de J. METHOD AND IMAGINATION IN COLERIDGE'S CRITI-CISM. London: Routledge and Kegan Paul, 1969.

> An important study moving from STC's philosophical orientation, through his theory and practice of literary criticism, to his use of literature "as a means to understanding and expounding philosophical and theological problems."

Lovejoy, A[rthur] O. "Coleridge and Kant's Two Worlds." In his ESSAYS IN THE HISTORY OF IDEAS. Baltimore: Johns Hopkins University Press, 1948.

> An essay (first published in ELH, 1940) which follows Wellek in showing the pervasive influence of Kant on STC's philosophical and religious writings.

Magnuson, Paul. COLERIDGE'S NIGHTMARE POETRY. Charlottesville: University of Virginia Press, 1974.

> Critical exploration of the "conversation poems" (briefly) and KUBLA KHAN, ANCIENT MARINER, REMORSE, CHRISTABEL, and "Dejection: An Ode."

Mallette, Richard. "Narrative Technique in the BIOGRAPHIA LITERARIA." MLR, 70 (1975), 32-40.

#Muirhead, John H. COLERIDGE AS PHILOSOPHER. London: George Allen and Unwin, 1930.

> For many years the standard summary of STC's philosophical thinking, this book is still useful, if read along with those by McFarland and Barfield (see Sec. D.1).

#Nethercot, Arthur H. THE ROAD TO TRYERMAINE. Chicago: University of Chicago Press, 1939.

> Attempts to do for CHRISTABEL what Lowes's ROAD TO XANADU did for KUBLA KHAN and THE ANCIENT MARINER.

#Orsini, Gian N.G. COLERIDGE AND GERMAN IDEALISM: A STUDY IN
THE HISTORY OF PHILOSOPHY, WITH UNPUBLISHED MATERIALS FROM
COLERIDGE'S MANUSCRIPTS. Carbondale: Southern Illinois University Press,
1969.

> Examines the influence on STC of "Kant and the post-Kantians
> . . . from approximately 1800 to approximately the eighteen-
> twenties."

Parker, Reeve. COLERIDGE'S MEDITATIVE ART. Ithaca, N.Y.: Cornell
University Press, 1975.

> Explores the artistic qualities of STC's "conversation poems."

Patterson, Charles I., Jr. "The Daemonic in KUBLA KHAN: Toward Interpretation." PMLA, 89 (1974), 1033-42.

> Argues that, viewed from the perspective of Plato's mythology of
> daemons, "KUBLA KHAN appears neither as a fragment nor as a
> poem about evil," but as "a poem about daemonic poetry."

Prickett, Stephen. COLERIDGE AND WORDSWORTH: THE POETRY OF
GROWTH. Cambridge: Cambridge University Press, 1970.

> A lucid, detailed exposition of the ideas of mental development
> shared by STC and WW, showing how STC eventually developed a
> more complete theory (if not practice) of "human integration"
> through the medium of his liberal Christian theology.

Purves, Alan C. "Formal Structure in 'Kubla Khan.'" SiR, 1 (1962), 187-91.

> One of the best "teaching essays" on STC, showing how every
> aspect of the poem's meaning is echoed by its metrics, rhyme
> scheme, and stanzaic divisions.

*Richards, I[vor] A. COLERIDGE ON IMAGINATION. London: Routledge
and Kegan Paul, 1934; 2nd ed., rev., 1950.

> Richards discovers in STC--and claims originality for him--many
> conceptions promoted by the New Critics and Modernist poets and
> critics of the twentieth century. (Richards was unaware of STC's
> debts to German thinkers.)

Sewell, Elizabeth. "Coleridge on Revolution." SiR, 11 (1972), 342-59.

> Traces through STC's publications, letters, and notebooks his am-
> bivalent feelings about the guilt and the necessity of (at least in-
> tellectual) revolutions.

Spatz, Jonas. "The Mystery of Eros: Sexual Initiation in Coleridge's 'Christabel.'" PMLA, 90 (1975), 107-16.

Ignores the Lesbian overtones, seeing Geraldine rather as the sex-
ually mature woman that Christabel must become.

#Suther, Marshall. THE DARK NIGHT OF SAMUEL TAYLOR COLERIDGE.
New York: Columbia University Press, 1960.

An exploration of STC's poetic decline, informed by the idea that
his loss of faith in radical humanism drove him from poetry to
philosophy and religion as a means of salvation.

_____. VISIONS OF XANADU. New York: Columbia University Press,
1965.

A detailed study of the images and symbols of KUBLA KHAN,
arguing for the unity and coherence not only of that poem but
STC's entire poetic output.

Tillyard, E[ustace] M.W. "Coleridge: The Rime of the Ancient Mariner,
1798." In his FIVE POEMS, 1470-1870: AN ELEMENTARY ESSAY ON THE
BACKGROUND OF ENGLISH LITERATURE. London: Chatto and Windus,
1948. Pp. 66-86.

A clearly written, sensible approach; valuable for students and
nonspecialist teachers.

Wendling, Ronald C. "Coleridge and the Consistency of 'The Eolian Harp.'"
SiR, 8 (1968), 26-42.

Finds in the apparent inconsistencies in the poem an epitome of
all STC's early intellectual and moral struggles, and argues that
his very failure to resolve them rationally illustrates his need to
subject such experiential inconsistencies to religious faith.

Whalley, George. "The Integrity of the BIOGRAPHIA LITERARIA." ESSAYS
AND STUDIES, 6 (1953), 85-101.

Wilson, Douglas Brownlow. "Two Modes of Apprehending Nature: A Gloss on
the Coleridgean Symbol." PMLA, 87 (1972), 42-52.

Analyzes STC's early ambivalence toward nature, his later (1816-
17) use of the distinction between natura naturata and natura
naturans, together with his definition of "symbol" and its relationship to the imagination; the key poem discussed is "The Eolian
Harp" in its two versions.

#Woodring, Carl R. POLITICS IN THE POETRY OF COLERIDGE. Madison:
University of Wisconsin Press, 1961.

The definitive study for STC's poetry of the implications of his
evolving political interests, this book complements Colmer's study
of the political prose above.

Yarlott, Geoffrey. COLERIDGE AND THE ABYSSINIAN MAID. London: Methuen, 1971.

> Focusing on the period 1800-02, Yarlott examines the great imaginative poems in terms of STC's emotional entanglements.

3. Collections of Miscellaneous Essays

#Beer, John, ed. COLERIDGE'S VARIETY: BICENTENARY STUDIES. Pittsburgh: University of Pittsburgh Press, 1975.

> Ten original essays, by Whalley, Griggs, Beer (2), Abrams, McFarland, Barfield, Dorothy Emmet, D.M. MacKinnon, and Coburn.

Blunden, Edmund, and Earl Leslie Griggs, eds. COLERIDGE: STUDIES BY SEVERAL HANDS ON THE HUNDREDTH ANNIVERSARY OF HIS DEATH. London: Constable, 1934.

> The contributions include chapters of E.H. Coleridge's unpublished life of STC, and essays on biographical and intellectual subjects by Blunden, A.J. Eagleston, Edith Morley, C.H. Wilkinson, J.L. Haney, G. McL. Harper, H. Beeley, J.H. Muirhead, Alice Snyder, and Griggs.

@Boulger, James D., ed. TWENTIETH CENTURY INTERPRETATIONS OF THE RIME OF THE ANCIENT MARINER: A COLLECTION OF CRITICAL ESSAYS. Englewood Cliffs, N.J.: Prentice-Hall, 1969.

> Includes a new essay by Boulger, besides reprinting important essays by Robert Penn Warren, House, Whalley, and A.M. Buchan.

#Brett, R.L., ed. S.T. COLERIDGE. Writers and Their Backgrounds. London: Bell, 1971.

> This important collection includes nine original essays by Whalley, Beer, A.R. Jones, Appleyard, Fogle, Brett, Dorothy Emmet, Willey, and Colmer that explore various aspects of STC's thought and writing.

@Coburn, Kathleen, ed. COLERIDGE: A COLLECTION OF CRITICAL ESSAYS. Twentieth Century Views. Englewood Cliffs, N.J.: Prentice-Hall, 1967.

> Besides Coburn's valuable introduction, this collection reprints essays by I.A. Richards, Whalley, D.W. Harding, Bostetter, Gerard, Elisabeth Schneider, Herbert Read, L.C. Knights, Yasunari Takahashi, Abrams, B.T. Sankey, Jr., W.F. Kennedy, R.O. Preyer, and D.M. Emmet.

#Hartman, Geoffrey H., ed. NEW PERSPECTIVES ON COLERIDGE AND WORDSWORTH. Selected Papers from the English Institute. New York: Columbia University Press, 1972.

>   Following papers on WW by Kenneth R. Johnston and John Hollander are five substantial studies of STC by Geoffrey H. Hartman, Angus Fletcher, Michael G. Cooke, Harold Bloom, and--of most permanent interest--Thomas McFarland's "The Origin and Significance of Coleridge's Theory of Secondary Imagination."

Chapter 5

GEORGE GORDON BYRON,

SIXTH BARON BYRON (1788-1824)

A. CONCORDANCES, BIBLIOGRAPHIES, AND STUDIES OF
   REPUTATION AND INFLUENCE

1. Concordances

#Hagelman, Charles W., Jr., and Robert J. Barnes, eds. A CONCORDANCE
TO BYRON'S "DON JUAN." Ithaca, N.Y.: Cornell University Press, 1967.

> Computer-index based on the variorum edition by Steffan and Pratt
> (Sec. B.4, below).

*Young, Ione Dodson, comp. A CONCORDANCE TO THE POETRY OF BYRON.
4 vols. Austin, Tex.: The Pemberton Press, 1965.

> An essential aid to all serious study of Byron's poetry, even though
> keyed to the text of the otherwise obsolescent Houghton Mifflin
> Cambridge Edition (Sec. B.2, below). The second revised print-
> ing is distributed by Mrs. Ione Young, 4107 Wildwood Road, Aus-
> tin, Texas 78722.

2. Bibliographies

*BIBLIOGRAPHICAL CATALOGUE OF FIRST EDITIONS, PROOF COPIES 8
MANUSCRIPTS OF BOOKS BY LORD BYRON EXHIBITED . . . JANUARY
1925. London: First Editions Club, 1925.

> A detailed description of the title page, contents, and binding of
> each of the copies exhibited (many of them from the British li-
> brary).

Pratt, Willis W. "A Decade of Byron Scholarship: 1946-1956, A Selective
Survey." K-SJ, 7 (1958), 69-85.

> A solid critical survey of standard sources, as well as newer mate-
> rials, showing (by contrast with the richness of subsequent publica-
> tions) how impoverished LB scholarship was on the eve of the
> appearance of Marchand's biography.

THE ROE-BYRON COLLECTION, NEWSTEAD ABBEY. Nottingham, Engl.: Corporation of Nottingham, 1937.

> A catalogue of one of the most important collections of LB's first editions, MSS, and memorabilia.

*Santucho, Oscar José. GEORGE GORDON, LORD BYRON: A COMPRE-HENSIVE BIBLIOGRAPHY OF SECONDARY MATERIALS IN ENGLISH, 1807-1974. With a Critical Review of Research by Clement Tyson Goode, Jr. Metuchen, N.J.: Scarecrow Press, 1977.

> By far the most comprehensive listing of secondary publications, with a full discussion of major works and trends, though without annotation of individual entries.

*Wise, Thomas James. BIBLIOGRAPHY OF THE WRITINGS IN VERSE AND PROSE OF GEORGE GORDON NOEL, BARON BYRON. 2 vols. London: Privately printed, 1932-33.

> Based on Wise's personal collection, most of which is now in the Ashley Collection of the British Library.

3. Studies of Reputation and Influence

Chambers, R[aymond] W[ilson]. RUSKIN (AND OTHERS) ON BYRON. Oxford: The English Association, 1925.

> On Ruskin's defense of LB and on the political interests of LB's other Victorian champions. Reprinted in Chambers' MAN'S UN-CONQUERABLE MIND (1939).

*Chew, Samuel C. BYRON IN ENGLAND: HIS FAME AND AFTER-FAME. London: John Murray, 1924.

> An exceedingly thorough and well-conceived discussion of LB's reputation in England from 1808 to ca. 1916, with voluminous bibliography; naturally, it is neither complete nor without error.

Estève, Edmond. BYRON ET LE ROMANTISME FRANÇAIS: ESSAI SUR LA FORTUNE ET L'INFLUENCE DE L'OEUVRE DE BYRON EN FRANCE DE 1812 À 1850. Paris: Hachette, 1907.

> Still authoritative for its topic, this study has been supplemented by E.P. Dargan's "Byron's Fame in France" (VIRGINIA QUAR-TERLY REVIEW, 1926), W.J. Phillips' FRANCE ON BYRON (1941), Robert Escarpit's "Misunderstanding in France" (BJ, 1975), and Marius-François Guyard's LA GRAND BRETAGNE DANS LE ROMAN FRANÇAIS, 1914-1940.

Hentschel, Cedric. THE BYRONIC TEUTON: ASPECTS OF GERMAN PES-
SIMISM, 1800-1933. London: Methuen, 1940.

> A study of themes in German literature with "Byronic" overtones.
> For more on LB's German reputation, see L.M. Price, RECEPTION
> OF ENGLISH LITERATURE IN GERMANY (1932).

#Leonard, William Ellery. BYRON AND BYRONISM IN AMERICA. Boston:
N.p., 1905.

> A perceptive, but not exhaustive survey of early influences. See
> also Samuel C. Chew, "Byron in America" (AMERICAN MERCURY,
> 1924).

*Moore, Doris Langley. THE LATE LORD BYRON: POSTHUMOUS DRAMAS.
London: John Murray, 1961.

> A fascinating story (based on and quoting from previously unpub-
> lished correspondence) of the in-fighting after LB's death, begin-
> ning with the decision to burn his "Memoirs" (1824) and continu-
> ing through the reactions and publications of many of LB's ac-
> quaintances from the years immediately following his death until
> they were dead or their claims to attention in connection with him
> had been resolved.

Peers, E. Allison. "Sidelights on Byronism in Spain." REVUE HISPANIQUE,
50 (1920), 359-66.

> By the author of an important HISTORY OF THE ROMANTIC
> MOVEMENT IN SPAIN (1935).

#Rutherford, Andrew, ed. BYRON: THE CRITICAL HERITAGE. London: Rout-
ledge and Kegan Paul, 1970.

> Excerpts, reviews, and comments on LB from 1808 to 1909.

B. EDITIONS

1. Collected Editions

Moore, Thomas, ed. THE WORKS OF LORD BYRON, WITH HIS LETTERS AND
JOURNALS AND LIFE BY THOMAS MOORE, ESQ. 17 vols. London: John
Murray, 1832-33.

> Murray issued many editions of LB's works, complete and selected,
> from one to seventeen volumes in various formats, based on this
> edition.

George Gordon Byron

*THE WORKS OF LORD BYRON. 13 vols. London: John Murray, 1898-1904. LETTERS AND JOURNALS, ed. Rowland E. Prothero, 6 vols.; POETRY, ed. Ernest Hartley Coleridge, 7 vols.

> The standard edition for those portions not yet superseded by Marchand's new edition of the letters and journals (Sec. C.1) and McGann's projected edition of the poetry (Sec. B.2). This edition will always be valuable to the student and scholar because of its expansive introductions, notes, bibliography of editions and translations of LB's poetry, and indexes.

2. Collected Poetry

*Coleridge, Ernest Hartley, ed. POETICAL WORKS . . . THE ONLY COMPLETE AND COPYRIGHT TEXT IN ONE VOLUME. London: John Murray, 1905.

> Based on the seven volumes of POETRY which Coleridge edited in the WORKS (see Sec. B.1, above), but "subjected to a fresh and, it is hoped, exhaustive revision in respect of punctuation and orthography," with an introductory memoir, notes, and index of first lines. Still the most authoritative one-volume edition of LB's poetry ever published.

@More, Paul E[lmer]. THE COMPLETE POETICAL WORKS. Cambridge Edition. Boston: Houghton Mifflin, 1905.

> Slightly revised by Robert F. Gleckner and reissued in 1975; this edition would be obsolescent if Ione Dodson Young had not keyed her CONCORDANCE to it.

Pinto, V[ivian] de Sola, ed. POEMS. 3 vols. Everyman Edition. London: J.M. Dent, 1963.

> Small print and sparse annotation prevent this collected edition from being entirely suitable for teaching use.

POETICAL WORKS OF LORD BYRON. Oxford Standard Authors Edition. London: Oxford University Press, 1904.

> Lacking material held in copyright by John Murray, this edition is completely outdated.

3. Selected Poetry and Prose

@Bostetter, Edward E., ed. BYRON: SELECTED WORKS. Rinehart Edition. New York: Rinehart, 1951; rev. ed. Holt, Rinehart, and Winston, 1972.

> A text suitable for undergraduates.

Bredvold, Louis I., ed. DON JUAN AND OTHER SATIRICAL POEMS. New York: Odyssey Press, 1935.

> A substantial, well-annotated selection (see Chew's companion volume, below).

Chew, Samuel C., ed. CHILDE HAROLD'S PILGIMAGE AND OTHER RO-MANTIC POEMS. New York: Odyssey Press, 1936.

> This (together with Bredvold's companion volume, above) is still an adequate teaching edition, with substantial, adequately anno-tated, uncut selections.

@Marchand, Leslie A., ed. SELECTED POETRY. Modern Library Edition. New York: Random House, 1951.

> A full though unannotated selection of all the poems except DON JUAN. Includes CHILDE HAROLD complete, and many lyrics, epigrams, and the domestic poems. Also includes the following, complete: ENGLISH BARDS, CURSE OF MINERVA, WALTZ, VISION, BEPPO, GIAOUR, BRIDE, CORSAIR, PRISONER, and MANFRED.

@Marshall, William H., ed. SELECTED POEMS AND LETTERS. Riverside Edi-tion. Boston: Houghton Mifflin, 1968.

> A full, well-annotated teaching selection of poems other than DON JUAN, plus thirty-five letters. In addition to selected lyrics and epigrams, includes the following, complete: CHILDE HAROLD, BRIDE, PRISONER, MANFRED, BEPPO, MAZEPPA, PROPHECY OF DANTE, VISION, CAIN, and HEAVEN AND EARTH.

Quennell, Peter, ed. BYRON: SELECTED VERSE AND PROSE WORKS, IN-CLUDING LETTERS AND EXTRACTS FROM LORD BYRON'S JOURNALS AND DIARIES. London: Collins, 1959.

> Leaves every major poem incomplete, while adding meaningless snippets of prose and letters.

————. BYRON: SELECTIONS FROM POETRY, LETTERS AND JOURNALS. London: Nonesuch, 1949.

> Contains ENGLISH BARDS, selections from CHILDE HAROLD and DON JUAN (cantos 1-3, 11-17), VISION, lyrics, and a generous selection of letters and journals, with a few notes at the end.

Rice, Richard Ashley, ed. THE BEST OF BYRON. New York: Ronald, 1933; rev. and enl., 1942.

A substantial selection with notes, but most individual titles have been cut. (BRIDE, PRISONER, MAZEPPA, VISION, and lyrics are complete.) Of the thirty-three letters, most are early.

4. Individual Titles

#Ashton, Thomas L. BYRON'S HEBREW MELODIES. Austin: University of Texas Press, 1972.

An edition with elaborate historical, biographical, and critical commentary; the most thorough study these poems are likely to receive (or require) for many years.

@Marchand, Leslie A., ed. DON JUAN. Riverside Edition. Boston: Houghton Mifflin, 1958.

Though based on the E.H. Coleridge text, this edition has long been a favorite student text because of its readability and excellent annotation.

#Steffan, Truman Guy. LORD BYRON'S CAIN: TWELVE ESSAYS AND A TEXT WITH VARIANTS AND ANNOTATIONS. Austin: University of Texas Press, 1968.

A wealth of useful information partly obscured by a lack of organizational and textual principles.

*Steffan, Truman Guy, and Willis W. Pratt, eds. BYRON'S DON JUAN: A VARIORUM EDITION. 4 vols. Austin: University of Texas Press, 1957; 2nd ed. (corrected), 1971.

The first volume--Steffan's THE MAKING OF A MASTERPIECE--is most useful for its appendixes; the two-volume VARIORUM EDITION and Pratt's annotations in volume 4 remain standard sources. For some later corrections, see the Penguin paperback redaction, below.

@Steffan, Truman Guy; E. Steffan; and Willis W. Pratt, eds. LORD BYRON: DON JUAN. Harmondsworth, Engl.: Penguin Books, 1973.

A redaction of the text and notes of the VARIORUM EDITION (above), in paperback suitable for use as a textbook.

5. Textual Sources and Studies

McGann, Jerome J. "Editing Byron's Poetry." BJ, 1 (1973), 5-10.

The first of several interim reports--the most recent in BJ, 5 (1977)--on McGann's forthcoming Oxford English Text edition of LB's poetry, the first comprehensive new edition since E.H. Coleridge's.

C. BIOGRAPHICAL SOURCES AND STUDIES

1. Primary Documents

Blaquiere, Edward. NARRATIVE OF A SECOND VISIT TO GREECE, INCLUD-
ING FACTS CONNECTED WITH THE LAST DAYS OF LORD BYRON. London:
George B. Whittaker, 1825.

> Primarily propaganda for the cause of Greek independence by the
> man who had persuaded LB to enlist in the cause.

#Byron, George Gordon. BYRON, A SELF-PORTRAIT: LETTERS AND DIARIES,
1798 TO 1824. Ed. Peter Quennell. London: John Murray, 1950.

> Before the publication of Marchand's edition of BYRON'S LETTERS
> AND JOURNALS (below), some valuable letters contained in these
> volumes were unavailable elsewhere.

* _____. BYRON'S LETTERS AND JOURNALS. Ed. Leslie A. Marchand.
London: John Murray; Cambridge, Mass.: Harvard University Press, 1973-- .

> Vol. 1, 1798-1810: "IN MY HOT YOUTH" (1973)
>
> Vol. 2, 1810-1812: "FAMOUS IN MY TIME" (1973)
>
> Vol. 3, 1813-1814: "ALAS! THE LOVE OF WOMEN" (1974)
>
> Vol. 4, 1814-1815: "WEDLOCK'S THE DEVIL" (1975)
>
> Vol. 5, 1816-1817: "SO LATE INTO THE NIGHT" (1976)
>
> Vol. 6, 1818-1819: "THE FLESH IS FRAIL" (1976)
>
> Vol. 7, 1820: "BETWEEN TWO WORLDS" (1977)
>
> > This edition, still in progress, meticulously transcribing
> > and restoring the expurgations of earlier editors, will
> > provide the standard text for many years. Fuller an-
> > notation for particular letters can be found in Prothero's
> > volumes in the WORKS (Sec. B.1) or in specialized
> > studies and editions (e.g., SHELLEY AND HIS CIRCLE,
> > Chap. 6.C.3).

@ _____. THE LETTERS OF LORD BYRON. Ed. R.G. Howarth, Introd. André
Maurois. Everyman Edition. London: J.M. Dent, 1962.

> A good selection, once useful as a textbook, though now partly
> outdated by Marchand's unexpurgated texts (see BYRON'S LETTERS
> AND JOURNALS, above).

@ _____. LORD BYRON IN HIS LETTERS: SELECTIONS FROM HIS LETTERS
AND JOURNALS. Ed. V.H. Collins. London: John Murray, 1927.

A substantial, annotated selection, with introduction and index.

\# _____ . LORD BYRON'S CORRESPONDENCE, CHIEFLY WITH LADY MEL-
BOURNE, . . . HOBHOUSE, . . . KINNAIRD, AND P.B. SHELLEY. Ed.
John Murray. 2 vols. London: John Murray, 1922.

> First publication of important letters, marred by the editor's cen-
> sorship of LB's language and sexual references.

_____ . THE SELECTED LETTERS OF LORD BYRON. Ed. Jacques Barzun.
Great Letters Series. New York: Farrar, Straus and Cudahy, 1953.

> An annotated selection, with introduction and index that was use-
> ful (before Marchand's unexpurgated edition, see BYRON'S LETTERS
> AND JOURNALS, above) for students and laymen.

Clinton, George. MEMOIRS OF THE LIFE AND WRITINGS OF LORD BYRON.
London: James Robins, 1825.

> Though dedicated to Lady Byron (and definitely partisan to her),
> these unauthoritative "memoirs" chiefly take advantage of that
> guise to reprint (with illustrations) large sections of LB's poems to
> which Murray held copyright.

[Dallas, Robert Charles]. CORRESPONDENCE OF LORD BYRON WITH A
FRIEND . . . ALSO RECOLLECTIONS OF THE POET. 3 vols. Paris: Galignani, 1825.

> More complete than an earlier London edition of 1824 (with an
> account of how certain portions were suppressed from that London
> edition), this work provided valuable information on the publica-
> tion of CHILDE HAROLD, Cantos I-II, and other early poems, by
> an older kinsman and sometime literary advisor of LB.

Galt, John. LIFE OF LORD BYRON. London: Henry Colburn and Richard
Bentley, 1830.

> A balanced and judicious account by the Scottish novelist, who
> had known LB slightly (from 1809) and who listened to opinions from
> all sides of disputed questions before recording his opinions.

Gamba, Count Peter [Pietro]. A NARRATIVE OF LORD BYRON'S LAST JOUR-
NEY TO GREECE. London: John Murray, 1825.

> First-hand account by Teresa Guiccioli's brother, who made the
> trip with LB.

Gordon, Sir Cosmo. LIFE AND GENIUS OF LORD BYRON. London: Knight
and Lacey, 1824.

A balanced, reasonably accurate life of no particular authority, published for quick sale at the time of LB's death. Chew suspected that "Sir Cosmo Gordon" was a pen name.

Guiccioli, Countess [Teresa]. MY RECOLLECTIONS OF LORD BYRON AND THOSE OF EYE-WITNESSES OF HIS LIFE. 2 vols. London: Richard Bentley, 1869.

Based on her (unpublished) life (Vie) of LB in French, this highly romanticized account also attacks those earlier biographies that had treated her badly.

[Hobhouse, John Cam], Baron Broughton. RECOLLECTIONS OF A LONG LIFE. Ed. Lady Dorchester. 6 vols. London: John Murray, 1909-11.

Greatly cut (and censored) version of Hobhouse's diaries; the first three volumes deal with LB.

[?lley, Matthew]. THE LIFE, WRITINGS, OPINIONS, AND TIMES OF . . . LORD BYRON, INCLUDING . . . ANECDOTES AND MEMOIRS OF . . . THE PRESENT POLISHED AND ENLIGHTED AGE AND COURT OF . . . KING GEORGE THE FOURTH. IN THE COURSE OF THE BIOGRAPHY IS ALSO SEPARATELY GIVEN, COPIOUS RECOLLECTIONS OF THE LATELY DESTROYED MS. . . . ENTITLED MEMOIRS OF MY OWN LIFE AND TIMES, BY THE RIGHT HON. LORD BYRON. 3 vols. London: Matthew lley, 1825.

An unauthoritative account (favorable to LB) drawn from contemporary gossip, which down-plays the scandal of the separation by asserting that its cause was an argument arising over Lady Byron's jealousy of actresses.

Kennedy, James. CONVERSATIONS ON RELIGION WITH LORD BYRON AND OTHERS, HELD IN CEPHALONIA. London: John Murray, 1830.

A humorless, badly edited record of LB's (possibly ironic) conversations indicating deep interest in orthodox Christianity.

*Lovell, Ernest J., Jr., ed. HIS VERY SELF AND VOICE: COLLECTED CONVERSATIONS OF LORD BYRON. New York: Macmillan, 1954.

This volume, together with Lovell's excellent editions of Medwin's and Blessington's CONVERSATIONS (see below), gives modern readers an almost complete account of the recorded conversations of LB.

* _____. LADY BLESSINGTON'S CONVERSATIONS OF LORD BYRON. Princeton: Princeton University Press, 1969.

Well edited and heavily annotated, with an excellent index.

* _____. MEDWIN'S CONVERSATIONS OF LORD BYRON. Princeton: Princeton University Press, 1966.

> Includes Medwin's manuscript revisions and notes and comments on the original edition by fourteen close friends of LB.

Millingen, Julius [M.]. MEMOIRS OF THE AFFAIRS OF GREECE, CONTAINING AN ACCOUNT OF THE MILITARY AND POLITICAL EVENTS WHICH OCCURED IN 1823 AND FOLLOWING YEARS. WITH VARIOUS ANECDOTES RELATING TO LORD BYRON, AND AN ACCOUNT OF HIS LAST ILLNESS AND DEATH. London: J. Rodwell, 1831.

> This colorless first-hand account of LB's last days by one of the physicians who bled him to death evoked Trelawny's fierce attack on the doctors, in the LONDON LITERARY GAZETTE (12 February 1831), containing excerpts from his unpublished journal.

Parry, William. THE LAST DAYS OF LORD BYRON, WITH HIS LORDSHIP'S OPINIONS ON VARIOUS SUBJECTS. London: Knight and Lacey, 1825.

> An artillery specialist's account of LB's last days (possibly ghost-written, in part, by Thomas Hodgskin—see William St. Clair in K-SJ, 1970) that has enjoyed a good reputation among later biographers.

#"Paston, George" [Emily M. Symonds], and Peter Quennell. "TO LORD BYRON": FEMININE PROFILES, BASED UPON UNPUBLISHED LETTERS, 1807-1824. London: John Murray, 1939.

> Letters to LB from twelve mistresses and female friends (including Elizabeth Pigot, Caroline Lamb, Harriette Wilson, Mary Chaworth, and Claire Clairmont), strung on a thin narrative.

#Polidori, John William. THE DIARY OF JOHN WILLIAM POLIDORI, 1816, RELATING TO BYRON, SHELLEY, ETC. Ed. W[illiam] M[ichael] Rossetti. London: Elkin Matthews, 1911.

> Edited by Polidori's nephew and of first importance for the sojourn in Switzerland.

#Wallis, Bruce, ed. BYRON: THE CRITICAL VOICE. 2 vols. Salzburg: University of Salzburg Studies in English, 1973.

> A useful (if rather unimaginative) selection of LB's critical comments comments on himself, his own writings, his contemporaries, earlier writers, and dozens of other subjects (e.g., Acting, Advice, Adulation, Allegory), drawn from his publications, letters, and reported conversations and arranged alphabetically, with cross-references. It is marred by including "opinions" from one totally spurious book-- "Captain Benson's" NARRATIVE OF LORD BYRON'S VOYAGE TO CORSICA AND SARDINIA.

2. Biographies

Drinkwater, John. THE PILGRIM OF ETERNITY: BYRON—A CONFLICT. London: Hodder and Stoughton, 1925.

> An interesting exploration of conflicting elements in LB's character, based on—but not always giving proper credence to—first-hand materials.

*Marchand, Leslie A. BYRON: A BIOGRAPHY. 3 vols. New York: Alfred A. Knopf, 1957.

> The standard biography, both readable and a first-rate work of scholarship.

* _____. BYRON: A PORTRAIT. New York: Alfred A. Knopf, 1970.

> Condensed (with additions and corrections) from Marchand's three-volume biography (above), this is the best one-volume biography and the standard one for general readers.

Maurois, André [Emile Salomon Wilhelm Herzog]. BYRON. Trans. Hamish Miles. New York: Appleton, 1930.

> A reasonably good popular biography for its day (much better than Maurois' fictionalized life of PBS).

#Mayne, Ethel Colburn. BYRON. 2 vols. New York: Charles Scribner's Sons, 1912; rev. and condensed, 1 vol., 1924.

> A full, sympathetic, and fair biography on the nineteenth-century model (i.e., with less documentation and more sentiment than is now customary).

#Moore, Thomas. THE LIFE, LETTERS AND JOURNALS OF LORD BYRON. 3 vols. London: John Murray, 1830.

> This "official" early biography by a close friend of LB pictured him as poet and drawing-room gentleman.

@Nichol, John. BYRON. English Men of Letters Series. London: Macmillan, 1880.

> A very good concise life of LB, which Swinburne and Samuel Chew both rated very highly.

Quennell, Peter. BYRON: THE YEARS OF FAME. London: Collins, 1935.

> A readable but relatively superficial account of LB's life through his separation from Lady Byron.

_____. BYRON IN ITALY. London: Collins, 1941.

> A popular account of LB's later years.

Vulliamy, C[olwyn] E[dward]. BYRON, WITH A VIEW OF THE KINGDOM OF CANT AND A DISSECTION OF THE BYRONIC EGO. London: M. Joseph, 1948.

> A large, loose, and brash defense of LB's life that labels any criticism of him or his works as evidence of cant and hypocrisy.

3. Studies of a Period or an Aspect of LB's Life

#Borst, William A. LORD BYRON'S FIRST PILGRIMAGE. New Haven: Yale University Press, 1948.

> A detailed biographical study of LB's trip to Iberia and the East, 1809-11.

Brogan, Howard O. "Byron So Full of Fun, Frolic, Wit, and Whim," HUNT-INGTON LIBRARY QUARTERLY, 37 (1974), 171-89.

> Places LB's conversation in the tradition of manners, capturing his spirit very well.

#Butler, E[liza] M. BYRON AND GOETHE: ANALYSIS OF A PASSION. London: Bowes and Bowes, 1956.

> A full account of the interrelations, centering on Goethe's interest in LB's life and works.

@Buxton, John. BYRON AND SHELLEY: THE HISTORY OF A FRIENDSHIP. London: Macmillan, 1968.

> A generally accurate retelling of the story of this famous friend-ship. For a more imaginative exploration of aspects of their lit-erary interrelations, see Robinson's SHELLEY AND BYRON (Chap. 6.D.2).

Chapman, John S. BYRON AND THE HONOURABLE AUGUSTA LEIGH. New Haven: Yale University Press, 1975.

> Weighs the evidence behind the charge of incest against LB and returns "the old Scottish verdict of 'not proven'" (compare Fox be-low).

#Cline, C[larence] L. BYRON, SHELLEY, AND THEIR PISAN CIRCLE. Cam-bridge: Harvard University Press, 1952.

Contains the fullest information on John Taaffe, a member of the circle, and the clearest account of the Masi affair (see also Cline's article in TSLL, 1968).

Clubbe, John. "Byron and Scott." TSLL, 15 (1973), 67-91.

The most thorough account of their personal and literary interactions, supplemented by Clubbe himself in LIBRARY CHRONICLE [University of Pennsylvania], 39 (1973), 18-33.

Edgcumbe, Richard. BYRON: THE LAST PHASE. London: John Murray, 1910.

This long, leisurely narrative covers the period from LB's arrival in Pisa (November 1821) until his death.

Elwin, Malcolm. LORD BYRON'S FAMILY: ANNABELLA, ADA AND AUGUSTA, 1816-1824. London: John Murray, 1975.

A fragmentary continuation of the study of the Lovelace papers begun in LORD BYRON'S WIFE (below).

* _____. LORD BYRON'S WIFE. London: Macdonald, 1962.

A detailed record--with generous quotations from otherwise unpublished documents in the Lovelace Collection--of Annabella Milbanke through the date of the separation.

Erdman, David V. "Byron and Revolt in England." SCIENCE AND SOCIETY, 11 (1947), 234-48.

Emphasizes LB's intention to join the people's side in the event of a civil war following "Peterloo."

_____. "Byron and 'the New Force of the People.'" K-SJ, 11 (1962), 47-64.

Explores LB's ambivalence to the rising working-class militance in the British reform movement after Waterloo (a companion piece to and modification of the previous item).

_____. "Byron's Stage Fright: The History of His Ambition and Fear of Writing for the Stage." ELH, 6 (1939), 219-43.

The best account of its subject, modified by Thomas L. Ashton's "The Censorship of Byron's MARINO FALIERO," HUNTINGTON LIBRARY QUARTERLY, 36 (1972), 27-44.

_____. "Lord Byron and the Genteel Reformers." PMLA, 56 (1941), 1065-94.

Treats LB's dealings with the Whigs in the Holland House circle; this article, together with three others by Erdman, provides the best analysis of LB's political development, a perspective integrated in Erdman's essay on LB's life in Volume 3 of SHELLEY AND HIS CIRCLE (Chap. 5.C.3).

_____. "Lord Byron as Rinaldo." PMLA, 57 (1942), 189-231.

On LB's career in the House of Lords and his intrigues (political and otherwise) with Lady Oxford and the Whigs.

Fox, Sir John C. THE BYRON MYSTERY. London: Grant Richards, 1924.

This solid analysis, by a legal mind, of the evidence on incest between LB and Augusta reaches a verdict of "guilty"; but see also Chapman, above.

Grebanier, Bernard. THE UNINHIBITED BYRON: AN ACCOUNT OF HIS SEXUAL CONFUSION. New York: Crown, 1970.

A sensationalized account of a serious topic that is better handled by Marchand and others.

Knight, G[eorge] Wilson. LORD BYRON'S MARRIAGE: THE EVIDENCE OF THE ASTERISKS. London: Routledge and Kegan Paul, 1957.

Argues that LB was essentially androgynous ("like Christ") and that what destroyed LB's marriage was his demand for anal sex.

Lovell, Ernest J., Jr. "Byron and Mary Shelley." K-SJ, 2 (1953), 35-49.

A detailed study of Mary Shelley's emotional attachment to LB. See also Lovell's "Byron and the Byronic Hero in the Novels of Mary Shelley" (TEXAS STUDIES IN ENGLISH, 1951).

Marchand, Leslie A. "John Hunt as Byron's Publisher." K-SJ, 8 (1959), 119-32.

Surveys not only LB's relations with John Hunt, but the financial and bibliographical details of their joint publications.

*Marshall, William H. BYRON, SHELLEY, HUNT, AND "THE LIBERAL." Philadelphia: University of Pennsylvania Press, 1960.

A detailed and thorough account of this short-lived periodical.

_____. "The Byron Will of 1809." LIBRARY CHRONICLE [University of Pennsylvania], 33 (1967), 97-114.

Transcribes and comments on the terms of the will, now in the Meyer H. Davis collection at Pennsylvania. See also related articles by Marshall in the LIBRARY CHRONICLE, 33 (1967), 8-29 (on Davis' Byron collection) and LIBRARY CHRONICLE, 34 (1968), 24-50 (on the sale of LB's library in 1816).

Milbanke, Ralph, Earl of Lovelace. ASTARTE: A FRAGMENT OF THE TRUTH CONCERNING GEORGE GORDON BYRON, SIXTH LORD BYRON, RECORDED BY HIS GRANDSON. London: Chiswick Press, 1905; new (enl.) ed., 1921.

These two privately financed, limited editions embody the strange attempt of LB's grandson to vindicate Lady Byron by proving the case of incest against LB and his half-sister Augusta.

#Moore, Doris Langley. LORD BYRON: ACCOUNTS RENDERED. London: John Murray, 1974.

Important study of previously unpublished financial documents and other evidence of LB's day-to-day existence in his later years.

@Nicholson, Harold. BYRON: THE LAST JOURNEY, APRIL 1823-APRIL 1824. London: Constable, 1924; new ed., with pref., 1948.

A moving popular account of LB's expedition to Greece and his death.

*Origo, Iris. THE LAST ATTACHMENT: THE STORY OF BYRON AND TERESA GUICCIOLI AS TOLD IN THEIR UNPUBLISHED LETTERS AND OTHER FAMILY PAPERS. London: John Murray, 1949.

Until the discovery of new documents now appearing in SHELLEY AND HIS CIRCLE (Chap. 6.C.3), Origo's account was definitive for this relationship; it remains a gripping and informative narrative.

@Parker, Derek. BYRON AND HIS WORLD. London: Thames and Hudson, 1968.

A picture-book with many fine illustrations held together by a readable (though brief) narrative.

#Pratt, Willis W. BYRON AT SOUTHWELL: THE MAKING OF A POET, WITH NEW POEMS AND LETTERS FROM THE RARE BOOK COLLECTION AT THE UNIVERSITY OF TEXAS. Austin: University of Texas Press, 1948.

The best study of this phase of Byron's early career.

Raymond, Dora Neill. THE POETICAL CAREER OF LORD BYRON. New York: Henry Holt, 1924.

The book's three parts narrate LB's political activities and writings in England, Italy, and Greece respectively. Outdated by more recent studies by Erdman and Woodring.

Strickland, Margot. THE BYRON WOMEN. London: Peter Owen, 1974.

Interestingly written, sane, popular short account of eight females important in his life (including Medora and Ada, but not his mother).

Vincent, E[ric] R. BYRON, HOBHOUSE AND FOSCOLO: NEW DOCU-MENTS IN THE HISTORY OF A COLLABORATION. Cambridge: University Press, 1949.

On Foscolo's collaboration in HISTORICAL ILLUSTRATIONS FOR CHILDE HAROLD, IV.

D. CRITICISM

1. General Studies

#Blackstone, Bernard. BYRON: A SURVEY. London: Longmans, 1975.

Though a collection of individual essays on aspects of LB, the volume coalesces into an illuminating (if mildly eccentric) critical view of LB's total achievement.

Calvert, William J. BYRON: ROMANTIC PARADOX. Chapel Hill: University of North Carolina Press, 1935.

In the spirit of his times, Calvert sought to understand the poems by exploring LB's personality—with considerable verve and some success.

#Cooke, Michael G. THE BLIND MAN TRACES THE CIRCLE: ON THE PAT-TERNS AND PHILOSOPHY OF BYRON'S POETRY. Princeton: Princeton University Press, 1969.

One of the three most influential recent American critical studies (along with books by Gleckner and McGann, both cited below) covering LB's entire career.

Doherty, Francis M. BYRON. Literary Critiques. London: Evans, 1968.

A brief but competent introduction to the works for the beginning student.

Elledge, W. Paul. BYRON AND THE DYNAMICS OF METAPHOR. Nashville, Tenn.: Vanderbilt University Press, 1968.

> A thin study containing some intelligent criticism (but also a complete misreading of THE PRISONER OF CHILLON).

*Gleckner, Robert F. BYRON AND THE RUINS OF PARADISE. Baltimore: Johns Hopkins University Press, 1967.

> A work of the first importance emphasizing LB's pessimism.

*Joseph, M[ichael] K. BYRON THE POET. London: Gollancz, 1964.

> An excellent book, more thorough than Rutherford on CHILDE HAROLD and DON JUAN, but not chronological; it entirely ignores LB's juvenilia.

Jump, John D. BYRON. Routledge Author Guide Series. London: Routledge and Kegan Paul, 1972.

> A thin, general, introductory study. Less satisfactory than those of Joseph, Rutherford, and Trueblood.

*McGann, Jerome J. FIERY DUST: BYRON'S POETIC DEVELOPMENT. Chicago: University of Chicago Press, 1968.

> Perhaps the best single book for the teacher and advanced student. Its eclectic approach and its emphasis on LB's optimism should be contrasted with the critical approaches of Cooke and Gleckner respectively (both cited above).

@Marchand, Leslie A. BYRON'S POETRY: A CRITICAL INTRODUCTION. Boston: Houghton Mifflin, 1965; Cambridge: Harvard University Press, 1968.

> Highly accurate but a little heavily weighted with biographical interpretations of the poetry.

Marshall, William H. THE STRUCTURE OF BYRON'S MAJOR POEMS. Philadelphia: University of Pennsylvania Press, 1962.

> A too-brief survey containing flashes of critical insight without sustained excellence.

@Rutherford, Andrew. BYRON: A CRITICAL STUDY. Edinburgh: Oliver and Boyd, 1961.

> A clearly written, balanced survey, excellent for beginning students and general readers.

George Gordon Byron

@Trueblood, Paul G. LORD BYRON. Twayne's English Authors Series. New York: Twayne, 1969.

> A clear, accurate, modest introduction to LB's life and works.

West, Paul. BYRON AND THE SPOILER'S ART. New York: St. Martin's Press, 1960.

> An impressionistic romp through LB's works, containing a number of shrewd insights amid a multitude of wrong guesses.

2. Studies of Particular Works, Periods, and Themes

Ashton, Thomas L. "MARINO FALIERO: Byron's 'Poetry of Politics.'" SiR, 13 (1974), 1-13.

> A profound essay correlating the sexual and political themes of LB's drama.

Beaty, Frederick L. "Byron on Malthus and the Population Problem." K-SJ, 18 (1969), 17-26.

> A thorough examination of LB's attitudes.

_____. "Byron's Imitations of Juvenal and Persius," SiR, 15 (1976), 333-55.

> The most recent and extended of many excellent articles on LB by Beaty.

Bostetter, Edward E. "Masses and Solids: Byron's View of the External World." MLQ, 35 (1974), 257-71.

> The final essay of one of the most influential Byronists, whose work is best seen in THE ROMANTIC VENTRILOQUISTS (Chap. 2.C).

*Boyd, Elizabeth French. BYRON'S DON JUAN: A CRITICAL STUDY. New Brunswick, N.J.: Rutgers University Press, 1945.

> An excellent study, especially strong on LB's reading and on parallels between DON JUAN and earlier literature.

Brisman, Leslie. "Byron: Troubled Stream from a Pure Source." ELH, 42 (1975), 623-50.

#Chew, Samuel C., Jr. THE DRAMAS OF LORD BYRON: A CRITICAL STUDY. Baltimore: Johns Hopkins University Press, 1915.

> For about fifty years this slim volume was the best work on LB's dramas.

Childers, William. "Byron's WALTZ: The Germans and Their Georges." K-SJ, 18 (1969), 81-95.

> A long step toward placing WALTZ within its sociopolitical context, supplemented by David V. Erdman in K-SJ, 19 (1970), 101-17.

Cooke, Michael G. "Byron's DON JUAN: The Obsession and Self-Discipline of Spontaneity." SiR, 14 (1975), 285-302.

> Seeks the form of DON JUAN in recurring repetitions and variations of the Juan-Julia episode.

Elton, Oliver. "The Present Value of Byron." RES, 1 (1925), 24-39; rpt. in ESSAYS AND ADDRESSES (1939).

> The last judgment on LB of one of the best scholar-critics of his generation.

England, A[nthony] B. BYRON'S DON JUAN AND EIGHTEENTH-CENTURY LITERATURE: A STUDY OF SOME RHETORICAL CONTINUITIES AND DISCONTINUITIES. Lewisburg, Pa.: Bucknell University Press, 1975.

> A sane examination of LB's relationship with Pope, Swift, Samuel Butler, and Fielding, concluding that there are more differences than similarities between LB and his predecessors.

Fischer, Doucet D., and Donald H. Reiman. BYRON ON THE CONTINENT: A MEMORIAL EXHIBITION, 1824-1974. New York: The Carl H. Pforzheimer Library and The New York Public Library, 1974.

> A catalogue--with extensive historical and critical commentary--of an exhibition held at the New York Public Library, February-April 1974.

Fuess, Claude M. LORD BYRON AS A SATIRIST IN VERSE. New York: Columbia University Press, 1912.

> A substantial historical survey, solid in its day and still worth consulting, though partly outdated.

Goldstein, Stephen L. "Byron's CAIN and the Painites." SiR, 14 (1975), 391-410.

> The reception--and promotion--of CAIN by Richard Carlile and other radical disciples of Thomas Paine.

Johnson, E[dward] D[udley] H. "Don Juan in England." ELH, 11 (1944), 135-53.

_____. "A Political Interpretation of Byron's MARINO FALIERO." MLQ, 3 (1942), 417-25.

> Sees LB's drama reflecting contemporary British and Italian politics.

Jones, Joseph Jay. "Lord Byron on America." TEXAS STUDIES IN ENGLISH, 1941, pp. 121-37.

Jump, John D., ed. BYRON: CHILDE HAROLD'S PILGRIMAGE AND DON JUAN--A CASEBOOK. London: Macmillan, 1973.

Klapper, M[olly] Roxana. THE GERMAN LITERARY INFLUENCE ON BYRON. Salzburg: University of Salzburg Studies in English, 1974.

> A useful exploration of LB's "Wertherism" and the influence on him of Gessner and other writers.

Knight, G[eorge] Wilson. BYRON AND SHAKESPEARE. London: Routledge and Kegan Paul, 1966.

> A lengthy exploration of Shakespeare's impact on LB, with an appendix on "The Separation Controversy" (see also Knight on LORD BYRON'S MARRIAGE, Sec. C.3).

_____. LORD BYRON: CHRISTIAN VIRTUES. London: Routledge and Kegan Paul, 1952.

> Intended as the first volume of an uncompleted "trilogy on Byron as man and poet" (the greatest in England "since Shakespeare"), this book almost parodies the method of bringing together all references on each one of LB's virtues (his love of animals, his internationalism, his good deeds as a patron, etc.).

[Lockhart, John Gibson]. JOHN BULL'S LETTER TO LORD BYRON. Ed. Alan Lang Strout. Norman: University of Oklahoma Press, 1947.

> One of the most influential contemporary critiques of LB (first published, 1821) that may have persuaded him to continue DON JUAN.

#Lovell, Ernest J., Jr. BYRON: THE RECORD OF A QUEST: STUDIES IN A POET'S CONCEPT AND TREATMENT OF NATURE. Austin: University of Texas Press, 1949.

> A major study of a crucial theme in LB's intellectual development.

#McGann, Jerome J. DON JUAN IN CONTEXT. Chicago: University of Chicago Press, 1976.

A brief but important exploration of the poetic style and thematic focus of LB's poem, set in the context of developments from his earlier life and poetry. See also a symposium by McGann, Ridenour, and Reiman in SiR 16 (1977), 563-94.

Marjarum, Edward Wayne. BYRON AS SKEPTIC AND BELIEVER. Princeton: Princeton University Press, 1938.

Examines briefly LB's early theism, his skeptical doubts, the influence of Lucretius, Spinoza, and various other "naturalists" (including PBS), and the attraction of Roman Catholicism.

Ogle, Robert B. "A Byron Contradiction: Some Light on His Italian Study." SiR, 12 (1973), 436-42.

LB's use of histories of Italian literature by Ginguené and Sismondi.

Pafford, Ward. "Byron and the Mind of Man: CHILDE HAROLD III-IV and MANFRED." SiR, 1 (1962), 105-27.

An important exploration of the influence of PBS (and, through him, WW) on LB during the sojourn in Switzerland and immediately thereafter.

*Ridenour, George M. THE STYLE OF DON JUAN. New Haven: Yale University Press, 1960.

The most ambitious argument for the thematic and stylistic unity of DON JUAN. For a later, equally important study, see McGann's DON JUAN IN CONTEXT, cited above.

Sperry, Stuart M. "Byron and the Meaning of MANFRED." CRITICISM, 16 (1974), 189-202.

Joins Pafford's (above) as one of the best periodical essays for teachers and students alike.

*Thorslev, Peter L., Jr. THE BYRONIC HERO: TYPES AND PROTOTYPES. Minneapolis: University of Minnesota Press, 1962.

A mature study tracing the various antecedents of LB's early heros and exploring LB's transformations of the traditions.

Trueblood, Paul Graham. THE FLOWERING OF BYRON'S GENIUS: STUDIES IN BYRON'S DON JUAN. Palo Alto, Calif.: Stanford University Press, 1945.

A thin study, largely superseded by Steffan and Pratt, Boyd, Ridenour, McGann, and the recent general critical books.

3. Collections of Miscellaneous Essays

@Bostetter, Edward E., ed. TWENTIETH CENTURY INTERPRETATIONS OF DON JUAN: A COLLECTION OF CRITICAL ESSAYS. Englewood Cliffs, N.J.: Prentice Hall, 1969.

> Reprints or excerpts from books, essays and reviews--on DON JUAN and LB generally--by Auden, Lovell, Joseph, Ridenour, Rutherford, Steffan, Wilkie, Alvin B. Kernan, Woolf, Yeats, T.S. Eliot, Boyd, Paul West, Kroeber, Hirsch, and Gleckner.

Briscoe, Walter A., ed. BYRON, THE POET: A COLLECTION OF ADDRESSES AND ESSAYS. London: G. Routledge and Sons, 1924.

> This interesting miscellany drawn from lectures (1915-23), news-paper articles, and other sources, gave the case for LB on the centenary of his death.

Jump, John D., ed. BYRON: A SYMPOSIUM. London: Macmillan, 1975.

> Brief sesquicentenary lectures by A.L. Rowse, Jump, Francis Berry, Gilbert Phelps, P.M. Yarker, A.B. England, W. Ruddick, Anne Barton, and P.D. Fleck.

@West, Paul, ed. BYRON: A COLLECTION OF CRITICAL ESSAYS. Englewood Cliffs, N.J.: Prentice-Hall, 1963.

> Includes, besides an original introduction, reprints of fourteen essays or portions of books, including those by G. Wilson Knight, W.W. Robson, Blackstone, Praz, West, Steffan, Leavis, Ridenour, Helen Gardner, Edmund Wilson, Gilbert Highet, Bertrand Russell, and John Wain.

Chapter 6
PERCY BYSSHE SHELLEY (1792-1822)

A. CONCORDANCES, BIBLIOGRAPHIES, AND STUDIES OF REPUTATION AND INFLUENCE

1. Concordances

*Ellis, F[rederick] S. A LEXICAL CONCORDANCE TO THE POETICAL WORKS OF PERCY BYSSHE SHELLEY. London: Bernard Quaritch, 1892.

> Keyed to Forman's two-volume edition of 1882 (Sec. B.1, below) this concordance does not include references to the poems in ORIGINAL POETRY BY VICTOR AND CAZIRE, THE ESDAILE NOTEBOOK, and other more recently published poetry and fragments.

2. Bibliographies

Cameron, Kenneth Neill. "Shelley Scholarship: 1940-1953, A Critical Survey." K-SJ, 3 (1954), 89-109.

> An important survey of scholarly materials available to the student through 1953 (including much published before 1940).

*Dunbar, Clement. A BIBLIOGRAPHY OF SHELLEY STUDIES: 1823-1950. New York: Garland, 1976.

> Very full list of substantive discussions of Shelley in books, articles, and reviews between the periods covered by White's UNEXTINGUISHED HEARTH and the annual bibliography in K-SJ.

*Forman, H[arry] Buxton. THE SHELLEY LIBRARY: AN ESSAY IN BIBLIOGRAPHY. London: Reeves and Turner, 1886.

> Still the best descriptive bibliography of first and early editions of PBS's poetry and prose.

#Granniss, Ruth S. A DESCRIPTIVE CATALOGUE OF THE FIRST EDITIONS IN BOOK FORM OF THE WRITINGS OF PERCY BYSSHE SHELLEY. New York: The Grolier Club, 1923.

> Supplements Forman (above) and contains facsimiles of the title pages of most first editions.

#White, Newman Ivey. THE UNEXTINGUISHED HEARTH: SHELLEY AND HIS CONTEMPORARY CRITICS. Durham, N.C.: Duke University Press, 1938.

> Reprints, with commentary, the reviews and periodical comments on PBS during his lifetime (to the end of 1822).

#Wise, Thomas James. A SHELLEY LIBRARY: A CATALOGUE OF PRINTED BOOKS, MANUSCRIPTS AND AUTOGRAPH LETTERS . . . COLLECTED BY THOMAS JAMES WISE. London: Privately printed, 1924.

> Though based on Wise's personal collection (now in the British Library), this catalogue is both broader in scope and less accurate in details than Forman's THE SHELLEY LIBRARY (above).

3. Studies of Reputation and Influence

Abdel-Hai, M. "Shelley and the Arabs: An Essay in Comparative Literature." JOURNAL OF ARABIC LITERATURE, 3 (1972), 72-89.

> After surveying the growth of PBS's reputation in the Arab world, the study offers "A Tentative Bibliography of Arabic Translations of Shelley's Poems."

Barcus, James E., ed. SHELLEY: THE CRITICAL HERITAGE. London: Routledge and Kegan Paul, 1975.

> Reprints selected reviews and excerpted comments on PBS from England and America, 1810-68. Most of the reviews represented here are found in full in White's UNEXTINGUISHED HEARTH (above) and/or in Reiman's THE ROMANTICS REVIEWED (Chap. 1.A.4).

Barton, Wilfred Converse. SHELLEY AND THE NEW CRITICISM: THE ANATOMY OF A CRITICAL MISVALUATION. Salzburg: University of Salzburg Studies in English, 1973.

> This spirited defense of PBS against the New Critics reflects the atmosphere of the 1950s and now seems dated.

#Bornstein, George. YEATS AND SHELLEY. Chicago: University of Chicago Press, 1970.

The most complete treatment of the subject. See also H.W.
Häusermann in THE MINT: A MISCELLANY, edited by G. Grigson (1946), and Harold Bloom's YEATS (1970).

#Duerksen, Roland A. SHELLEYAN IDEAS IN VICTORIAN LITERATURE. The
Hague: Mouton, 1966.

Traces the impact of PBS on the major Victorians (through Shaw),
particularly in their political thinking.

Fogarty, Nancy. SHELLEY IN THE TWENTIETH CENTURY: A STUDY OF THE
DEVELOPMENT OF SHELLEY CRITICISM IN ENGLAND AND AMERICA, 1916-
1971. Salzburg: University of Salzburg Studies in English, 1976.

Liptzin, Solomon. SHELLEY IN GERMANY. New York: Columbia University
Press, 1924.

Sketches PBS's reputation and influence in Germany through 1922.

@Norman, Sylva. FLIGHT OF THE SKYLARK: THE DEVELOPMENT OF SHEL-
LEY'S REPUTATION. London: Max Reinhardt, 1954.

A very readable account of the reputation of PBS during the nineteenth century (and his heirs' attempts to keep it that way). See
supplementary essays by Carl Woodring in K-SJ (1960) and by
Sylva Norman in TSLL (1967).

#Peyre, Henri. SHELLEY ET LA FRANCE: LYRISME ANGLAIS ET LYRISME
FRANÇAIS AU XIXe SIECLE. Cairo: Paul Barbey, 1935.

A thorough, scholarly account of lasting value.

Pollin, Burton R. MUSIC FOR SHELLEY'S POETRY: AN ANNOTATED BIBLI-
OGRAPHY OF MUSICAL SETTINGS OF SHELLEY'S POETRY. New York: Da
Capo, 1974.

An exhaustive listing of works by composers based on or suggested
by PBS's words.

Pottle, Frederick A. SHELLEY AND BROWNING: A MYTH AND SOME
FACTS. Chicago: Pembroke Press, 1923; rpt. with a new pref., 1965.

A slim but perceptive account of Browning's early enthusiasm for
PBS.

#Power, Julia. SHELLEY IN AMERICA IN THE NINETEENTH CENTURY. Lin-
coln: University of Nebraska Press, 1940.

A full account of American response to PBS and his poetry during
the century.

Reiman, Donald H. "Shelley in the Encyclopedias." K-SJ, 12 (1963), 55-65.

> Traces PBS's fortune (and, incidentally, those of other Romantics) in nineteenth-century British (and some American) encyclopedias.

B. EDITIONS

1. Collected Editions

*Forman, H[arry] Buxton, ed. THE POETICAL WORKS OF PERCY BYSSHE SHELLEY. 4 vols. London: Reeves and Turner, 1876; PROSE WORKS. 4 vols. Library Edition. 1880. POETICAL WORKS. Republished in 2 vols., 1882; 5 vols., 1892.

> Though this edition can no longer be considered "complete," it is probably the most carefully planned and executed edition of PBS's writings ever published and it remains the best source of information on some MSS that have since been lost sight of. Ellis' CONCORDANCE (Sec. A.1, above) is keyed to the 1882 text; the Aldine Edition of 1892 contains a few additions and corrections.

*Ingpen, Roger, and Walter E. Peck, eds. THE COMPLETE WORKS OF PERCY BYSSHE SHELLEY. 10 vols. Julian Edition. London: Ernest Benn, 1924-30.

> The nearest thing to a complete edition, its three volumes of PBS's prose will remain standard until the new Oxford edition, being edited by Timothy Webb and E.B. Murray, appears.

#Shelley, Mary W., ed. ESSAYS, LETTERS FROM ABROAD, TRANSLATIONS AND FRAGMENTS. 2 vols. London: Edward Moxon, 1840.

> The first publication of much of PBS's prose and the first selection of his letters. The text, reset in double columns, was bound with the one-volume second edition of the POETICAL WORKS during the 1840s (see entry, below), 1850s, and 1860s to form Moxon's one-volume edition of PBS's WORKS.

_____. THE POETICAL WORKS OF PERCY BYSSHE SHELLEY. 4 vols. London: Edward Moxon, 1839; 2nd, enl. ed., 1 vol., 1840.

> The second, one-volume edition contains poems not included in the first. Both editions are basic sources for a study of the texts of PBS's poetry.

2. Collected Poetry and Collected Prose

Clark, David Lee, ed. SHELLEY'S PROSE; OR, THE TRUMPET OF A PROPHECY. Albuquerque: University of New Mexico Press, 1954.

An unreliable edition both in text and in annotation. Until a much-needed new edition is published (two are now in process), scholars must depend on volumes 5-7 of the Julian Edition, cited under Ingpen and Peck, above.

*Hutchinson, Thomas, ed. THE COMPLETE POETICAL WORKS OF SHELLEY. Oxford: Clarendon Press, 1904; London: Oxford University Press, 1905. (Reset 1943; second ed., corrected by G.M. Matthews, 1970.)

Though its texts of many poems are seriously outdated and though it lacks annotation, this edition remains the most nearly complete one-volume edition of the poetry still in print.

#Locock, C[harles] D., ed. THE POEMS OF PERCY BYSSHE SHELLEY. Introd. A. Clutton-Brock. 2 vols. London: Methuen, 1911.

Useful primarily for its notes--including some that examine textual as well as critical cruxes.

Rogers, Neville, ed. THE COMPLETE POETICAL WORKS OF PERCY BYSSHE SHELLEY. 4 vols. projected. Oxford: Clarendon Press, 1972-- .

Volume 1 appeared in 1972, volume 2 in 1975. No edition of PBS's works has ever met with such a storm of criticism from scholars and reviewers. This edition takes a step backwards in editing PBS, being both inadequate and erroneous in its canon, textual principles, accuracy of execution, and critical annotation.

Rossetti, William Michael, ed. THE POETICAL WORKS OF PERCY BYSSHE SHELLEY. 2 vols. London: Edward Moxon, 1870; rev. ed., 3 vols., 1878.

Though reprinted in three volumes and one volume throughout the nineteenth century and historically important, Rossetti's texts are now outdated and only sporadically useful, even to the scholar.

Woodberry, George Edward, ed. THE COMPLETE POETICAL WORKS OF PERCY BYSSHE SHELLEY. Centenary Edition. 4 vols. Boston: Houghton Mifflin, 1892. (Condensed into 1 vol. as the Cambridge Edition, 1901; slightly rev., with new errors, by Newell F. Ford in 1975.)

The four-volume Centenary Edition is still useful to the scholar for its collations and notes. The Cambridge Edition is now badly outdated and of little value.

3. Selected Poetry and Prose

a. GENERAL EDITIONS

Bloom, Harold, ed. SELECTED POETRY. Signet Classic Poetry Series. New York: New American Library, 1966.

> A substantial selection, with an introduction and a few notes.

Spender, Stephen, ed. A CHOICE OF SHELLEY'S VERSE. London: Faber and Faber, 1971.

> A small selection, with a brief and not very good introduction.

b. TEACHING EDITIONS

@Barnard, Ellsworth, ed. SELECTED POEMS, ESSAYS, AND LETTERS. New York: Odyssey, 1944.

> A well-annotated teaching edition for its day. Although this volume is dated, some of its notes are still useful.

@Butter, P[eter] H. ALASTOR AND OTHER POEMS, PROMETHEUS UNBOUND WITH OTHER POEMS, ADONAIS. Collins Annotated Student Texts. London: Collins, 1970.

> A well-edited and fully annotated edition of three complete volumes arranged as PBS published them.

Cameron, Kenneth Neill, ed. SELECTED POETRY AND PROSE. Rinehart Edition. New York: Rinehart, 1951.

> Selections arranged by categories, with an introduction and with notes at the end of the book.

@Duerksen, Roland A., ed. POLITICAL WRITINGS, INCLUDING A DEFENCE OF POETRY. Crofts Classics. New York: Appleton-Century-Crofts, 1970.

> A generous selection of the prose, with an introduction and a few notes.

Holloway, John, ed. SELECTED POEMS. London: Heinemann, 1960.

> A rather small (mildly eccentric) selection, enhanced by an intelligent introduction and substantial annotation.

@McElderry, Bruce R., Jr., ed. SHELLEY'S CRITICAL PROSE. Regents Critics Series. Lincoln: University of Nebraska Press, 1967.

An excellent edition, including annotated texts of A DEFENCE OF POETRY, all PBS's Prefaces and reviews, selections from the letters, the dialogue between PBS and Byron on HAMLET, and Peacock's FOUR AGES, with introduction, bibliography, and--most important-- substantial index.

@Matthews, G[eoffrey] M., ed. SHELLEY: SELECTED POEMS AND PROSE. New Oxford English Series. London: Oxford University Press, 1964.

A slender selection, but containing original textual material and very valuable annotation.

*Reiman, Donald H., and Sharon B. Powers, eds. SHELLEY'S POETRY AND PROSE: A NORTON CRITICAL EDITION. New York: W.W. Norton, 1977.

Provides new texts, based on primary authorities, of most of the major poems and three prose works, as well as both the most detailed annotation available for most of the works included and a selection of recent criticism.

Rogers, Neville, ed. SELECTED POETRY. Riverside Editions. Boston: Houghton Mifflin, 1968; London: Oxford University Press, 1969.

The introduction and notes are riddled with factual as well as interpretive errors; not recommended.

@Webb, Timothy, ed. SELECTED POEMS. London: J.M. Dent, 1977.

A brief but very well edited selection; "Julian and Maddalo," EPIPSYCHIDION, and ADONAIS are the longest poems included complete, but there are good (reedited) selections from PBS's poetic translations.

4. Individual Titles

*Cameron, Kenneth Neill, ed. THE ESDAILE NOTEBOOK: A VOLUME OF EARLY POEMS. New York: Alfred A. Knopf, 1964; corrected ed., London: Faber and Faber, 1965.

The best annotated edition. For the most accurate text, see SHELLEY AND HIS CIRCLE, volume 4, edited by K.N. Cameron (Sec. C.3, below).

#Dobell, Bertram, ed. THE WANDERING JEW: A POEM. Shelley Society's Publications. London: Reeves and Turner, 1887.

Still one of the basic sources of textual and background information on the poem.

Duerksen, Roland A., ed. THE CENCI. Library of the Liberal Arts. Indianapolis: Bobbs-Merrill, 1970.

> A paperback text with study aids.

EPIPSYCHIDION, 1821, TOGETHER WITH SHELLEY'S MANUSCRIPT DRAFT. Menston, Yorks, Engl.: Scolar Press, 1970.

> A photo-facsimile reprint of the rare first edition, with the portions of the draft of the poem found in Bodleian MS. Shelley d.1.

#Forman, H[arry] Buxton, ed. THE MASK OF ANARCHY . . .: FAC-SIMILE OF THE HOLOGRAPH MANUSCRIPT. Shelley Society's Publications. London: Reeves and Turner, 1887.

> Important photofacsimile of PBS's intermediate draft (now in the British Library) from which Mary Shelley copied (and PBS corrected) the final press-copy (now in the Library of Congress).

_____. A PROPOSAL FOR PUTTING REFORM TO THE VOTE THROUGHOUT THE KINGDOM: FACSIMILE OF THE HOLOGRAPH MANUSCRIPT. Shelley Society's Publications. London: Reeves and Turner, 1887.

> Important early photofacsimile of PBS's prose tract of 1817.

Hicks, Arthur C., and R. Milton Clarke, eds. A STAGE VERSION OF SHELLEY'S CENCI, BASED UPON THE BELLINGHAM THEATRE GUILD'S PRODUCTION . . . MARCH . . . 1940. Caldwell, Idaho: Caxton Printers, 1945.

> An acting text based on (and with the history of) a production of the play at Bellingham, Washington.

Hughes, A[rthur] M[ontague] D[urban], ed. POEMS PUBLISHED IN 1820. Oxford: Clarendon Press, 1910.

> Though useful in its day, this student's edition of PROMETHEUS UNBOUND . . . WITH OTHER POEMS has been superseded by Butter's edition (Sec. B.3.b, above).

@Jordan, John E., ed. A DEFENCE OF POETRY: PERCY BYSSHE SHELLEY, THE FOUR AGES OF POETRY: THOMAS LOVE PEACOCK. Library of the Liberal Arts. Indianapolis: Bobbs-Merrill, 1965.

> An excellent edition, showing hard work and mature judgment in both texts and notes.

Rogers, Neville, ed. THE ESDAILE POEMS: EARLY MINOR POEMS FROM THE ESDAILE NOTEBOOK. Oxford: Clarendon Press, 1966.

> Though this edition corrected a few textual errors in Cameron's edition of 1964 (above), its annotation is inferior to that edition

and its text was superseded in volume 4 of SHELLEY AND HIS
CIRCLE (Sec. C.3, below).

#Zillman, Lawrence John, ed. SHELLEY'S PROMETHEUS UNBOUND: THE
TEXT AND THE DRAFTS. New Haven, Conn.: Yale University Press, 1968.

> Helpful, but based on a mistaken theory of editing PROMETHEUS
> UNBOUND.

5. Textual Sources and Studies

#Forman, H[arry] Buxton, ed. NOTE BOOKS OF PERCY BYSSHE SHELLEY
FROM . . . THE LIBRARY OF W.K. BIXBY. 3 vols. Boston: Bibliophile
Society, 1911.

> Transcriptions, with running commentary, of large portions of three
> of PBS's rough-draft notebooks now in the Huntington Library.

Garnett, Richard, ed. RELICS OF SHELLEY. London: Edward Moxon, 1862.

> Contains previously unpublished fragments from PBS's rough-draft
> MSS. Its importance is now entirely historical.

Koszul, A[ndré] H., ed. SHELLEY'S PROSE IN THE BODLEIAN MANUSCRIPTS.
London: Henry Frowde, 1910.

> Annotated transcriptions from Lady Jane Shelley's first bequest of
> MSS to the Bodleian Library, Oxford.

Locock, C[harles] D. AN EXAMINATION OF THE SHELLEY MANUSCRIPTS
IN THE BODLEIAN LIBRARY. Oxford: Clarendon Press, 1903.

> Describes--and collates with published texts--the first group of
> PBS's poetic notebooks given to the Bodleian Library, Oxford.

#Massey, Irving. POSTHUMOUS POEMS OF SHELLEY: MARY SHELLEY'S FAIR
COPY BOOK, BODLEIAN MS. SHELLEY ADDS D. 9. Montreal: McGill-
Queens University Press, 1969.

> Transcribes and collates with published texts and other MSS one of
> Mary Shelley's chief copy books that she used to transcribe poetry
> from PBS's MSS after his death.

Notopoulos, James A. "The Dating of Shelley's Prose." PMLA, 58 (1943),
477-98.

> Still a valuable corrective to the erroneous dates in David Lee
> Clark's edition of the prose.

Shelley-Rolls, Sir John C.E., and Roger Ingpen, eds. VERSE AND PROSE, FROM THE MANUSCRIPTS OF PERCY BYSSHE SHELLEY. London: Privately printed, 1934.

> Prints for the first time additional fragments from the "Boscombe" (now Bodleian) Shelley MSS.

#Taylor, Charles H., Jr. THE EARLY COLLECTED EDITIONS OF SHELLEY'S POEMS: A STUDY IN THE HISTORY AND TRANSMISSION OF THE PRINTED TEXT. New Haven: Yale University Press, 1958.

> Studies various pirated and unauthorized editions between 1824 and 1839, showing their influence on Mary Shelley's editions.

#Woodberry, George Edward. THE SHELLEY NOTEBOOK IN THE HARVARD COLLEGE LIBRARY. Cambridge, Mass.: John Barnard Associates, 1929.

> Photofacsimile of an important copy book containing some of PBS's best poems; the notes are flawed because Woodberry could not distinguish between PBS's and Mary Shelley's handwriting.

C. BIOGRAPHICAL SOURCES AND STUDIES

1. Primary Documents

Blunden, Edmund, ed. SHELLEY AND KEATS, AS THEY STRUCK THEIR CONTEMPORARIES: NOTES PARTLY FROM MANUSCRIPT SOURCES. London: C.W. Beaumont, 1925.

> The first two-thirds of this slim volume concern PBS, including Thornton Hunt's important memoir, "Shelley--By One Who Knew Him" (pp. 11-53).

*Clairmont, Claire. THE JOURNALS OF CLAIRE CLAIRMONT. Ed. Marion Kingston Stocking. Cambridge: Harvard University Press, 1968.

> A very accurate and well-annotated edition of a crucial document in PBS's biography.

*Gisborne, Maria, and Edward E. Williams. MARIA GISBORNE & EDWARD E. WILLIAMS: THEIR JOURNALS AND LETTERS. Ed. Frederick L. Jones. Norman: University of Oklahoma Press, 1951.

> Valuable for PBS's biography for the period 1819-22. However, this text of Gisborne's journal contains substantial errors.

Hogg, Thomas Jefferson. THE LIFE OF PERCY BYSSHE SHELLEY. 2 vols. London: Edward Moxon, 1858; ed. Edward Dowden, 1906.

PBS's college friend purposely caricatured PBS and corrupted the texts of PBS's letters to make himself look superior to PBS; amusing but unreliable.

#Hunt, Leigh. LORD BYRON AND SOME OF HIS CONTEMPORARIES. London: Henry Colburn, 1828.

The material on PBS appears also (with some revisions) in Hunt's AUTOBIOGRAPHY (1850).

#Medwin, Thomas. THE LIFE OF PERCY BYSSHE SHELLEY, REVISED FOR A SECOND EDITION. Ed. H[arry] Buxton Forman. London: Oxford University Press, 1913.

Though erroneous on many details, this biography, first published in 1847 by PBS's cousin and school friend, is the only early life of PBS to concentrate on his literary interests.

#Peacock, Thomas Love. PEACOCK'S MEMOIRS OF SHELLEY WITH SHELLEY'S LETTERS TO PEACOCK. Ed. H.F.B. Brett-Smith. London: Oxford University Press, 1909.

Peacock comments on and corrects the lives of PBS by Hogg, Trelawny, Lady Jane Shelley, and others. These memoirs and letters were first published in three parts in FRASER'S MAGAZINE (June 1858; January 1860; March 1862).

Shelley, Lady Jane. SHELLEY MEMORIALS: FROM AUTHENTIC SOURCES. London: Henry King, 1859; 3rd ed., with new pref., 1875.

The Shelley family took their MSS away from Hogg after he had misused them in his LIFE (see above), printing a selection, with commentary, in this small volume.

Shelley, Mary W. THE LETTERS OF MARY W. SHELLEY. Ed. Frederick L. Jones. 2 vols. Norman: University of Oklahoma Press, 1944.

Still valuable but incomplete. A new edition by Betty T. Bennett will soon be published by Johns Hopkins.

_____. MARY SHELLEY'S JOURNAL. Ed. Frederick L. Jones. Norman: University of Oklahoma Press, 1947.

Based on the incomplete (and often garbled) text in SHELLEY AND MARY (below). A new edition is in progress, to be published by Oxford University Press.

*Shelley, Percy Bysshe. THE LETTERS OF PERCY BYSSHE SHELLEY. Ed. Frederick L. Jones. 2 vols. Oxford: Clarendon Press, 1964.

Corrections and additional letters appear in SHELLEY AND HIS CIRCLE, edited by Cameron and Reiman (cited in Sec. C.3).

SHELLEY AND MARY. 3 vols., occasionally 4 vols. London: Privately printed, 1882.

These continuously paginated volumes contain partially accurate texts of letters, journals, and documents, issued by the poet's son and daughter-in-law, now useful chiefly as a record of materials available among the Abinger and Bodleian MSS.

#Trelawny, Edward John. RECOLLECTIONS OF THE LAST DAYS OF SHELLEY AND BYRON. London: Edward Moxon, 1858; rev. as RECORDS OF SHELLEY, BYRON AND THE AUTHOR, 2 vols., 1878.

Trelawny, who lied wildly about his own life, seems to have stuck as close to the truth in writing about PBS as good story telling would permit.

*Wolfe, Humbert, ed. THE LIFE OF PERCY BYSSHE SHELLEY, AS COMPRISED IN [the lives by Hogg, Trelawny, and Peacock, see above]. 2 vols. London: J.M. Dent, 1933.

A useful (though not totally accurate) reprinting of three basic sources, with a sparse but helpful unified index.

2. Biographies

@Blunden, Edmund. SHELLEY: A LIFE STORY. London: Collins, 1946.

A readable, popular narrative but overly dependent on Dowden's biography of sixty years earlier (see below).

*Dowden, Edward. THE LIFE OF PERCY BYSSHE SHELLEY. 2 vols. London: Kegan Paul, Trench, 1886; rev. and abridged, 1 vol., 1896.

The official life by a distinguished scholar, somewhat inhibited by restrictions imposed by PBS's heirs and by Dowden's own limited sympathy for PBS.

@Holmes, Richard. SHELLEY: THE PURSUIT. London: Weidenfedd and Nicolson, 1974.

A substantial popular biography by a well-read amateur with no appreciation of PBS's greater poetry. For a detailed appraisal, see K.N. Cameron's review, K-SJ, 25 (1976), 162-69.

*Ingpen, Roger. SHELLEY IN ENGLAND: NEW FACTS AND LETTERS FROM THE SHELLEY-WHITTON PAPERS. 2 vols. paginated as 1. London: Kegan Paul, Trench, Trübner, 1917.

Sane throughout but especially valuable on PBS's legal and financial dealings with his father and on the fate of his children
Charles and Ianthe.

Maurois, André [Emile S.W. Herzog]. ARIEL: THE LIFE OF SHELLEY. Trans.
Ella D'Arcy. New York: Appleton, 1924.

A readable but extremely distorted fictionalized life that, widely
circulated, warped general readers' view of PBS for two generations.

#Peck, Walter E. SHELLEY: HIS LIFE AND WORK. 2 vols. Boston: Hough-
ton Mifflin, 1927.

A valuable storehouse of information partly distorted by the author's
personal predilections.

Rossetti, William Michael. MEMOIR OF SHELLEY. London: E. Moxon,
Son, 1870.

The biographical introduction to Rossetti's edition of PBS's poetry
(1870), this brief memoir was the fairest and best brief account
before White's PORTRAIT OF SHELLEY (see below).

*White, Newman Ivey. SHELLEY. 2 vols. New York: Alfred A. Knopf,
1940.

Abridged as A PORTRAIT OF SHELLEY (1945), this title is still
the standard biography, though correctable in parts by scholarship
of the past thirty-five years (see especially Cameron and Reiman,
SHELLEY AND HIS CIRCLE, in Sec. C.3).

3. Studies of a Period or an Aspect of PBS's Life

Angeli, Helen Rossetti. SHELLEY AND HIS FRIENDS IN ITALY. London:
Methuen, 1911.

Remains a valuable source book and interesting narrative of the
years in Italy.

Cameron, Kenneth Neill. "Shelley vs. Southey: New Light on an Old Quar-
rel." PMLA, 57 (1942), 489-512.

A detailed analysis of the entire course of relations between the
two men, with important suggestions for the impact on ADONAIS
of their final animosity.

*Cameron, Kenneth Neill, and Donald H. Reiman, eds. SHELLEY AND HIS
CIRCLE, 1773-1822. 12 vols. projected. Cambridge: Harvard University
Press, Vols. 1-2, 1961; Vols. 3-4, 1971; Vols. 5-6, 1973.

A catalogue-edition of MSS in The Carl H. Pforzheimer Library, with elaborate commentaries and essays, this is a very important repository of biographical information on PBS, LB, Hunt, Peacock, Mary Shelley, and other contemporaries not found in the standard biographies and reference works, as well as of bibliographical and critical material.

#Cline, C[larence] L. BYRON, SHELLEY, AND THEIR PISAN CIRCLE. Cambridge: Harvard University Press, 1952.

A detailed account of the gathering, interactions, and dispersal of the group, 1820-22, with new information (particularly on John Taaffe).

Matthews, G[eoffrey] M. "Shelley and Jane Williams." RES, n.s. 12 (1961), 40-48.

Argues for a passionate love affair between PBS and Jane Williams, based on MS evidence (but see Reiman below).

Reiman, Donald H. "Shelley's 'The Triumph of Life': The Biographical Problem." PMLA, 78 (1962), 404-13.

A detailed refutation of Matthews' "Shelley and Jane Williams" (above) and discussion of PBS's use of Rousseau's JULIE in "The Triumph."

Roe, Ivan. SHELLEY: THE LAST PHASE. London: Hutchinson, 1953.

A detailed, popular narrative of the last days of PBS at Casa Magni, Lerici.

Small, Christopher. ARIEL LIKE A HARPY: SHELLEY, MARY, AND FRANKENSTEIN. London: Victor Gollancz, 1972.

Reprinted in America (1973) as MARY SHELLEY'S FRANKENSTEIN: TRACING THE MYTH, this is an interesting critique of the interactions of PBS and Mary Shelley, suggesting that Victor Frankenstein is based on PBS.

D. CRITICISM

1. General Studies

*Baker, Carlos. SHELLEY'S MAJOR POETRY: THE FABRIC OF A VISION. Princeton: Princeton University Press, 1948.

Fine interpretations of the poems from ALASTOR to "The Triumph of Life," emphasizing PBS's use of earlier British literature and his symbolic mode.

#Butter, Peter H. SHELLEY'S IDOLS OF THE CAVE. Edinburgh: Edinburgh University Press, 1954.

> Explores perceptively PBS's characteristic patterns of symbols and modes of thought.

*Cameron, Kenneth Neill. SHELLEY: THE GOLDEN YEARS. Cambridge: Harvard University Press, 1974.

> In this sequel to THE YOUNG SHELLEY (below), Cameron examines in detail a few biographical cruxes before outlining in detail the factual background and thought of Shelley's mature prose and poems.

* _____. THE YOUNG SHELLEY: GENESIS OF A RADICAL. New York: Macmillan, 1950.

> The best account of Shelley's intellectual development through the writing of QUEEN MAB.

Campbell, Olwen Ward. SHELLEY AND THE UNROMANTICS. London: Methuen, 1924.

> Important during the 1920s and 1930s as a sane and balanced account of Shelley's thought and poetic achievement.

@Carey, Gillian. SHELLEY. London: Evans, 1975.

> A very brief but reasonably accurate and entirely sensible introduction for students.

#Curran, Stuart. SHELLEY'S ANNUS MIRABILIS: THE MATURING OF AN EPIC VISION. San Marino, Calif.: Huntington Library, 1975.

> Excellent, original study of the poems of late 1818 and 1819, emphasizing the Zoroastrian-Manichaean elements.

#Grabo, Carl. THE MAGIC PLANT: THE GROWTH OF SHELLEY'S THOUGHT. Chapel Hill: University of North Carolina Press, 1936.

> The first important study of PBS's thought and art in the mid-century revival of his critical reputation.

King-Hele, Desmond. SHELLEY: HIS THOUGHT AND WORK. London: Macmillan, 1960.

> A substantial introduction to PBS for the general reader, strongest on the relationship of PBS's thought and images to the scientific knowledge of his day.

Kurtz, Benjamin P. THE PURSUIT OF DEATH: A STUDY OF SHELLEY'S POETRY. New York: Oxford University Press, 1933.

> An intelligent and readable account of PBS's thought, emphasizing his concern with death and his maturing attitude toward it.

*Reiman, Donald H. PERCY BYSSHE SHELLEY. Twayne's English Authors Series. New York: Twayne, 1969; corrected paperback ed., New York: St. Martin's, 1974.

> The standard introduction for students, nonspecialist teachers, and general readers. Based on primary materials.

Reiter, Seymour. A STUDY OF SHELLEY'S POETRY. Albuquerque: University of New Mexico Press, 1967.

> An introduction to PBS's works that attempts to relate his poetry to later literature and thought.

Stovall, Floyd H. DESIRE AND RESTRAINT IN SHELLEY. Durham, N.C.: Duke University Press, 1931.

> Explores PBS's maturing understanding of the relation between his will and the resistance of society and the physical world.

*Wasserman, Earl R. SHELLEY: A CRITICAL READING. Baltimore: Johns Hopkins University Press, 1971.

> This book, a massive and exhaustive study of most of PBS's major completed poems within the framework of an elaborate and original theory of his philosophical orientation, is indispensible reading for scholars, teachers, and advanced students.

Woodman, Ross Grieg. THE APOCALYPTIC VISION IN THE POETRY OF SHELLEY. Toronto: University of Toronto Press, 1964.

> A mature study, more valuable for its sensitive readings of individual poems than for its thesis.

2. Studies of Particular Works, Periods, and Themes

Allsup, James O. THE MAGIC CIRCLE: A STUDY OF SHELLEY'S CONCEPT OF LOVE. Port Washington, N.Y.: Kennikat, 1976.

> A challenging, compact study showing, through readings of several poems, how PBS harmonized Platonic eros and Christian agape.

#Barnard, Ellsworth. SHELLEY'S RELIGION. Minneapolis: University of Minnesota Press, 1937.

A full and lucid treatment of PBS's religious thought, slightly dated by the fervor of Barnard's attacks on hostile critics of PBS from the 1920s and 1930s.

Barrell, Joseph. SHELLEY AND THE THOUGHT OF HIS TIME. New Haven: Yale University Press, 1947.

This attempt to find PBS's place in the history of ideas has some very good passages, but the student should first read Pulos' THE DEEP TRUTH (below).

#Bloom, Harold. SHELLEY'S MYTHMAKING. New Haven: Yale University Press, 1959.

Brilliant individual insights tangled in a web of fallacious theorizing. The parallel between PBS and Martin Buber is ludicrous.

Brazell, James. SHELLEY AND THE CONCEPT OF HUMANITY: A STUDY OF HIS MORAL VISION. Salzburg: University of Salzburg Studies in English, 1972.

A concise exploration of PBS's moral ideas.

Caldwell, Richard S. "'The Sensitive Plant' as Original Fantasy." SiR, 15 (1976), 221-52.

An illuminating psychoanalytic reading of the poem that breaks new ground in PBS criticism.

*Chernaik, Judith. THE LYRICS OF SHELLEY. Cleveland: Case Western Reserve University Press, 1972.

The best critical study of PBS as a lyric poet, with newly edited texts of many of his short poems.

*Curran, Stuart. SHELLEY'S CENCI: SCORPIONS RINGED WITH FIRE. Princeton: Princeton University Press, 1970.

A thorough and brilliant study of the play's stage history, language, characterizations, and theme. Curran here tends to take PBS and his play out of their historical contexts.

Delisle, Fanny. A STUDY OF SHELLEY'S A DEFENCE OF POETRY: A TEXTUAL AND CRITICAL EXAMINATION. 2 vols. Salzburg: University of Salzburg Studies in English, 1974.

A significant examination of various aspects of PBS's essay.

Firkins, O[scar] W. POWER AND ELUSIVENESS IN SHELLEY. Minneapolis: University of Minnesota Press, 1937.

A brief, suggestive study of patterns of images in PBS's poetry.

Flagg, John Sewell. PROMETHEUS UNBOUND AND HELLAS--AN APPROACH TO SHELLEY'S LYRICAL DRAMAS. Salzburg: University of Salzburg Studies in English, 1972.

An intelligent study of the two works as Aeschylean dramas.

_____. "Shelley and Aristotle: Elements of the POETICS in Shelley's Theory of Poetry." SiR, 9 (1970), 44-67.

The fullest treatment of an important topic.

Ford, Newell F. "The Symbolism of Shelley's Swans." SiR, 1 (1962), 175-83.

This interesting exploration, like Ford's other pieces, "The Symbolism of Shelley's Nightingales" (MLR, 1960) and "Shelley's 'To a Skylark'" (KSMB, 1960), derive from his (unpublished) book on bird symbolism in English poetry.

Grabo, Carl. THE MEANING OF THE WITCH OF ATLAS. Chapel Hill: University of North Carolina Press, 1935.

Emphasizes neo-Platonic elements in the poem but fails to solve most of the interpretive problems.

_____. PROMETHEUS UNBOUND: AN INTERPRETATION. Chapel Hill: University of North Carolina Press, 1935.

Though now of chiefly historical interest, this book--emphasizing scientic and neo-Platonic imagery in PROMETHEUS UNBOUND-- stimulated much important thinking about PBS's poetry.

Hartley, Robert A. "The Uroboros in Shelley's Poetry." JEGP, 73 (1974), 524-42.

The most thorough study of the sources and symbolism of the tail-eating serpent in PBS's poetry.

Hildebrand, W[illiam] H. "Shelley's Early Vision Poems." SiR, 8 (1969), 198-215.

A competent (if overwritten) analysis of PBS's early poems incorporating a dream-vision.

_____. SHELLEY'S POLAR PARADISE: A READING OF PROMETHEUS UN-BOUND. Salzburg: University of Salzburg Studies in English, 1974.

An explication of PBS's masterpiece without much reference to its political, scientific, religio-philosophical contexts or levels of meaning.

Hodgson, John A. "The World's Mysterious Doom: Shelley's THE TRIUMPH OF LIFE." ELH, 42 (1975), 595-622.

Challenging and original (though possibly unsound) reading of the poem.

Hughes, A[rthur] M.D. THE NASCENT MIND OF SHELLEY. Oxford: Clarendon Press, 1947.

A mature exploration centering on PBS's early development. Overshadowed by Cameron's THE YOUNG SHELLEY (Sec. D.1, above), which is a much more thorough scholarly study.

Hughes, Daniel J. "Coherence and Collapse in Shelley, with Particular Reference to EPIPSYCHIDION." ELH, 28 (1961), 260-83.

Shows how PBS integrates the themes of sexual desire, the processes of thought, and the act of composing poetry; Hughes explores the latter two processes also in "Kindling and Dwindling: The Poetic Process in Shelley" (K-SJ, 1964) and in the entry below.

_____. "Potentiality in PROMETHEUS UNBOUND." SiR, 2 (1963), 107-126.

This important essay, reprinted by Reiman and Powers in their Norton Critical Edition of Shelley (Sec. B.3, above) and by Woodings (Sec. D.3, below), is the best of several good essays that have established Hughes as an important critic of PBS even though he has never published a book on him; his other essays include a paper about PBS's poem on the supposed Leonardo da Vinci painting of Medusa (CRITICISM, 1970) and two in the previous entry.

Jones, Frederick L. "Shelley and Milton." SP, 49 (1952), 488-519.

A full, old-fashioned listing of parallels between PBS's and Milton's writings, since supplemented by others (see, especially, MLQ, 1955; NOTES AND QUERIES, 1960 and 1961; RES, 1963; K-SJ, 1962, 1965, 1972-73; and Wittreich's ROMANTICS ON MILTON, Chap. 1.C.2)

Keach, William. "Reflexive Imagery in Shelley." K-SJ, 24 (1975), 49-69.

Explores an important aspect of the diction and syntax of PBS's major poems.

Klapper, M[olly] Roxana. THE GERMAN LITERARY INFLUENCE ON SHELLEY. Salzburg: University of Salzburg Studies in English, 1975.

A significant exploration of a neglected topic.

#Kroeber, Karl. "Experience as History: Shelley's Venice, Turner's Carthage." ELH, 41 (1974), 321-39.

> A seminal essay on the role of history in the thought of PBS and the Romantics generally. See also Jerrold Ziff, "J.M.W. Turner on Poetry and Painting," SiR, 3 (1964), 193-215.

Leyda, Seraphia DeVille. "THE SERPENT IS SHUT OUT FROM PARADISE": A REVALUATION OF ROMANTIC LOVE IN SHELLEY. Salzburg: University of Salzburg Studies in English, 1972.

> A serious (but not fully matured) examination of PBS's ideas of eros and agape. See also Allsup's THE MAGIC CIRCLE (above); and the study of sexuality in PBS's works by Nathaniel Brown, forthcoming from Harvard University Press.

McNiece, Gerald. "The Poet as Ironist in 'Mont Blanc' and 'Hymn to Intellectual Beauty.'" SiR, 14 (1975), 311-36.

> Discussion helpful for students and nonspecialist teachers.

#_____. SHELLEY AND THE REVOLUTIONARY IDEA. Cambridge: Harvard University Press, 1969.

> Detailed analysis of the impact of the events and literature of the French Revolution and of British radical thinkers on PBS's poetry.

Male, Roy R., Jr. "Shelley and the Doctrine of Sympathy." UNIVERSITY OF TEXAS STUDIES IN ENGLISH, 29 (1950), 183-203.

> Explores the influence of one important aspect of eighteenth-century philosophy and psychology on PBS's thought.

#Matthews, G[eoffrey] M. "'Julian and Maddalo': The Draft and the Meaning." STUDIA NEOPHILOLOGICA, 35 (1963), 57-84.

> Important analysis of the significance, for dating and meaning, of the extant draft MSS of the poem.

_____. "On Shelley's 'The Triumph of Life.'" STUDIA NEOPHILOLOGICA, 34 (1962), 104-34.

> A valuable exploration of Rousseau's writings (other than JULIE) on PBS's poem (see also Reiman in Sec. C.3).

#_____. "A Volcano's Voice in Shelley." ELH, 24 (1957), 191-228.

> A widely acclaimed and influential essay, reprinted by Woodings and, in part, by Ridenour (both in Sec. D.3, below). Matthews also wrote an excellent essay entitled "Shelley's Lyrics," reprinted by Reiman and Powers in the Norton Shelley (Sec. B.3, above).

*Notopoulos, James A. THE PLATONISM OF SHELLEY. Durham, N.C.: Duke University Press, 1949.

This exhaustive study of PBS's knowledge and use of Platonic ideas also contains corrected texts of PBS's translations from Plato, supplemented by Notopoulos in K-SJ, 15 (1966), 99-115.

O'Malley, Glenn. SHELLEY AND SYNESTHESIA. Evanston, III.: Northwestern University Press, 1964.

Detailed study of synesthetic imagery in ALASTOR, EPIPSYCHIDION, ADONAIS, and PROMETHEUS UNBOUND.

Orel, Harold. "Another Look at THE NECESSITY OF ATHEISM." MOSAIC, 2 (1969), 27-37.

A significant examination of the meaning of PBS's tract in the light of its intellectual and biographical background.

Perrin, Jean. "The Achtaeon Myth in Shelley's Poetry." ESSAYS AND STUDIES (by Members of the English Association), 28 (1975), 29-46.

A significant study by a scholar who has written a substantial book in French on PBS.

*Pulos, C[hristos] E. THE DEEP TRUTH: A STUDY OF SHELLEY'S SCEPTICISM. Lincoln: University of Nebraska Press, 1962.

This brief book is the best introduction to PBS's intellectual development.

_____. "Shelley and Malthus." PMLA, 67 (1952), 113-24.

The impact of Malthus' theory on PBS's thought and writings.

Raine, Kathleen. "A Defense of Shelley's Poetry." SOUTHERN REVIEW, 3 (1967), 856-73.

Reiman, Donald H. "Roman Scenes in PROMETHEUS UNBOUND III.iv." PQ, 46 (1967), 69-78.

Demonstrates that PBS had in mind specific scenes in Rome when writing two of the most apparently abstruse passages in PROMETHEUS. Also explores PBS's ideas on classical verses Baroque architecture and sculpture and the artistry of his travel letters to Peacock.

* _____. SHELLEY'S "THE TRIUMPH OF LIFE": A CRITICAL STUDY, BASED ON A TEXT NEWLY EDITED FROM THE BODLEIAN MANUSCRIPT. Urbana: University of Illinois Press, 1965.

A comprehensive study of the poem's text, prosody, imagery, and meaning, in the light of PBS's earlier poetic theory and practice.

Rieger, James. THE MUTINY WITHIN: THE HERESIES OF PERCY BYSSHE SHELLEY. New York: George Braziller, 1967.

A stimulating but basically wrong-headed attempt to find the sources and motivation for PBS's literary career in occult philosophies and heretical theologies. The best chapter is on THE CENCI.

#Robinson, Charles E. SHELLEY AND BYRON: THE SERPENT AND THE EAGLE WREATHED IN FIGHT. Baltimore: Johns Hopkins University Press, 1976.

An illuminating (though perhaps slightly over-relentless) demonstration of LB's intellectual, aesthetic, and personal impact on PBS as man and poet, as well as a number of crucial instances of the influence of PBS on LB.

#Rogers, Neville. SHELLEY AT WORK: A CRITICAL INQUIRY. Oxford: Clarendon Press, 1956; 2nd ed., 1967.

A useful exploration of PBS's thought and poetry by reference to his rough-draft notebooks, partially marred by erroneous transcriptions and overemphasis on the Platonic elements.

Rubin, David. "A Study of Antimonies in Shelley's THE WITCH OF ATLAS." SiR, 8 (1969), 216-28.

One of the few studies to explore concrete details in one of the most elusive of PBS's major poems.

Schulze, Earl J. SHELLEY'S THEORY OF POETRY: A REAPPRAISAL. The Hague: Mouton, 1966.

Though flawed by significant factual errors, this study remains one of the important studies of PBS's poetics.

Scott, William O. "Shelley's Admiration for Bacon." PMLA, 73 (1958), 228-36.

The best source of information on Bacon's impact on PBS's thought and poetry.

Silverman, Edwin B. POETIC SYNTHESIS IN SHELLEY'S ADONAIS. The Hague: Mouton, 1972.

An attempt (only sporadically successful) to synthesize recent critical perspectives on the poem.

Story, Patrick. "Pope, Pageantry, and Shelley's 'Triumph of Life.'" K-SJ, 21-22 (1972-73), 145-59.

> Treats Pope's (pervasive) influence on one of PBS's poems, as well as PBS's adaptation of elements from traditional London masques and triumphs.

Thurston, Norman. "Author, Narrator, and Hero in Shelley's ALASTOR." SiR, 14 (1975), 119-31.

> A judicious, balanced explication taking cognizance of recent criticism. Perhaps the best starting place for nonspecialist teacher or student.

Turner, Paul. "Shelley and Lucretius." RES, n.s. 10 (1959), 269-82.

> The best study of PBS's interest in and use of DE RERUM NATURA.

Ullman, James Ramsey. MAD SHELLEY. Princeton: Princeton University Press, 1930.

> A brilliantly conceived and written undergraduate thesis showing, in a few pages, great sympathy for and understanding of PBS's supposed eccentricities.

Wasserman, Earl R. SHELLEY'S PROMETHEUS UNBOUND: A CRITICAL READING. Baltimore: Johns Hopkins University Press, 1965.

> A provocative, controversial reading, later incorporated into Wasserman's SHELLEY: A CRITICAL READING (Sec. D.1).

_____. THE SUBTLER LANGUAGE: CRITICAL READINGS OF NEOCLASSIC AND ROMANTIC POEMS. Baltimore: Johns Hopkins University Press, 1965.

> The influential chapters on "Mont Blanc," "The Sensitive Plant," and ADONAIS were revised and incorporated into Wasserman's SHELLEY: A CRITICAL READING (Sec. D.1).

Weaver, Bennett. TOWARD THE UNDERSTANDING OF SHELLEY. Ann Arbor: University of Michigan Press, 1932.

> An examination of PBS's knowledge and use of the Bible leads to an analysis of his place in the biblical prophetic tradition.

*Webb, Timothy. THE VIOLET IN THE CRUCIBLE: SHELLEY AND TRANSLATION. Oxford: Clarendon Press, 1977.

> A thorough study of PBS's theory and practice as a translator.

#Wilson, Milton. SHELLEY'S LATER POETRY: A STUDY OF HIS PROPHETIC IMAGINATION. New York: Columbia University Press, 1959.

> An important study of PBS's later poetic style as well as his mature ideas, centering on PROMETHEUS UNBOUND.

Wright, John W. SHELLEY'S MYTH OF METAPHOR. Athens: University of Georgia Press, 1970.

> Supplements Schulze's book (above) by demonstrating the modernity of PBS's aesthetics.

Yeats, William Butler. "The Philosophy of Shelley's Poetry." In his IDEAS OF GOOD AND EVIL. London: A.H. Bullen, 1903; collected in ESSAYS AND INTRODUCTIONS (1961).

> A seminal essay for the study of recurrent symbolism in PBS's poetry.

Young, Arthur P. SHELLEY AND NONVIOLENCE. The Hague: Mouton, 1975.

> Explores PBS's ideas on nonviolence (which Young contrasts with pure pacificism) in the light of later experiences and theories of Gandhi, Tolstoi, King, Chavez, and others.

*Zillman, Lawrence John, ed. SHELLEY'S PROMETHEUS UNBOUND: A VARIORUM EDITION. Seattle: University of Washington Press, 1959.

> Though the textual information has some value, the chief usefulness of this mammoth compilation lies in the excerpts from earlier critics that are arranged by topics and speech by speech through the text of the poem.

3. Collections of Miscellaneous Essays

@Ridenour, George M., ed. SHELLEY: A COLLECTION OF CRITICAL ESSAYS. Englewood Cliffs, N.J.: Prentice-Hall, 1965.

> Contains original essays by Ridenour and F.A. Pottle, as well as reprints of essays or chapters by Fogle, Leone Vivante, Humphry House, Carlos Baker, Wasserman, Melvin M. Rader, Matthews, G. Wilson Knight, Milton Wilson, and Bloom.

@Woodings, R[obert] B., ed. SHELLEY: MODERN JUDGEMENTS. London: Macmillan, 1968.

> Reprints, in whole or in part, essays or chapters of books by Pottle, Pulos, Rogers, O'Malley, Bloom (2), Cameron, Wasserman, Hughes, Matthews, Joseph Raben, Baker, Wilson, Bostetter, and McGann.

Chapter 7
JOHN KEATS (1795-1821)

A. CONCORDANCES, BIBLIOGRAPHIES, AND STUDIES OF REPUTATION AND INFLUENCE

1. Concordances

*Baldwin, Dane L., Leslie N. Broughton, L.C. Evans, J.W. Hebel, B.F. Stelter, and Mary Rebecca Thayer. A CONCORDANCE TO THE POEMS OF JOHN KEATS. Washington, D.C.: The Carnegie Institution, 1971.

> Based on Forman's Oxford edition of 1907.

2. Bibliographies

*MacGillivray, J[ames] R. KEATS: A BIBLIOGRAPHY AND REFERENCE GUIDE, WITH AN ESSAY ON KEATS' REPUTATION. Toronto: University of Toronto Press, 1949.

> Includes first editions; later editions of collected, selected, and separate poems, letters, and prose; criticisms in periodicals and elsewhere through 1946; translations; and creative works based on JK's life and works, through ca. 1946.

Schwartz, Lewis M. KEATS REVIEWED BY HIS CONTEMPORARIES: A COLLECTION OF NOTICES FOR THE YEARS 1816-1821. Metuchen, N.J.: Scarecrow Press, 1973.

> An essay precedes the reprinted texts, more complete here than elsewhere, but marred by a number of errors.

3. Studies of Reputation and Influence

Ford, George H. KEATS AND THE VICTORIANS: A STUDY OF HIS INFLUENCE AND RISE TO FAME, 1821-1895. New Haven: Yale University Press, 1944.

Centers on JK's impact on major Victorian writers--particularly Arnold, Rossetti, Morris, and Swinburne.

Harwell, Thomas Meade. KEATS AND THE CRITICS, 1848-1900. Salzburg: University of Salzburg Studies in English, 1972.

#Matthews, G[eoffrey] M., ed. KEATS: THE CRITICAL HERITAGE. London: Routledge and Kegan Paul, 1971.

The introduction traces JK's reputation (briefly) into the twentieth century. The critical selections are limited to the period 1816-63.

#Rollins, Hyder E. KEATS' REPUTATION IN AMERICA TO 1848. Cambridge: Harvard University Press, 1946.

The fullest study of a slim topic.

B. EDITIONS

1. Collected Editions

*Forman, H[arry] Buxton, and Maurice Buxton Forman, eds. THE POETICAL WORKS AND OTHER WRITINGS OF JOHN KEATS. Introd. John Masefield. 8 vols. Hampstead Edition. New York: Charles Scribner's Sons, 1938-39.

2. Collected Poetry

*Allott, Miriam, ed. THE POEMS OF JOHN KEATS. London: Longmans, 1970.

Reedited and annotated in detail. On the limitations of the text, see Stillinger, THE TEXTS OF KEATS'S POEMS (Sec. B.5).

@Barnard, John, ed. JOHN KEATS: THE COMPLETE POEMS. Penguin English Poets. Harmondsworth, Engl.: Penguin, 1973.

A good edition, with reasonably sound text, informative textual and critical notes, and useful appendixes.

#de Selincourt, E[rnest], ed. THE POEMS OF JOHN KEATS. London: Methuen, 1905; rev. ed., 1907.

A well-annotated edition, but its text is now obsolete.

Forman, H[arry] Buxton, ed. THE POETICAL WORKS OF JOHN KEATS. Oxford: Clarendon Press, 1906.

Based on Forman's earlier editions of JK's poetry dating from 1884.

_____. THE COMPLETE POETICAL WORKS OF JOHN KEATS. Oxford Edition [later, Oxford Standard Authors Edition]. London: Oxford University Press, 1907.

Frequently reprinted. Virtually the same text as the previous entry.

#Garrod, H[eathcote] W., ed. THE POETICAL WORKS OF JOHN KEATS. Oxford English Text Edition. Oxford: Clarendon Press, 1939; 2nd ed., 1958.

Once thought to contain accurate texts and collations of the poems, this edition has been shown to be too faulty for scholarly use, and it is too expensive and cumbersome for use by students and general readers. It will be superseded by Jack Stillinger's edition forthcoming from Harvard University Press.

_____. THE POETICAL WORKS OF JOHN KEATS. Oxford Standard Authors Edition. London: Oxford University Press, 1956.

Not truly based on Garrod's thoroughly reedited Oxford English Text Edition (above), this volume is rather, an imperfect redaction of H. Buxton Forman's earlier Oxford Standard Authors Edition (1908).

Scudder, Horace, ed. THE POETICAL WORKS OF KEATS. Cambridge Edition. Boston: Houghton Mifflin, 1899; rev. Paul D. Sheats, 1975.

This edition, also including a large number of JK's letters, has long been out of date in both its texts and its annotations. The limitations have not been fully repaired by Sheats's valiant tinkering.

@Thorpe, Clarence DeWitt, ed. JOHN KEATS: COMPLETE POEMS AND SELECTED LETTERS. New York: Odyssey Press, 1935.

An excellent student text edition by the standards of its day, still useful for some of its annotations.

3. Selected Poetry and Prose

Baker, Carlos, ed. POEMS AND SELECTED LETTERS. New York: Bantam Books, 1962; Charles Scribner's Sons, 1970.

Compact paperback with introduction, brief notes, and bibliography.

@Bush, Douglas, ed. SELECTED POEMS AND LETTERS. Riverside Edition. Boston: Houghton Mifflin, 1959.

An excellent selection, with full annotation that is strong on the facts of JK's life and on the sources of allusions, but limited in its comments on JK's aims and achievements in individual poems.

Downer, Arthur C., ed. THE ODES OF KEATS, WITH NOTES AND ANALY-SES AND A MEMOIR. Oxford: Clarendon Press, 1897.

A teaching edition, now outdated.

Fogle, Richard Harter, ed. SELECTED POETRY AND LETTERS. Rinehart Edition. New York: Rinehart, 1951; 2nd ed., Holt, Rinehart, and Winston, 1969.

A solid, if unexciting, teaching edition.

#Gittings, Robert, ed. THE ODES OF KEATS AND THEIR EARLIEST MANU-SCRIPTS. London: Heinemann, 1970.

Facsimiles of the MSS and a valuable introduction.

@_____. SELECTED POEMS AND LETTERS OF JOHN KEATS. New York: Barnes and Noble, 1966.

A surprisingly full, well-annotated student's edition, with poems and letters arranged together chronologically.

Man, Paul de, ed. SELECTED POETRY. Signet Classic Poetry Series. New York: New American Library, 1966.

A paperback edition with introduction.

Sharrock, Roger, ed. KEATS: SELECTED POEMS AND LETTERS. New Oxford English Series. London: Oxford University Press, 1964.

A useful annotated selection--about what one finds in "major author" editions of general anthologies.

Ward, Aileen, ed. THE POEMS OF JOHN KEATS. Illus. by David Gentleman. Cambridge, Engl.: Printed for Members of the Limited Editions Club at the University Printing House, 1966.

A selection containing an introduction, some notes, and indexes of titles and first lines.

4. Individual Titles

#de Selincourt, E[rnest], ed. HYPERION: A FACSIMILE OF KEATS'S AUTO-GRAPH MANUSCRIPT, WITH A TRANSLITERATION OF THE MANUSCRIPT OF THE FALL OF HYPERION. Oxford: Clarendon Press, 1905.

A large, thin folio volume of interest to all and of great value to the textual scholar.

#Forman, Maurice Buxton, ed. JOHN KEATS: ANATOMICAL AND PHYSIO-LOGICAL NOTE BOOK. PRINTED FROM THE HOLOGRAPH IN THE KEATS MUSEUM, HAMPSTEAD. London: Oxford University Press, 1934.

A sixty-eight-page text casting light on JK's medical studies.

Notcutt, H. Clement, ed. ENDYMION: A POETIC ROMANCE. TYPE-FACSIMILE OF THE FIRST EDITION, WITH INTRODUCTION AND NOTES. London: Oxford University Press, 1927.

According to Stillinger, this type-facsimile contains a number of typographical errors or alterations of the first-edition text and cannot be relied on; the notes and introduction retain some value.

Robertson, M., ed. KEATS: POEMS PUBLISHED IN 1820. Oxford: Clarendon Press, 1909.

A "page for page and line for line" reprint of the first edition of the LAMIA volume, with notes to make it suitable for use as a student text (in 1909).

5. Textual Sources and Studies

Jones, Leonidas. "The Dating of the Two HYPERIONS." STUDIES IN BIBLIOGRAPHY, 30 (1977), 120-35.

Argues (on the basis of new evidence in the Reynolds-Hood Commonplace Book in the Bristol Central Library) that recent biographers are wrong and that the Introduction to THE FALL OF HYPERION was written well before the end of 1818.

Sperry, Stuart M., Jr. "Richard Woodhouse's Interleaved and Annotated Copy of Keats's POEMS (1817)." In LITERARY MONOGRAPHS. Ed. Eric Rothstein and Thomas K. Dunseath. Madison: University of Wisconsin Press, 1967. I, 101-64.

Analyzes one of the basic textual authorities.

*Stillinger, Jack. THE TEXTS OF KEATS'S POEMS. Cambridge: Harvard University Press, 1974.

Analyzes in lucid detail the substantive features of the text of each poem and its transmission in various holograph manuscripts, transcripts by JK's friends and early editors, and publication in periodicals and books through Allott's edition of 1970.

Swennes, Robert H. "Keats's Own Annotated Copy of ENDYMION." K-SJ, 20 (1971), 14-17.

> Provides important holograph corrections of the text.

C. BIOGRAPHICAL SOURCES AND STUDIES

1. Primary Documents

Brawne, Fanny. LETTERS OF FANNY BRAWNE TO FANNY KEATS, 1820-1824. Ed. Fred Edgcumbe. Pref. Maurice Buxton Forman. London: Oxford University Press, 1937.

> Letters from JK's fiancee to his young sister, revealing the characters of both women.

#Brown, Charles Armitage. THE LETTERS OF CHARLES ARMITAGE BROWN. Ed. Jack Stillinger. Cambridge, Mass.: Harvard University Press, 1966.

> An excellent edition of the letters of one of JK's closest friends.

_____. LIFE OF JOHN KEATS. Ed. Dorothy Hyde Bodurtha and Willard Bissell Pope. London: Oxford University Press, 1937.

> The text of an important first-hand biography that, though used by Houghton, had remained unpublished until this date.

*Keats, John. THE LETTERS OF JOHN KEATS. Ed. Hyder Edward Rollins. 2 vols. Cambridge: Harvard University Press, 1958.

> Besides its excellent texts of JK's letters and full annotation, these volumes contain a detailed chronology of his life (to be checked against the later biographies--particularly Gittings, cited in Sec. C.2).

* _____. LETTERS OF JOHN KEATS: A NEW SELECTION. Ed. Robert Gittings. Oxford Paperbacks. London: Oxford University Press, 1970.

> This carefully checked and precisely annotated selection corrects or supplements information in Rollins' edition (see above) for many of the 170 letters it includes.

*Rollins, Hyder Edward, ed. THE KEATS CIRCLE: LETTERS AND PAPERS. Cambridge: Harvard University Press, 1948; 2nd ed., 1965.

> The second edition incorporates MORE LETTERS AND POEMS OF THE KEATS CIRCLE, edited by Rollins (1955). This well-edited selection of letters by JK's friends gives valuable information about both him and them.

2. Biographies

*Bate, Walter Jackson. JOHN KEATS. Cambridge: Harvard University Press, 1963; paperback rpt., New York: Oxford University Press, 1966.

A masterful, sensitive biography that is especially strong on the relations of JK's life to his development as a poet.

@Bush, Douglas. JOHN KEATS: HIS LIFE AND WRITINGS. Masters of World Literature Series. New York: Macmillan, 1966.

A good, short biography, heavily indebted to Bate's more comprehensive work (above).

#Colvin, Sidney. JOHN KEATS: HIS LIFE AND POETRY, HIS FRIENDS, CRITICS, AND AFTER-FAME. London: Macmillan, 1917; 2nd ed., corrected, 1918.

A full, mature biography building on Colvin's earlier short life (KEATS, 1887) in the English Men of Letters series.

*Gittings, Robert. JOHN KEATS. London: Heinemann, 1968.

The most factually accurate and meticulously researched biography of JK, this work incorporates the biographical discoveries Gittings had first published in JOHN KEATS: THE LIVING YEAR (1954) and THE MASK OF KEATS: A STUDY OF PROBLEMS (1956)—both of which, however, retain interest because their readings of certain poems are not repeated in the later full biography—and THE KEATS INHERITANCE (1964), which remains a fascinating story of the tangles of English Chancery law on the road toward BLEAK HOUSE.

@Hewlett, Dorothy. ADONAIS: A LIFE OF JOHN KEATS. London: Hurst and Blackett, 1937; 2nd ed., 1950; 3rd ed., 1970.

A lucid, readable, and moving popular biography.

Houghton, Lord [Richard Monckton Milnes, first Baron Houghton]. LIFE, LETTERS, AND LITERARY REMAINS OF JOHN KEATS. 2 vols. London: Edward Moxon, 1848.

This pioneer life and edition of theretofore unpublished poems and letters laid the foundation for a growing appreciation of JK's life and art.

#Lowell, Amy. JOHN KEATS. 2 vols. Boston: Houghton Mifflin, 1925.

Still useful as storehouse of information on JK's literary sources and analogues, as well as (in its time) a powerful vindication of JK as a poet of the modern spirit.

Rossetti, William Michael. LIFE OF JOHN KEATS. London: Walter Scott, 1887.

> This brief biography in the Great Writers Series is sympathetic, balanced, and perceptive. Many of its factual statements have, of course, been rendered obsolete by almost a century of further research.

#Ward, Aileen. JOHN KEATS: THE MAKING OF A POET. New York: Viking, 1963.

> This full, sensitive, and well-written critical biography, with a tactful psychoanalytic perspective, has suffered somewhat from unwarranted comparisons with Bate and Gittings (cited above). But it makes positive contributions that are not within the scope of the other two biographies (one immersed in the poet's calling and JK's style and the other in the external facts of JK's life), and all three should be read by the serious student and teacher.

3. Studies of a Period or an Aspect of JK's Life

Hilton, Timothy. KEATS AND HIS WORLD. London: Thames and Hudson, 1971.

> Lavish portraits, maps, and photos of JK's MSS and books, tied together with a thin narrative.

Murchie, Guy. THE SPIRIT OF PLACE IN KEATS: SKETCHES OF PERSONS AND PLACES KNOWN BY HIM AND HIS REACTION TO THEM. London: Newman Neame, 1955.

> Harmless, popular antiquarianism (illustrated).

Parson, Donald. PORTRAITS OF KEATS. Cleveland: World, 1954.

> The fullest compilation of portraits of JK--those done from life, memory, and imagination.

Richardson, Joanna. THE EVERLASTING SPELL: A STUDY OF KEATS AND HIS FRIENDS. London: Jonathan Cape, 1963.

> Traces the influence of JK in and through the lives of his friends who survived him.

D. CRITICISM

1. General Studies

#Blackstone, Bernard. THE CONSECRATED URN: AN INTERPRETATION OF KEATS IN TERMS OF GROWTH AND FORM. London: Longmans, Green, 1959.

A rich, provocative study of JK's poetry and thought in the context of the growth of interest in biological images, as opposed to the mechanistic patterns of thinking deriving from Newton.

Crawford, Alexander W. THE GENIUS OF KEATS: AN INTERPRETATION. London: Arthur H. Stockwell, 1932.

A pioneer argument for JK's powers of mind and his intellectual as well as aesthetic grasp of art.

Dickstein, Morris. KEATS AND HIS POETRY: A STUDY IN DEVELOPMENT. Chicago: University of Chicago Press, 1971.

A book difficult to read but profitable to those sympathetic with recent academic criticism.

Evans, B[enjamin] Ifor. KEATS. London: Duckworth, 1934.

A well-written brief introduction to JK's life and works by a scholar who wrote frequently on him.

*Evert, Walter H. AESTHETIC AND MYTH IN THE POETRY OF KEATS. Princeton: Princeton University Press, 1965.

A major study centered on JK's mythology of Apollo as god of poetry and imagination.

Fausset, Hugh I'Anson. KEATS: A STUDY IN DEVELOPMENT. London: Martin Secker, 1922.

Important historically as a strong voice arguing that JK matured to an ideal balance between sensations and thoughts.

*Finney, Claude Lee. THE EVOLUTION OF KEATS'S POETRY. 2 vols. Cambridge: Harvard University Press, 1936.

A detailed chronological study of JK's poetry, so thorough and rich (especially in exploring JK's literary sources) that it has not been made obsolete by changes of fashion or the growth of factual knowledge on various points.

#Ford, Newell F. THE PREFIGURATIVE IMAGINATION OF JOHN KEATS: A STUDY OF THE BEAUTY-TRUTH IDENTIFICATION AND ITS IMPLICATIONS. Palo Alto, Calif.: Stanford University Press, 1951.

A historically important demonstration that has been accepted (and absorbed and deepened) by later critics.

Garrod, H[eathcote] W. KEATS. Oxford: Clarendon Press, 1926; 2nd ed., 1939.

A brief book (deriving from lectures) that holds to the older view that JK is a great poet "only when the senses capture him."

Goldberg, Milton A. THE POETICS OF ROMANTICISM: TOWARD A READ-ING OF JOHN KEATS. Yellow Springs, Ohio: Antioch Press, 1969.

Attempts to set JK's poetic theory and practice in a lightly sketched context stretching from Plato to Joyce and Eliot.

Hudson, William Henry. KEATS AND HIS POETRY. London: George G. Harrap, 1911.

Inglis, Fred. KEATS. London: Evans, 1966.

A brief, undistinguished (though not totally unscholarly) look at JK from a Leavisite perspective.

#Jones, John. JOHN KEATS'S DREAM OF TRUTH. London: Chatto and Windus, 1969.

A subtle examination of the relationship between realism and dreamy eroticism in JK's poetry.

Mayhead, Robin. JOHN KEATS. Cambridge: Cambridge University Press, 1967.

A brief, useful introduction for students (directed at those in Brit-ish secondary schools and those for whom English is a second lan-guage).

#Murry, John Middleton. KEATS AND SHAKESPEARE: A STUDY OF KEATS' POETIC LIFE FROM 1816 to 1820. London: Oxford University Press, 1925.

A detailed but readable study of JK's active career as a poet, now partly absorbed and outdated by more recent studies.

Owen, F.M. JOHN KEATS: A STUDY. London: C. Kegan Paul, 1880.

Mrs. Owen's study was one of the earliest to recognize JK as a thinker and to attempt an allegorical interpretation of ENDYMION.

Pettet, E.C. ON THE POETRY OF KEATS. Cambridge: Cambridge Univer-sity Press, 1957.

This sprawling book of ten chapters and six appendixes argues, in a somewhat amateurish way, that JK was a poet of sensation rather than thought.

*Sperry, Stuart M. KEATS THE POET. Princeton, N.J.: Princeton University Press, 1973.

The standard synthesis of recent scholarship and criticism on JK's poetry (including Sperry's own original contributions). The best place for upper-level students and nonspecialist teachers to begin their study.

Talbot, Norman. THE MAJOR POEMS OF JOHN KEATS. Sydney, Australia: Sydney University Press, 1968.

A brief, undistinguished introductory survey.

#Thorpe, Clarence DeWitt. THE MIND OF JOHN KEATS. New York: Oxford University Press, 1926.

A landmark study that first demonstrated JK's intellectual powers to be equal to his sensations.

*Wasserman, Earl R. THE FINER TONE: KEATS' MAJOR POEMS. Baltimore: Johns Hopkins University Press, 1953.

A study of JK's ideas and poetic technique and achievement is compressed into studies of five poems--"Grecian Urn," "La Belle Dame," "Eve of St. Agnes," LAMIA, and "Nightingale." This controversial book has been one of the most influential studies thus far in the twentieth century; necessary reading for advanced students and their teachers.

Wigod, Jacob. THE DARKENING CHAMBER: THE GROWTH OF TRAGIC CONSCIOUSNESS IN KEATS. Salzburg: University of Salzburg Studies in English, 1972.

A mature general study of JK's poetry.

2. Studies of Particular Works, Periods, and Themes

Beaudry, Harry R. THE ENGLISH THEATRE AND JOHN KEATS. Salzburg: University of Salzburg Studies in English, 1973.

A workmanlike study of JK's circle and the contemporary theater.

Bell, Arthur H. "'The Depth of Things': Keats and Human Space." K-SJ, 23 (1974), 77-94.

An interesting original approach to JK's metaphorical use of space.

Benvenuto, Richard. "'The Ballance of Good and Evil' in Keats's Letters and 'Lamia.'" JEGP, 71 (1972), 1-11.

A sane interpretation of LAMIA, harmonizing with those by Slote and Reiman (below).

Beyer, Werner W. KEATS AND THE DAEMON KING. New York: Oxford University Press, 1947.

> A detailed study of the influence on JK of the German poem OBERON by Christoph Martin Wieland, as known to JK through the English translation of William Sotheby.

Brown, Leonard S. "The Genesis, Growth, and Meaning of ENDYMION." SP, 30 (1933), 618-53.

> Argues that ENDYMION was an answer and corrective to PBS's ALASTOR.

Caldwell, James Ralston. JOHN KEATS' FANCY: THE EFFECT ON KEATS OF THE PSYCHOLOGY OF HIS DAY. Ithaca, N.Y.: Cornell University Press, 1945.

> Examines most of JK's poems in light of the ideas of David Hartley and Archibald Alison.

Crawford, Alexander W. THE GENIUS OF KEATS: AN INTERPRETATION. London: Arthur H. Stockwell, 1932.

> Examines in detail "La Belle Dame," the odes, LAMIA, and the two HYPERIONS from the viewpoint that JK's growth in philosophical thinking helped his poetry.

@Danzig, Allan, ed. TWENTIETH CENTURY INTERPRETATIONS OF THE EVE OF ST. AGNES. Englewood Cliffs, N.J.: Prentice-Hall, 1971.

> Contains an original essay by Clifford Adelman, as well as essays or excerpts from books by Wasserman, Stillinger, Bate, and Gittings.

D'Avanzo, Mario L. KEATS'S METAPHORS FOR THE POETIC IMAGINATION. Durham, N.C.: Duke University Press, 1967.

> Traces the significance of figures repeatedly used by JK as metaphors for imagination and poetic creativity.

Eggers, J. Phillip. "Memory in Mankind: Keats's Historical Imagination." PMLA, 86 (1971), 990-98.

> Traces the development of JK's sense of history from juvenile hero-worship to a sense of history as a collective memory, closely related to the memory that brings forth poetry.

Ende, Stuart A. KEATS AND THE SUBLIME. New Haven: Yale University Press, 1977.

Sets JK in a context of ideas on the sublime ranging from Milton and his eighteenth-century imitators through Freud and Yeats.

Ford, Newell F. "Holy Living and Holy Dying in Keats's Poetry." K-SJ, 20 (1971), 37-61.

JK's use of religious imagery that parallels Christian doctrine and ritual.

Fraser, G.S. JOHN KEATS: "ODES"--A CASEBOOK. London: Macmillan, 1971.

Gorell, Lord [Ronald Gorell Barnes]. JOHN KEATS: THE PRINCIPLE OF BEAUTY. London: Sylvan Press, 1948.

A general study, independent in approach but not very deep.

Hartman, Geoffrey H. "Spectral Symbolism and the Authorial Self: An Approach to Keats's HYPERION." ESSAYS IN CRITICISM, 24 (1974), 1-19.

Visible through Hartman's difficult prose lies an important reading of JK's HYPERION poems.

Haworth, Helen E. "Keats and the Metaphor of Vision." JEGP, 67 (1968), 371-94.

An important cautionary essay, urging readers not to take literally JK's poetic metaphors.

#Jack, Ian. KEATS AND THE MIRROR OF ART. Oxford: Clarendon Press, 1967.

Detailed examination of JK's interest in an knowledge of the visual arts and their impact on his poetry.

Jones, James Land. ADAM'S DREAM: MYTHIC CONSCIOUSNESS IN KEATS AND YEATS. Athens: University of Georgia Press, 1975.

Beginning with the theories of Cassirir and Eliade on "mythic consciousness," this provocative study examines the mythic systems of JK and Yeats as parallel attempts to recapture that consciousness.

Kauvar, Gerald B. THE OTHER POETRY OF KEATS. Rutherford, N.J.: Fairleigh Dickinson University Press, 1969.

Contains substantial quotations of JK's minor poems and of other critics' comments on them, lightly seasoned with original explication.

Leoff, Eve. A STUDY OF JOHN KEATS'S ISABELLA. Salzburg: University of Salzburg Studies in English, 1972.

> The most thorough study to date of this poem.

Little, Judy. KEATS AS A NARRATIVE POET: A TEST OF INVENTION. Lincoln: University of Nebraska Press, 1975.

> Explores JK's interest in and his various attempts to produce long narrative poems.

Lyon, Harvey T., ed. KEATS' WELL-READ URN: AN INTRODUCTION TO LITERARY METHOD. New York: Henry Holt, 1958.

> A convenient summary, with selected excerpts, of critical commentary on "Ode to a Grecian Urn" from 1828 to 1957.

Matthey, François. THE EVOLUTION OF KEATS'S STRUCTURAL IMAGERY. Bern, Switzerland: Francke, 1974.

> An interesting but rather too-neat diagramming of the structure of JK's major poems.

Notcutt, H[enry] Clement. AN INTERPRETATION OF KEATS'S ENDYMION. N.p.: [1919].

> An eighty-four-page allegorical reading of the poem, treated "primarily as a record of the personal experience of Keats" (p. 47), later revised as the introduction to Notcutt's type-facsimile reprint of the poem (Sec. B.4).

#Patterson, Charles I. THE DAEMONIC IN THE POETRY OF JOHN KEATS. Urbana: University of Illinois Press, 1970.

> Explores and shows the impact on JK's poetry of his knowledge of the Greek and Celtic traditions of nonmalicious daemons.

Pereira, E[rnest]. JOHN KEATS: THE POET AS CRITIC. Pretoria: Communications of the University of South Africa, 1969.

> A lecture by a critic who has published frequently on JK in South Africa and who is now at work on a book-length study of this topic.

Ragussis, Michael. "Narrative Structure and the Problem of the Divided Reader in THE EVE OF ST. AGNES." ELH, 42 (1975), 378-94.

> Explores the narrative viewpoint in terms of the reader's response, while showing how the poem's theme parallels that of ROMEO AND JULIET.

Reiman, Donald H. "Keats and the Humanistic Paradox: Mythological History in LAMIA." SEL, 11 (1971), 656-69.

> Discusses the sense of disillusionment in JK's later poetry in terms of the "humanistic paradox"--when the human mind is seen to be the source of all values, those values become as mutable as the mind's moods.

#Ricks, Christopher. KEATS AND EMBARRASSMENT. Oxford: Clarendon Press, 1974.

> Traces JK's mentions of blushing and other signs of embarrassment, and attempts to show how JK transmuted his discomfort into great artistic images.

#Ridley, M[aurice] R. KEATS' CRAFTMANSHIP: A STUDY IN POETIC DEVEL-OPMENT. Oxford: Clarendon Press, 1933.

> Detailed study of chronological progress in diction, rhythms, formal organization, patterns of sound, and similar aspects of JK's poems, including analysis of changes and additions in the rough-draft MSS.

#Ryan, Robert M. KEATS: THE RELIGIOUS SENSE. Princeton: Princeton University Press, 1976.

> A thorough, nondogmatic exploration of religious (or philosophical) ideas in JK's writings, together with information on where and how they came to him.

Sinson, Janice C. KEATS AND THE ANATOMY OF MELANCHOLY. London: Keats-Shelley Memorial Association, 1971.

> A slender study carrying examination of Burton's influence on JK at least as far as it need go.

*Slote, Bernice. KEATS AND THE DRAMATIC PRINCIPLE. Lincoln: University of Nebraska Press, 1958.

> After examining JK's theory of poetry and his interest in the theater and in writing plays, this well-researched and sane study concludes with a detailed reading of LAMIA as a dramatic poem.

Southam, B[rian] C. "The Ode 'To Autumn.'" K-SJ, 9 (1960), 91-98.

> A clear, effective reading of the poem (indebted to Unger, below).

#Spurgeon, Caroline F.E. KEATS'S SHAKESPEARE: A DESCRIPTIVE STUDY. London: Oxford University Press, 1928.

Studies the edition of Shakespeare that JK owned, as well as the Shakespearean elements in his poetry.

@Stillinger, Jack, ed. TWENTIETH CENTURY INTERPRETATIONS OF KEATS'S ODES: A COLLECTION OF CRITICAL ESSAYS. Englewood Cliffs, N.J.: Prentice-Hall, 1968.

Reprints essays or excerpts from books by Fogle, Cleanth Brooks and Robert Penn Warren, Gerard, Bate, Perkins, Bloom, Bateson, Bush, and Abrams.

Thekla, Sister. THE DISINTERESTED HEART: THE PHILOSOPHY OF JOHN KEATS. Newport Pagnell, Bucks., Engl.: Greek Orthodox Monastery of the Assumption, 1973.

Unger, Leonard. "Keats and the Music of Autumn." In his THE MAN IN THE NAME. Minneapolis: University of Minnesota Press, 1956.

A perceptive reading of "To Autumn."

Vendler, Helen. "The Experiential Beginnings of Keats's Odes." SiR, 12 (1973), 591-606.

Attempts to discover for each of JK's odes which idea or image—perhaps in a later stanza of the final poem—was the germ from which the poem developed.

Vitoux, Pierre. "Keats's Epic Design in HYPERION." SiR, 14 (1975), 165-83.

A significant analysis (by a leading French student of the English Romantics) of elements in JK's fragments that provide clues for the poem's possible development into a complete epic.

Wilson, Katharine M. THE NIGHTINGALE AND THE HAWK: A PSYCHO-LOGICAL STUDY OF KEATS' ODE. London: George Allen and Unwin, 1964.

A Jungian reading of images through JK's poems, culminating in "Ode to a Nightingale."

Zillman, Lawrence John. JOHN KEATS AND THE SONNET TRADITION: A CRITICAL AND COMPARATIVE STUDY. Los Angeles: Lymanhouse, 1939.

An attempt to dissect the technical and formal elements of JK's sonnets in relation to the development of the English sonnet from Wyatt and Surrey through the eighteenth and the early nineteenth centuries.

3. Collections of Miscellaneous Essays

@Bate, Walter Jackson, ed. KEATS: A COLLECTION OF CRITICAL ESSAYS.
Twentieth Century Views. Englewood Cliffs, N.J.: Prentice-Hall, 1964.

> Reprints essays or parts of books by T.S. Eliot, Bush, Fogle, Bate
> (2), Stillinger, Bloom, Perkins (2), Wasserman, and D.G. James.

#Muir, Kenneth, ed. JOHN KEATS: A REASSESSMENT. Liverpool: Liver-
pool University Press, 1958; 2nd ed., 1969.

> An important collection of ten original essays by scholars at the
> University of Liverpool, including Muir (3), Kenneth Allott, Miriam
> Allott, Arnold Davenport, R.T. Davies, Clarisse Godfrey, Joan
> Grundy, and David Masson.

#Murry, John Middleton. STUDIES IN KEATS. London: Oxford University
Press, 1930; rev. and enl. as STUDIES IN KEATS, OLD AND NEW, 1939;
as THE MYSTERY OF KEATS, 1949; and as KEATS, 1955.

> Influential explorations of various biographical and critical prob-
> lems, including chapters on "Keats and Milton," "Keats and Words-
> worth," and "Keats and Blake."

O'Neill, Judith, comp. CRITICS ON KEATS. Readings in Literary Criticism
Series. Coral Gables, Fla.: University of Miami Press, 1967.

> Brief snippets from important critics of the nineteenth and twen-
> tieth centuries. Useful chiefly for inveterate name droppers.

#Stillinger, Jack. THE HOODWINKING OF MADELINE AND OTHER ESSAYS
ON KEATS'S POEMS. Urbana: University of Illinois Press, 1971.

> In the title-essay on "The Eve of St. Agnes" and in other essays
> on "Isabella," ENDYMION, the Odes, and other poems, Stillinger
> upholds the view that JK soon outgrew his youthful idealism to
> become a hard-headed realist. The study is a reaction against the
> books by Wasserman and others who see JK as a dedicated (if dis-
> illusioned) visionary.

Chapter 8

SECONDARY AND MINOR POETS

A. GENERAL WORKS

1. Bibliographies

*Houtchens, Carolyn Washburn, and Lawrence Huston Houtchens, eds. THE ENGLISH ROMANTIC POETS AND ESSAYISTS: A REVIEW OF RESEARCH AND CRITICISM. 2nd ed. New York: Published for the Modern Language Association by New York University Press, 1966.

> The latest revision of a volume (1st ed., 1957) treating Blake, Lamb, Hazlitt, De Quincey, and Carlyle, as well as the following poets treated in this chapter: Scott, Southey, Campbell, Moore, Landor, and Hunt. For details, see the bibliographical references under these individual writers (below).

2. Anthologies and Joint Editions

Bennett, Betty T., ed. BRITISH WAR POETRY IN THE AGE OF ROMANTICISM: 1793-1815. New York: Garland, 1976.

> The only nonreprint in Reiman's ROMANTIC CONTEXT: POETRY series (see below), this anthology, with a 67-page historical and critical introduction, includes over 300 poems published in contemporary British newspapers and periodicals about the French Revolutionary and Napoleonic wars, culled from over 2,000 poems identified and collected by Bennett.

@Hayward, John, ed. THE OXFORD BOOK OF NINETEENTH-CENTURY ENGLISH VERSE. Oxford: Clarendon Press, 1964.

> No study aids, but a selection of a few well-known poems by eighty-four poets, major and minor, including (besides Blake, WW, STC, LB, PBS, and JK) Rogers, Bloomfield, Scott, Southey, Landor, Campbell, Galt, Moore, Hunt, Kirke White, Peacock, Keble, Hemans, Clare (14), Darley, Hartley Coleridge, Reynolds, Hood, and Beddoes.

#Miles, Alfred H., ed. THE POETS AND POETRY OF THE CENTURY. 10 vols. London: Hutchinson, 1891-97; enl. ed., 12 vols., London and New York, 1905-07.

> The most extensive anthology of English poets (major and minor) of the nineteenth century. The earlier volumes are arranged chronologically, the later ones by type (e.g., humorous verse, religious verse).

Milford, H[umphrey] S., ed. THE OXFORD BOOK OF ENGLISH VERSE OF THE ROMANTIC PERIOD, 1798-1837. Oxford: Clarendon Press, 1935.

> A reissue of a volume originally published in 1928 as THE OXFORD BOOK OF REGENCY VERSE, this selection, though generally inferior to Hayward's (above), includes examples from many more minor and obscure poets, including Baillie, Barbauld, Combe, Croly, Cunningham, Elliott, Frere, Grahame, Hogg, the Lambs, Lockhart, Luttrell, Milman, Montgomery, Moxon, the Smith brothers, Thurlow, Wilson, and Wolfe.

Oliver, John W., and J.C. Smith, eds. A SCOTS ANTHOLOGY, FROM THE THIRTEENTH TO THE TWENTIETH CENTURY. Edinburgh: Oliver and Boyd, 1949.

> Besides the work of major figures like Burns, this volume includes examples of Scots dialect poems of James Hogg, Allan Cunningham, and a number of lesser contemporaries of the Romantics--Thomas Pringle, Hew Ainslie, William Watt, William Motherwell, William Thom, Alex Smart, W.A. Foster, George Outram, Lady John Scott, and William Miller.

THE POETICAL WORKS OF MILMAN, BOWLES, WILSON, AND BARRY CORNWALL: COMPLETE IN ONE VOLUME. Paris: A. and W. Galignani, [1829].

> A very large volume, in small print, with a biographical-critical introduction for each poet.

THE POETICAL WORKS OF ROGERS, CAMPBELL, MONTGOMERY, LAMB, AND KIRKE WHITE. Paris: A. and W. Galignani, 1829.

> Reissued in Philadelphia by Carey and Lea, 1830, and kept in print first by Grigg and later Lippincott in Philadelphia at least through 1859.

Reeves, James, ed. FIVE LATE ROMANTIC POETS: GEORGE DARLEY, HARTLEY COLERIDGE, THOMAS HOOD, THOMAS LOVELL BEDDOES, EMILY BRONTË. London: Heinemann, 1974.

> A limited selection, with introduction and commentary.

*Reiman, Donald H., ed. THE ROMANTIC CONTEXT: POETRY. 128 vols. New York: Garland, 1976-78.

> Besides including Betty T. Bennett's edition cited above, this series reprints, with critical introductions, 321 first or other early editions of the chief minor poets (some of them best sellers or influential in their day) that influenced and/or reflected the work of the great Romantic poets. The authors reprinted are Baillie, Barrett, Barton, Bayly, Beck, Betham, Bland, Bloomfield (2), Booth, Bowles, Patrick Brontë, Brydges, Burges, Canning and Gifford, Carr, Cary, Claris ("Brooke"), Colman, Conder, Cottle, Croker, Croly, Dacre, Dallas (2), Darley, Darwin, Dermody, Dyer, Elliott, Fitzgerald, Frere, Gent, Hayley, Heber, Hemans, Hitchener, Hobhouse, Hodgson, Lloyd, Mant, Medwin, Merivale, Milman, James Montgomery, Opie, Tighe, Procter ("Cornwall"), Quillinan, Reynolds, Smith brothers, Sotheby, Thelwall, Thurlow, Walker, Webb, Wells, White, Wiffen, Wilson ("North"), Wolfe, and Wrangham.

Rice-Oxley, L[eonard], ed. POETRY OF THE ANTI-JACOBIN. The Percy Reprints. Oxford: Basil Blackwell, 1924.

> The poetry of the Tory wits--Canning, Frere, and others--who in 1798 helped sustain British support for Pitt's war against revolutionary France.

Rogers, Charles, ed. THE MODERN SCOTTISH MINISTREL: OR THE SONGS OF SCOTLAND OF THE PAST HALF CENTURY. 6 vols. Edinburgh: A. and C. Black, 1855-57.

> Besides publishing a wide range of Scots poetry of the period, these volumes also include biographical sketches of the poets and translations from Gaelic into English verse.

Stephens, James; Edwin L. Beck; and Royall H. Snow, eds. ENGLISH ROMANTIC POETS. New York: American Book Co., 1933.

> This old standby teaching anthology has a good selection of WW, STC, LB, PBS, and JK (no Blake), plus a generous sampling of minor poets--Beddoes, Campbell, Clare, Hartley Coleridge, Cunningham, Hawker, Hemans, Hood, Hunt, Lamb, Landor, Mangan, Moore, Motherwell, Peacock, Praed, Rogers, Scott, Southey, White, and Wolfe.

3. Studies of Two or More Secondary or Minor Poets

Harvey, A.D. "The English Epic in the Romantic Period." PQ, 55 (1976), 241-59.

Names, classifies, and briefly characterizes the numerous epics by secondary and minor poets between PARADISE LOST and ca. 1820.

Saintsbury, George E[dward] B[ateman]. ESSAYS IN ENGLISH LITERATURE, 1780-1860. New York: Charles Scribner's Sons, 1895.

Contains essays on (among other topics) Southey, Landor, Hood, Campbell, and political satires.

Sambrook, A.J. "A Romantic Theme: The Last Man." FORUM FOR MODERN LANGUAGE STUDIES, 2 (1965), 25-33.

Treats works by LB, Campbell, Beddoes, Mary Shelley, and Hood.

B. INDIVIDUAL POETS

In this section on individual poets I treat separately twelve significant secondary figures--Beddoes, Campbell, Clare, Hogg, Hood, Hunt, Landor, Moore, Peacock, Rogers, Scott, and Southey--and works on their lives, thought, and poetry (not prose of fiction). In treating such writers as Scott upon whom a great deal has been written and for whom there are relatively full bibliographies of secondary sources, I have been more selective and have listed lesser publications only if they are too recent to be covered in NCBEL and other standard bibliographies.

Because the scholarship on several of the twelve secondary poets is much less complete than that on the five major poets treated in Chapters 3-7, it has not proven necessary to annotate or evaluate every item, especially when the title describes the subject matter and there are not several competing publications covering the same ground. Primary and secondary resources for these poets are grouped under the following headings: Bibliography; Editions; Biographical Sources and Studies; and Criticism.

1. Thomas Lovell Beddoes (1803-49)

a. BIBLIOGRAPHY

D[onner] H[enry] W. "Thomas Lovell Beddoes." In NCBEL. Ed. George Watson. Cambridge: Cambridge University Press, 1969. III, 409-11.

Lists principal materials through 1967.

b. EDITIONS

Burwick, Frederick. "Beddoes, Bayern, und Die Burschenschaften." COMPARATIVE LITERATURE, 21 (1969), 289-306.

Reprints the (German) texts of two articles Beddoes published in the BAYERISCHEN VOLKBLATT (1831-32).

*Donner, H[enry] W., ed. PLAYS AND POEMS OF THOMAS LOVELL BEDDOES. London: Routledge and Kegan Paul, 1950.

The standard scholarly edition.

_____. "Two German Poems Attributed to T.L. Beddoes." STUDIA NEO-PHILOLOGICA, 37 (1965), 360-66.

Gosse, Edmund, ed. POETICAL WORKS OF THOMAS LOVELL BEDDOES. 2 vols. London: J.M. Dent, 1890.

Reedited by Gosse as THE COMPLETE WORKS OF THOMAS LOVELL BEDDOES (2 vols., London: Fanfrolico Press, 1928), with Gosse's "Memoir" of Beddoes.

[Kelsall, Thomas Forbes, ed.]. POEMS BY THE LATE THOMAS LOVELL BEDDOES, . . . WITH A MEMOIR. 2 vols. London: William Pickering, 1851.

According to Roger Ingpen, the second volume of this edition consists of remaining sheets of the first edition of DEATH'S JEST BOOK, and a reprint of THE BRIDE'S TRAGEDY, paginated consecutively with DEATH'S JEST BOOK. When those sheets were exhausted, Pickering had the two works in the second volume reprinted, numbered them consecutively with the poems in the original first volume, and bound the POEMS as one volume.

c. BIOGRAPHICAL SOURCES AND STUDIES

Donner, H[enry] W. "T.L. Beddoes to Leonhard Tobler: Eight German Letters." STUDIA NEOPHILOLOGICA, 35 (1963), 227-55.

*Gosse, Edmund, ed. THE LETTERS OF THOMAS LOVELL BEDDOES. London: Elkin Mathews and John Lane, 1894.

Reissued with Gosse's edition of THE COMPLETE WORKS . . . , 1928 (see below).

Lundin, Jon. "T.L. Beddoes at Gottingen." STUDIA NEOPHILOLOGICA, 43 (1971), 484-99.

Analyzes Beddoes' studies in esoteric sciences, philosophy, and mythography at Gottingen, 1825-29.

Scarlett, E.P. "The Doctor of the Dance of Death." ARCHIVES OF INTERNAL MEDICINE (Chicago), 117 (1966), 300-04.

d. CRITICISM

"Beddoes and His Contemporaries." TLS, 13 December 1928, pp. 973-74.

> A leading review article, appraising Beddoes' place in the Romantic movement.

Hoyt, Charles Alva. "Themes and Imagery in the Poetry of T.L. Beddoes." STUDIA NEOPHILOLOGICA, 35 (1963), 85-103.

> The major recent critical discussion.

2. Thomas Campbell (1777-1844)

a. BIBLIOGRAPHY

Bierstadt, Albert Morton. "Unacknowledged Poems by Thomas Campbell." MLN, 37 (1922), 343-45.

> Bierstadt is also known as Albert Morton Turner; this article derives from his (unpublished) Harvard dissertation (1920). See also his essay on GERTRUDE OF WYOMING (JEGP, 1921).

Duffy, Charles. "An Epigraph by Thomas Campbell." NOTES AND QUERIES, n.s. 6 (1959), 14.

> See also Duffy's "'Hymen's Ball': An Unpublished Poem by Thomas Campbell" (NOTES AND QUERIES, 1940) and his (unpublished) Cornell dissertation, "Thomas Campbell: A Critical Biography," (1939).

Jordan, Hoover, H. "Thomas Campbell." In THE ENGLISH ROMANTIC POETS AND ESSAYISTS. 2nd ed. Ed. C.W. Houtchens and L.H. Houtchens. New York: MLA, 1966. Pp. 185-96.

> This, the best published critical survey, can be supplemented by NCBEL.

b. EDITIONS

Campbell, Lewis, ed. POEMS OF THOMAS CAMPBELL. Golden Treasury Series. London: Macmillan, 1904.

> A good selection, showing Campbell at his best.

Campbell, Thomas. AN ESSAY ON ENGLISH POETRY, WITH NOTICES OF THE BRITISH POETS. London: John Murray, 1848.

Hill, W. Alfred, ed. THE POETICAL WORKS OF THOMAS CAMPBELL. Memoir by W.E. Aytoun. Aldine Edition. London: George Bell and Sons, 1875; rev. ed. with a memoir by William Allingham, 1890.

Hill was Campbell's "nephew-in-law."

*Robertson, James Logie, ed. THE COMPLETE POETICAL WORKS OF THOMAS CAMPBELL. London: Oxford University Press, 1907.

> Not really complete, because Robertson omits poems he doesn't like.

Sargent, Epes, ed. THE COMPLETE POETICAL WORKS OF THOMAS CAMPBELL, WITH AN ORIGINAL BIOGRAPHY AND NOTES. Boston: Phillips, Sampson, 1854.

c. BIOGRAPHICAL SOURCES AND STUDIES

Beattie, William. THE LIFE AND LETTERS OF THOMAS CAMPBELL. 3 vols. London: Edward Moxon, 1849.

> The official Victorian biography, by Campbell's physician (and enthusiastic admirer).

Hadden, J[ames] Cuthbert. THOMAS CAMPBELL. Famous Scots Series. Edinburgh: Oliphant, Anderson, and Ferrier, 1899.

> A valuable short biography, compressing and giving perspective to those of Beattie (above) and Redding (below).

Redding, Cyrus. LITERARY REMINISCENCES AND MEMOIRS OF THOMAS CAMPBELL. 2 vols. London: C.J. Skeet, 1860.

> Valuable anecdotal account by a journalist who worked closely with Campbell on the NEW MONTHLY MAGAZINE.

d. CRITICISM

Duffy, Charles. "Thomas Campbell and America." AMERICAN LITERATURE, 13 (1942), 346-55.

> Discusses biographical connections and Campbell's great literary popularity in America.

Stillinger, Jack. "Whittier's Early Imitation of Thomas Campbell." PQ, 38 (1959), 502-04.

> Whittier's "The Exile's Departure" derives from Campbell's "Exile of Erin."

#Symons, Arthur. "Thomas Campbell. In his THE ROMANTIC MOVEMENT IN ENGLISH POETRY. London: Constable, 1909.

Rated by Hoover Jordan "the most scintillating" critical essay on Campbell.

3. John Clare (1793-1864)

a. BIBLIOGRAPHY

Chapple, A.J.V. "Some Unpublished Poetical Manuscripts of John Clare." YALE UNIVERSITY LIBRARY GAZETTE, 31 (1956), 34-48.

*Crossan, G[reg] D. "John Clare: A Chronological Bibliography." BULLETIN OF BIBLIOGRAPHY, 32 (1975), 55-62.

According to some scholars, this bibliography--also published in Crossan's A RELISH FOR ETERNITY: THE PROCESS OF DIVINIZA- TION IN THE POETRY OF JOHN CLARE (Salzburg, 1976)--is the best available on Clare.

*Grainger, Margaret. A DESCRIPTIVE CATALOGUE OF THE JOHN CLARE COLLECTION IN PETERBOROUGH MUSEUM AND ART GALLERY. Petersbor- ough, Engl.: Peterborough Museum and Art Gallery, 1973.

Contains indexes to the poems in the large collection of MSS.

Powell, David. "A Bibliography of the Writings of John Clare, with a Selec- tion of Critical Material after 1893."

Dissertation in librarianship, University of London, 1953.

_____. CATALOGUE OF THE JOHN CLARE COLLECTION IN THE NORTH- AMPTON PUBLIC LIBRARY. Northampton, Engl.: Northampton Public Library, 1964.

#Todd, Janet M. "John Clare: A Bibliographical Essay." BRITISH STUDIES MONITOR, 4 (Winter 1974), 3-18.

The most recent full survey of Clare bibliography, supplemented by Eric Robinson's "A Note on John Clare," BRITISH STUDIES MONI- TOR, 5 (Fall 1974), 36-38.

b. EDITIONS

Green, David Bonnell. "John Clare, John Savage, and 'The Scientific Recep- tacle.'" REVIEW OF ENGLISH LITERATURE, 8 (1966), 87-98.

Includes hitherto unreprinted texts of three of eight poems that Clare contributed to this periodical in 1825, together with three letters from Savage (one of its editors) to Clare.

Grigson, Geoffrey, ed. POEMS OF JOHN CLARE'S MADNESS. London: Routledge and Kegan Paul, 1949.

> An intelligent introduction to Clare's later poetry, but the texts are unreliable. See also Robinson and Summerfield (below).

Park, Julian, ed. "Unpublished Poems by John Clare." UNIVERSITY OF BUFFALO STUDIES, 14, No. 3 (1937), 57-67.

Reeves, James, ed. SELECTED POEMS BY JOHN CLARE. London: Heinemann, 1954.

*Robinson, Eric, and Geoffrey Summerfield, eds. THE LATER POEMS OF JOHN CLARE. Manchester: Manchester University Press, 1964.

> Includes a number of the interesting poems of Clare's madness, including "Childe Harold" and "Don Juan" (which Clare wrote under the delusion he was Byron), edited from Clare's holograph MSS.

* _____. SELECTED POEMS AND PROSE OF JOHN CLARE. London: Oxford University Press, 1967.

> A selection of Clare's accessible shorter poems, reedited from the MSS, that (unsuccessfully) attempts to present him as a major poet, in the class of WW, STC, LB, PBS, and JK. There are no notes and few study aids.

* _____. THE SHEPHERD'S CALENDAR. London: Oxford University Press, 1964.

> An attractive, illustrated edition of one of Clare's most interesting poems, here reedited from the MSS, but without the other poems that were published with it in the original edition of 1827.

Tibble, Anne, ed. BIRDS NEST: POEMS BY JOHN CLARE. N.p.: Mid-Northumberland Arts Group, 1973.

> Includes twenty previously unpublished poems.

*Tibble J[ohn] W. THE POEMS OF JOHN CLARE. 2 vols. London: J.M. Dent, 1935.

> Long the standard edition, this is being replaced by newer texts based more closely on Clare's MSS. Tibble has included a selection (of the same inadequate texts) in JOHN CLARE: SELECTED POEMS (Everyman's Library, 1965).

c. BIOGRAPHICAL SOURCES AND STUDIES

#Blunden, Edmund, ed. SKETCHES IN THE LIFE OF JOHN CLARE. London: Cobden-Sanderson, 1931.

> A selection from Clare's voluminous autobiographical notes and fragments.

Cherry, J[ohn] L[aw]. THE LIFE AND REMAINS OF JOHN CLARE. London: Frederick Warne, 1873.

> Includes some 200 pages of selections from Clare's later prose and poetry.

Grainger, Margaret. JOHN CLARE, COLLECTOR OF BALLADS. Occasional Papers No. 3. Peterborough, Engl.: Peterborough Museum Society, 1964.

> A twenty-three-page pamphlet.

Green, David Bonnell. "New Letters of John Clare to Taylor and Hessey." SP, 44 (1967), 720-34.

> Seven letters revealing Clare's relations with the LONDON MAGA-ZINE circle.

Martin, Frederick W. THE LIFE OF JOHN CLARE. London: Macmillan, 1865; 2nd ed., with notes by Eric Robinson and Geoffrey Summerfield, 1964.

> The best of the earlier biographies, with up-to-date scholarly notes.

Robinson, Eric, and Geoffrey Summerfield. "John Clare: An Interpretation of Certain Asylum Letters." RES, n.s. 13 (1962), 135-46.

Storey, Mark. "Letters of John Clare, 1821: Revised Datings." NOTES AND QUERIES, 16 (1969), 58-64.

> Solves dating problems by means of the Taylor-Hessey correspondence in the British Library (Egerton MS. 2245).

_____. "Some Previously Unpublished Letters from John Clare." RES, n.s. 25 (1974), 177-85.

> Four of the five letters are to Taylor and Hessey.

*Tibble, J.W., and Anne Tibble. JOHN CLARE: HIS LIFE AND POETRY. London: Heinemann, 1956.

> A newly revised redaction of the same authors' earlier JOHN CLARE, A LIFE (1932). This is the standard biography thus far.

* , eds. THE LETTERS OF JOHN CLARE. London: Routledge and Kegan Paul, 1951.

> The only substantial collection of Clare's correspondence.

Wilson, June. GREEN SHADOWS: THE LIFE OF JOHN CLARE. London: Hodder and Stoughton, 1951.

d. CRITICISM

Barrell, John. THE IDEA OF LANDSCAPE AND THE SENSE OF PLACE, 1730–1840: AN APPROACH TO THE POETRY OF JOHN CLARE. Cambridge: Cambridge University Press, 1972.

> Approaches Clare's early poems about Helpston through the historical changes from the eighteenth-century ideal of landscape to the later ideas of "improving" the land for higher-yield agriculture.

Frosch, Thomas R. "The Descriptive Style of John Clare." SiR, 10 (1971), 137–49.

> An interesting article, weakened by the use of unreliable texts as the basis of the stylistic analysis.

Jack, Ian. "Poems of John Clare's Sanity." In SOME BRITISH ROMANTICS. Ed. James V. Logan, John E. Jordan, and Northrop Frye. Columbus: Ohio State University Press, 1966. Pp. 191–232.

> Argues that THE SHEPHERD'S CALENDAR (1827) contains Clare's best and most significant poetry.

Murry, John Middleton. JOHN CLARE AND OTHER STUDIES. London: Peter Nevill, 1950.

> Murry treats Clare again in "Clare Revisited," UNPROFESSIONAL ESSAYS, 1956, pages 53–111.

#Storey, Mark, ed. CLARE: THE CRITICAL HERITAGE. London: Routledge and Kegan Paul, 1973.

> Includes all the highlights of Clare criticism from the beginning through 1964.

* . THE POETRY OF JOHN CLARE: A CRITICAL INTRODUCTION. London: Macmillan, 1974.

> A substantial volume that is the first critical book devoted entirely to Clare's works.

Swingle, L[arry] J. "Stalking the Essential John Clare: Clare in Relation to His Contemporaries." SiR, 14 (1975), 273-84.

> An important analysis.

Todd, Janet M. IN ADAM'S GARDEN: A STUDY OF JOHN CLARE'S PRE-ASYLUM POETRY. Gainesville: University of Florida Press, 1973.

> A thin study that tends to paste labels onto, rather than analyze, the poems.

_____. "'Very copys of nature': John Clare's Descriptive Poetry." PQ, 53 (1974), 84-99.

4. James Hogg (1770-1835)

a. BIBLIOGRAPHY

Adam, R[obert] B[orthwick]. WORKS, LETTERS, AND MANUSCRIPTS OF JAMES HOGG, "THE ETTRICK SHEPHERD." Buffalo, N.Y.: Privately printed, 1930.

> A valuable but curious bibliography done as a gift book to Adam's son on his twelfth birthday, with illustrations both of Hogg's times and of the Scottish border country where Hogg (and the elder Adam) grew up, as well as transcriptions of several of Hogg's letters.

Batho, Edith C. "Notes on the Bibliography of James Hogg, the Ettrick Shepherd." LIBRARY, 4th Ser., 16 (1935), 309-26.

> Contains the fullest list of Hogg's unreprinted periodical contributions.

Hogg, William Dodds. THE FIRST EDITIONS OF THE WRITINGS OF JAMES HOGG, THE ETTRICK SHEPHERD. Publications of the Edinburgh Bibliographical Society, No. 12. Edinburgh: Edinburgh Bibliographical Society, 1924.

> The standard primary bibliography.

Law, Derek. "The Bibliography of James Hogg: Five Unrecorded Items." BIBLIOTHECK, 7 (1974), 79-80.

Pache, Walter. "'Der Ettrickschafter Hoggs': A Scotsman's Literary Reputation in Germany." STUDIES IN SCOTTISH LITERATURE, 8 (1970), 109-17.

b. EDITIONS

*Mack, Douglas S., ed. JAMES HOGG: SELECTED POEMS. Oxford: Clarendon Press, 1971.

A reliable text of what the editor believes to be Hogg's best poems.

Oliver, J[ohn] W., ed. POEMS OF JAMES HOGG. Edinburgh: Oliver and Boyd, 1946.

A sixty-eight-page selection for the Saltire Society.

THE POETICAL WORKS OF THE ETTRICK SHEPHERD. 6 vols. Glasgow: Blackie, 1838-40.

*Thomson, Thomas, ed. THE WORKS OF THE ETTRICK SHEPHERD. 2 vols. Glasgow: Blackie, 1865-66.

The second volume includes Hogg's "Autobiography," as well as Thomson's "Biographical Sketch of the Ettrick Shepherd." The texts of poetry are (according to Louis Simpson) better than those of the prose in this edition.

c. BIOGRAPHICAL SOURCES AND STUDIES
See also Thomson's edition of the WORKS, above.

Batho, Edith C. THE ETTRICK SHEPHERD. Cambridge: Cambridge University Press, 1927.

The most valuable parts of this work (weak on criticism) are its factual treatment of biographical details and its bibliography.

Carswell, Donald. SIR WALTER: A FOUR-PART STUDY IN BIOGRAPHY. London: John Murray, 1930.

Treats Scott, Hogg, Lockhart, and Joanna Baillie.

Douglas, George. JAMES HOGG. Edinburgh: Oliphant, Anderson and Ferrier, 1899.

Garden, Mary Gray Hogg, ed. MEMORIALS OF JAMES HOGG, THE ETTRICK SHEPHERD. London: Alexander Gardner, 1885.

Mrs. Garden was Hogg's daughter.

Mack, Douglas S., ed. JAMES HOGG: MEMOIRS OF THE AUTHOR'S LIFE AND FAMILIAR ANECDOTES OF SIR WALTER SCOTT. Edinburgh: Scottish Academic Press, 1973.

Stephenson, H.T. THE ETTRICK SHEPHERD: A BIOGRAPHY. Bloomington: Indiana University Press, 1922.

*Strout, Alan Lang. THE LIFE AND LETTERS OF JAMES HOGG, THE ETTRICK SHEPHERD. Vol. 1: 1770-1825. Lubbock: Texas Technical College Press, 1947.

> The only volume published. The most detailed and scholarly account of Hogg's earlier years.

d. CRITICISM

Mack, Douglas S. "James Hogg and the Ettrick Shepherd." LIBRARY REVIEW, 22 (1970), 307-09.

*Simpson, Louis. JAMES HOGG: A CRITICAL STUDY. Edinburgh: Oliver and Boyd, 1962.

> The fullest account of Hogg's writings, with a sketch of his life. Simpson devotes almost sixty pages to the poetry.

Veitch, John. THE HISTORY AND POETRY OF THE SCOTTISH BORDER. Glasgow: James Maclehose, 1878.

5. Thomas Hood (1799-1845)

a. BIBLIOGRAPHY

C[ollins], R[owland] L., "Thomas Hood." In NCBEL. Ed. George Watson. Cambridge: Cambridge University Press, 1969. III, 359-62.

> A convenient listing of Hood's works and of secondary studies through 1964.

b. EDITIONS

Ainger, Alfred, ed. POEMS OF THOMAS HOOD. Vol. I: SERIOUS POEMS. London: Macmillan, 1897.

> There were no other volumes to complete this edition.

*Clubbe, John, ed. SELECTED POEMS OF THOMAS HOOD. Cambridge: Harvard University Press, 1970.

> An excellent selection, with introduction, extensive annotation, index, and many of Hood's own illustrations.

[Hood, Thomas, Jr., and Frances Freeling Broderip, eds.]. THE WORKS OF THOMAS HOOD, EDITED BY HIS SON AND DAUGHTER. 10 vols. London: Edward Moxon, 1869-73.

Based on an earlier Moxon edition (8 vols., 1862-69) "edited, with notes, by his son."

*Jerrold, Walter, ed. THE COMPLETE POETICAL WORKS OF THOMAS HOOD. London: Oxford University Press, 1906.

Reprinted several times.

Rossetti, William Michael, ed. THE POETICAL WORKS OF THOMAS HOOD. With a Critical Memoir. London: Routledge, 1873.

c. BIOGRAPHICAL SOURCES AND STUDIES

#Clubbe, John. VICTORIAN FORERUNNER: THE LATER CAREER OF THOMAS HOOD. Durham, N.C.: Duke University Press, 1968.

A mature study with useful bibliography of relevant materials, published and unpublished.

#[Hood, Thomas, Jr., and Frances Freeling Broderip, eds.] MEMORIALS OF THOMAS HOOD, COLLECTED, ARRANGED, AND EDITED BY HIS DAUGHTER, WITH A PREFACE AND NOTES BY HIS SON. 2 vols. London: Edward Moxon, 1860.

A basic biographical source.

Jerrold, Walter. THOMAS HOOD: HIS LIFE AND TIMES. London: Alston Rivers, 1907.

A bulky, rambling life in the nineteenth-century manner.

_____. THOMAS HOOD AND CHARLES LAMB: THE STORY OF A FRIEND-SHIP. London: E. Benn, 1930.

Hood's reminiscences, with interpolations and additions by Jerrold.

Marchand, Leslie A., ed. LETTERS OF THOMAS HOOD, FROM THE DILKE PAPERS IN THE BRITISH MUSEUM. New Brunswick, N.J.: Rutgers University Press, 1945.

Morgan, Peter F. "Charles Lamb and Thomas Hood: Records of a Friendship." TENNESSEE STUDIES IN LITERATURE, 9 (1964), 71-85.

_____. "John Hamilton Reynolds and Thomas Hood." K-SJ, 11 (1962), 83-95.

*_____, ed. THE LETTERS OF THOMAS HOOD. Toronto: University of Toronto Press, 1973.

A full, annotated edition of Hood's letters.

*Reid, J[ohn] C[lowie]. THOMAS HOOD. London: Routledge and Kegan Paul, 1963.

The most complete modern biography. See also Clubbe, above.

Whitley, Alvin. "Hood and Dickens: Some New Letters." HUNTINGTON LIBRARY QUARTERLY, 14 (1951), 385-413.

d. CRITICISM

Ades, John I. "Thomas Hood: 'Two Parts Methodist to One of Humourist.'" CHARLES LAMB BULLETIN, 7 (1974), 141-46.

Blunden, Edmund. "The Poet Hood." REVIEW OF ENGLISH LITERATURE, 1 (1960), 26-34.

Brander, Laurence. THOMAS HOOD. Writers and Their Works. London: Published for the British Council and the National Book League by Longmans, Green, 1963.

A concise (40-page) generous appraisal, with a select biography.

@Jeffrey, Lloyd N. THOMAS HOOD. Twayne's English Authors Series. New York: Twayne, 1972.

Whitley, Alvin. "Keats and Hood." K-SJ, 5 (1956), 33-47.

Discusses their personal connections (through the Reynolds family) and the influence of JK's poetry on Hood's.

6. [James Henry] Leigh Hunt (1784-1859)

a. BIBLIOGRAPHY

#Brack, O.M., Jr., and D.H. Stefanson. A CATALOGUE OF THE LEIGH HUNT MANUSCRIPTS IN THE UNIVERSITY OF IOWA LIBRARIES. Iowa City: Friends of the University of Iowa Libraries, 1973.

Lists 169 manuscripts and proofs.

*Brewer, Luther A. MY LEIGH HUNT LIBRARY: THE FIRST EDITIONS. Cedar Rapids, Iowa: Privately printed, 1932.

Contains a useful chronology of Hunt's life and a chronological list of Hunt's many residences, as well as descriptions of the first editions (with lively anecdotes and illustrations).

Mitchell, Alexander. "A Bibliography of the Writings of Leigh Hunt, with Critical Notes." BOOKMAN'S JOURNAL, 3rd Ser., 18 (1931), 9–73.

Collates and comments briefly on first and second editions of Hunt's publications, both verse and prose.

Nowell-Smith, Simon. "Leigh Hunt as Bellman." TIMES LITERARY SUPPLE-MENT , 2 April 1970, p. 367.

Identifies anonymous "bellman's verses" that Hunt wrote while imprisioned, 1814–16. See also Betty T. Bennett's comment, TIMES LITERARY SUPPLEMENT, 16 April 1970, p. 430.

b. EDITIONS

Hudnall, Clayton E. "Leigh Hunt on Keats: Two New Poems." SOUTHERN HUMANITIES REVIEW, 4 (1970), 358–62.

Uncollected poems that appeared in the weekly MIRROR OF LITER-ATURE (1830).

Johnson, Reginald Brimley, ed. POEMS OF LEIGH HUNT, WITH PREFACES FROM SOME OF HIS PERIODICALS. The Temple Library. London: J.M. Dent, 1891.

This companion volume to ESSAYS OF LEIGH HUNT, edited by R.B. Johnson, includes 138 pages of original poetry and another 25 pages of poetic translations.

Kent, Charles, ed. LEIGH HUNT AS POET AND ESSAYIST, BEING THE CHOICEST PASSAGES FROM HIS WORKS. The Chandos Classics. London: Frederick Warne, 1891.

Includes about seventy-five pages of Hunt's occasional and shorter poetry (compared with about 450 pages of his essays).

Lee, S[amuel] Adams, ed. THE POETICAL WORKS OF LEIGH HUNT, NOW FIRST ENTIRELY COLLECTED, REVISED BY HIMSELF. 2 vols. Boston: Ticknor and Fields, 1857.

For this edition Hunt included of his characteristic early poems-- more, in fact, than he thought worthy of republication. The same basic selection, edited by Thornton Hunt, was published in London in 1860.

*Milford, H[umphrey] S., ed. THE POETICAL WORKS OF LEIGH HUNT. London: Oxford University Press, 1923.

> Although it omits the juvenilia, this is the only edition of Hunt's poetry even approaching completeness. Includes valuable study aids.

#THE POETICAL WORKS OF LEIGH HUNT. London: Edward Moxon, 1832.

> A generous selection of Hunt's earlier poetry, with a long, chatty introduction by Hunt.

c. BIOGRAPHICAL SOURCES AND STUDIES

*Blunden, Edmund. LEIGH HUNT: A BIOGRAPHY. London: Cobden-Sanderson, 1930.

> Published in New York the same year under the title LEIGH HUNT AND HIS CIRCLE, this biography remains--in spite of some paucity of fact and detail--the fullest and best in English. Blunden is sympathetic and critically perceptive. For the best biography, see Landré (below); and for additional facts, see Cameron and Reiman, SHELLEY AND HIS CIRCLE (Chap. 6.C.3).

*Brewer, Luther A. MY LEIGH HUNT LIBRARY: THE HOLOGRAPH LETTERS. Iowa City: University of Iowa Press, 1938.

> Quotes in full most of the letters belonging to Brewer at his death in 1933, together with comments. There is a good index.

#Fogle, Stephen F., ed. LEIGH HUNT'S AUTOBIOGRAPHY: THE EARLIEST SKETCHES. Gainesville: University of Florida Monographs, 1959.

> Carefully edited, with introduction and notes.

*Hunt, Thornton, ed. THE CORRESPONDENCE OF LEIGH HUNT. 2 vols. London: Smith, Elder, 1862.

> An important collection, but most of the letters have passages deleted; some have since been published in full (e.g., those to Shelley, in Cameron and Reiman, SHELLEY AND HIS CIRCLE, cited in Chap. 6.C.3).

Kendall, Kenneth E. LEIGH HUNT'S REFLECTOR. The Hague: Mouton, 1971.

> Studies Hunt's early (1811-12) short-lived periodical and its contributors, including Lamb, Barnes, Field, Mitchell, Scholefield, Aikin, Dyer, and Gilchrist, on all of whom Kendall provides convenient biographical data.

*Landré, Louis. LEIGH HUNT (1784-1859): CONTRIBUTION À L'HISTOIRE DU ROMANTISME ANGLAIS. 2 vols. Paris: Société D'Edition "Les Belles-Lettres," 1935-36.

> The most thorough biography and scholarly study of Hunt's writings, with full bibliographies and notes. A monumental study of enduring value.

Miller, Barnette. LEIGH HUNT'S RELATIONS WITH BYRON, SHELLEY, AND KEATS. New York: Columbia University Press, 1910.

> A pioneering study, now largely superseded by later research, including especially William H. Marshall's BYRON, SHELLEY, HUNT AND THE LIBERAL (Chap. 5.C.3) and Cameron and Reiman, SHELLEY AND HIS CIRCLE (Chap. 6.C.3).

Monkhouse, Cosmo. LIFE OF LEIGH HUNT. Great Writers Series. London: Walter Scott, 1893.

> A useful brief life, with a bibliography by John P. Anderson.

*Morpurgo, J.E., ed. THE AUTOBIOGRAPHY OF LEIGH HUNT. London: Cresset Press, 1948.

> A convenient edition, with introduction and notes, of this famous-- and invaluable--document, first published in three volumes (1860) and edited in two volumes by Roger Ingpen (London, 1903). For an earlier (less mellow) account of some of the same people and events, see Hunt's LORD BYRON AND SOME OF HIS CONTEM-PORARIES (London, 1828, and various subsequent editions).

Severn, Derek. "Leigh Hunt v. the Tories and the Prince Regent." CORN-HILL MAGAZINE, No. 1066 (1970-71), pp. 288-312.

> Valuable account of the years of the EXAMINER'S reform journalism, 1808-12.

#Tatchell, Molly. LEIGH HUNT AND HIS FAMILY IN HAMMERSMITH. London: Hammersmith Local History Group, 1969.

> A valuable account of Hunt and some of his children in the later years of his life.

d. CRITICISM

There has been very little criticism on Leigh Hunt as a poet (rather than as a journalist, essayist, and friend of other poets). Most of the best criticism of his poetry is to be found in the biographies (particularly Landré's, Sec. B.6.c) and in articles and books on Keats, Shelley, and their circles.

Fenner, Theodore. LEIGH HUNT AND OPERA CRITICISM: THE EXAMINER YEARS. Lawrence: University of Kansas Press, 1972.

> A substantial discussion of Hunt's musical interests as well as of a neglected area of his prose writing.

Fogle, Stephen F. "Leigh Hunt and the End of Romantic Criticism." In SOME BRITISH ROMANTICS. Ed. James V. Logan, John E. Jordan, and Northrop Frye. Columbus: Ohio State University Press, 1966. Pp. 119–39.

> Shows that Hunt's IMAGINATION AND FANCY (1844) marks the end of the important critical distinctions and precision that marked the criticism of the major Romantic poets.

Short, Clarice. "The Composition of Hunt's THE STORY OF RIMINI." K–SJ, 21–22 (1972–73), 207–18.

> Analyzes in detail the draft MSS in the Ashley Collection of the British Library and the Keats Memorial Library, Keats House, Hampstead.

7. Walter Savage Landor (1775-1864)

a. BIBLIOGRAPHY

*Super, R[obert] H[enry]. THE PUBLICATION OF LANDOR'S WORKS. London: The Bibliographical Society, 1954.

> A monograph describing the circumstances of his publications and quoting the relevant correspondence, documents, and secondary sources.

_____. "Walter Savage Landor." In NCBEL. Ed. George Watson. Cambridge: Cambridge University Press, 1969. III, 1210–16.

> Carries the list of secondary sources through 1964, with listings as late as 1967. See also Super's critical survey of Landor criticism in Houtchens and Houtchens, THE ENGLISH ROMANTIC POETS AND ESSAYISTS (Sec. A.1, above).

*Wise, Thomas James, ed. A LANDOR LIBRARY: A CATALOGUE OF THE PRINTED BOOKS, MANUSCRIPTS AND AUTOGRAPH LETTERS BY WALTER SAVAGE LANDOR COLLECTED BY THOMAS JAMES WISE. London: Privately printed, 1928.

> Part of Wise's Ashley Library, now in the British Library.

*Wise, Thomas James, and Stephen Wheeler, eds. A BIBLIOGRAPHY OF THE WRITINGS IN PROSE AND VERSE OF WALTER SAVAGE LANDOR. London: Printed for the Bibliographical Society by Blades, East and Blades, 1919.

Records the literary contents as well as physical properties of the first editions, periodical publications, collected editions, and major biographical and critical publications to 1919.

b. EDITIONS

This selected list of editions of Landor's poetry omits selections that include both his poetry and prose. The best known of those were edited by Sidney Colvin (1882) and E.K. Chambers (1946).

Buxton, Richard, compiler. THE SCULPTURED GARLAND: A SELECTION FROM THE LYRICAL POEMS OF WALTER SAVAGE LANDOR. Illus. by Iain MacNab. London: Dropmore Press, 1948.

*Crump, Charles G., ed. POEMS, DIALOGUES IN VERSE, AND EPIGRAMS BY WALTER SAVAGE LANDOR. 2 vols. London: J.M. Dent, 1892.

These volumes from Volumes 7-8 of Crump's edition of Landor's works (IMAGINARY CONVERSATIONS, 6 vols., 1891; LONGER PROSE WORKS, with index to entire set, 2 vols., 1892-93). This is still the best collective edition of Landor's works, though it lacks some poems found in the Welby-Wheeler edition, below.

#Forster, John. THE WORKS AND LIFE OF WALTER SAVAGE LANDOR. 8 vols. London: Chapman and Hall, 1876.

The official edition (and life) by Landor's literary executor.

Foster, Finley M.K., ed. POEMS TO IANTHE BY WALTER SAVAGE LANDOR. Newark, Del.: The Craftsmen of Kells, 1922.

@Grigson, Geoffrey, ed. POEMS BY WALTER SAVAGE LANDOR. London: Centaur Press, 1964.

A full selection, with introduction, chronology, some notes, and indexes. The text is handled casually, but the selection fills the nonspecialists needs.

LOVE POEMS OF LANDOR. London: John Lane, 1901.

Proudfit, Charles L. "An Earlier Version of W.S. Landor's Poem 'Lyons.'" NOTES AND QUERIES, n.s. 18 (1971), 247-48.

See also Proudfit's "More Unrecorded Periodical Contributions of Walter Savage Landor," NOTES AND QUERIES, n.s. 18 (1971), 90-91, which identifies fourteen letters and articles published in provincial newspapers, 1848-56.

Radford, Ernest, ed. THE POEMS OF WALTER SAVAGE LANDOR. London: Walter Scott, 1889.

Sidgwick, J.B., ed. THE SHORTER POEMS OF WALTER SAVAGE LANDOR. Cambridge: Cambridge University Press, 1946.

*Welby, T[homas] Earle, and Stephen Wheeler, eds. THE COMPLETE WORKS OF WALTER SAVAGE LANDOR. 16 vols. London: Chapman and Hall, 1927-36.

> The poems occupy Volumes 13-16. The set was limited to 525 copies; the text of the prose is unsatisfactory, but Wheeler's edition of the poetry is (virtually) complete, accurate, well annotated, and fully indexed.

*Wheeler, Stephen, ed. THE POETICAL WORKS OF WALTER SAVAGE LANDOR. 3 vols. Oxford: Clarendon Press, 1937.

> Reprints Volumes 13-16 of THE COMPLETE WORKS edited by T. Earle Welby and Wheeler (see above).

c. BIOGRAPHICAL SOURCES AND STUDIES

Colvin, Sidney. LANDOR. English Men of Letters Series. London: Macmillan, 1881.

> A brief biography, based largely on Forster.

@Elwin, Malcolm. LANDOR: A REPLEVIN. London: Macdonald, 1958.

> A passionate defense of Landor, partly in reaction to the scholarly objectivity of Super's great biography (below). Elwin's earlier, popularized biography entitled SAVAGE LANDOR was published in 1941.

#Forster, John. WALTER SAVAGE LANDOR: A BIOGRAPHY. 2 vols. London: Chapman and Hall, 1869.

> The official biography by Landor's friend and literary executor.

Proudfit, Charles L. "Southey and Landor: A Literary Friendship." WC, 5 (1974), 105-12.

> In the special Southey issue of WC.

#Ruoff, A. La Vonne. "Landor's Letters to His Family 1802-1829." BULLETIN OF THE JOHN RYLANDS LIBRARY, 53 (1971), 465-500; 54 (1972), 398-433; 58 (1976), 467-507.

The first installment covers the years 1802–25, the second, 1826–29, the third, 1830–32.

_____. "Landor's Letters to the Reverend Walter Birch." BULLETIN OF THE JOHN RYLANDS LIBRARY, 51 (1968), 200–61.

*Super, R[obert] H[enry]. WALTER SAVAGE LANDOR: A BIOGRAPHY. New York: New York University Press, 1954.

A carefully researched, intelligently written, full biography, useful to students of the period whether or not they are seeking information especially about Landor.

Van Thal, Herbert, ed. LANDOR: A BIOGRAPHICAL ANTHOLOGY. London: George Allen and Unwin, 1973.

Wheeler, Stephen, ed. LETTERS OF WALTER SAVAGE LANDOR, PRIVATE AND PUBLIC. London: Duckworth, 1899.

Contains many of the letters Landor published in periodicals, as well as a small number of personal letters.

d. CRITICISM

Bradley, William. THE EARLY POEMS OF WALTER SAVAGE LANDOR: A STUDY OF HIS DEVELOPMENT AND DEBT TO MILTON. London: Printed by Bradbury, Agnew, 1914.

A valuable study.

Davie, Donald. "Landor's Shorter Poems." In his PURITY OF DICTION IN ENGLISH VERSE. London: Chatto and Windus, 1952.

An influential critical appraisal that first appeared in ESSAYS IN CRITICISM, 1 (1951), 345–55.

@Dilworth, Ernest N. WALTER SAVAGE LANDOR. Twayne's English Authors Series. New York: Twayne, 1971.

The first two chapters of this brief introduction treat Landor's poetry.

Evans, Edward Waterman, Jr. WALTER SAVAGE LANDOR: A CRITICAL STUDY. New York: G.P. Putnam's Sons, 1892.

Hamilton, G. Rostrevor. WALTER SAVAGE LANDOR. London: Published for the British Council and the National Book League by Longmans, Green, 1960.

A brief pamphlet providing an intelligent introduction to the man and his writings.

Kelly, Andrea. "The Latin Poetry of Walter Savage Landor." In THE LATIN POETRY OF THE ENGLISH POETS. Ed. J.W. Binns. London: Routledge and Kegan Paul, 1974. Pp. 150-93.

A careful account and analysis of Latin poetry in Landor's career.

Kestner, Joseph. "The Genre of Landor's GEBIR: 'Eminences Excessively Bright.'" WC, 5 (1974), 41-49.

Argues persuasively that GEBIR is an epyllion à la Catullus, not an epic.

Mercier, Vivian. "The Future of Landor Criticism." In SOME BRITISH RO-MANTICS. Ed. James V. Logan, John E. Jordan, and Northrop Frye. Columbus: Ohio State University Press, 1966. Pp. 43-85.

*Pinsky, Robert. LANDOR'S POETRY. Chicago: University of Chicago Press, 1968.

A perceptive study that attempts to gauge the significance of Landor's poetry both in its own right and for its relevance to Modernist poets like Yeats, Pound, and Davie.

Proudfit, Charles L. "Landor's Hobbyhorse: A Study in Romantic Orthography." SiR, 7 (1968), 207-17.

On Landor's lifelong (unsuccessful) struggle to introduce an original system of English orthography into his writings.

*Vitoux, Pierre. L'OEUVRE DE WALTER SAVAGE LANDOR. Paris: Presses Universitaires de France, 1964.

After a biographical section, this excellent scholarly work devotes over 110 densely packed pages to discussion and analysis of Landor's poetry, before turning to his prose. There is a thorough bibliography in this, the best critical study of Landor's works.

8. Thomas Moore (1779-1852)

The life and career of Moore are so closely connected with those of LB that general books on LB and his circle should be consulted--e.g., Marchand's BYRON (Chap. 5.C.2) and D.L. Moore's THE LATE LORD BYRON (Chap. 5.A.3).

a. BIBLIOGRAPHY

Jordan, Hoover H. "Thomas Moore." In THE ENGLISH ROMANTIC POETS AND ESSAYISTS. 2nd ed. Ed. C.W. Houtchens and L.H. Houtchens. New York: MLA, 1966. Pp. 199-208.

> The best evaluative survey of secondary materials on Moore. See also NCBEL and the annual scholarly bibliographies covering the period.

*MacManus, M.J. A BIBLIOGRAPHICAL HAND-LIST OF THE FIRST EDITIONS OF THOMAS MOORE. Dublin: n.p., 1934.

> Originally published in the DUBLIN MAGAZINE for 1933 (n.s.8, April 1933, pp. 55-61; July, pp. 60-65; Oct., 56-63), this remains the standard checklist of Moore's publications; but see also the first section of Hoover Jordan (above) for a record of disputed attributions to Moore of various prose works.

Muir, Percy H. "Thomas Moore's Irish Melodies, 1808-1834." THE COLOPHON, Part 15, 1933, unpaged.

> Examines the bibliographical complexities of the early editions.

Thomas, Allen Burdett. MOORE EN FRANCE: CONTRIBUTION À L'HISTOIRE DE LA FORTUNE DES OEUVRES DE THOMAS MOORE DANS LA LITTÉRATURE FRANÇAISE, 1819-1830. Paris: H. Champion, 1911.

> Includes a bibliography (pp. 169-71).

b. EDITIONS

*Godley, A[lfred] D[enis]. THE POETICAL WORKS OF THOMAS MOORE. London: Henry Frowde, Oxford University Press, 1910.

> The standard reedited text, with some additions to Moore's own text, below.

#THE POETICAL WORKS OF THOMAS MOORE, COLLECTED BY HIMSELF. 10 vols. London: Longman, Orme, Brown, Green and Longmans, 1840-41.

> Reprinted in England, France, and America in one to ten volumes, throughout the century.

Shepherd, Richard Herne, ed. PROSE AND VERSE, HUMOROUS, SATIRICAL, AND SENTIMENTAL, BY THOMAS MOORE. WITH SUPPRESSED PASSAGES FROM THE MEMOIRS OF LORD BYRON, CHIEFLY FROM THE AUTHOR'S MANUSCRIPT. London: Chatto and Windus, 1878.

> Supplements the ten-volume edition of Moore's POETICAL WORKS (above).

c. BIOGRAPHICAL SOURCES AND STUDIES

Croker, J[ohn] W[ilson]. CORRESPONDENCE BETWEEN . . . J.W. CROKER AND . . . LORD JOHN RUSSELL ON SOME PASSAGES IN MOORE'S DIARY. WITH A POSTSCRIPT BY MR. CROKER, EXPLANATORY OF MR. MOORE'S ACQUAINTANCE AND CORRESPONDENCE WITH HIM. London: John Murray, 1854.

> A bitter reflection by Croker on how Moore used him, while despising Croker (as Russell's edition of Moore's MEMOIRS, below, revealed).

Dowden, Wilfred S. "Let Erin Remember': A Re-examination of the Journal of Thomas Moore." RICE UNIVERSITY STUDIES, 61 (1975), 39-50.

> Describes the recently rediscovered MS of Moore's journal and its significance. Dowden is now preparing an unexpurgated text of the journal.

* _____, ed. THE LETTERS OF THOMAS MOORE. 2 vols. Oxford: Clarendon Press, 1964.

> Though less complete and less well edited than it should be, this edition will probably remain standard for the letters for some time. For additional letters, see Croker (above) and NOTES FROM THE LETTERS OF THOMAS MOORE TO . . . JAMES POWER (below); for corrections to Dowden's dating of letters, see Pearsall (below).

Gwynn, Stephen. THOMAS MOORE. English Men of Letters Series. London: Macmillan, 1905.

> A sketchy but balanced biography.

@Jones, Howard Mumford. "THE HARP THAT ONCE--": A CHRONICLE OF THE LIFE OF THOMAS MOORE. New York: Henry Holt, 1937.

> Long the standard biography, this study has now been supplanted by Jordan (below).

*Jordan, Hoover H. BOLT UPRIGHT: THE LIFE OF THOMAS MOORE. 2 vols. Salzburg: University of Salzburg Studies in English, 1975.

> Now the standard biography. An excellent work, but unfortunately lacking an index.

MacCall, Seamus. THOMAS MOORE. Noted Irish Lives. London: George Duckworth, 1935.

McClary, Ben Harris. "The Moore-Irving Letter File." NOTES AND QUERIES, n.s. 13 (1966), 181-82.

Adds to Dowden's edition four (previously published) letters from Moore to Irving. See also McClary's "Another Moore Letter," NOTES AND QUERIES, n.s. 14 (1967), 24-25.

#NOTES FROM THE LETTERS OF THOMAS MOORE TO HIS MUSIC PUBLISHER, JAMES POWER. With an Introductory Letter from Thomas Crofton Croker. London and New York: Redfield, 1854.

Includes passages omitted from Dowden's collected edition.

#Pearsall, Robert Brainard. "Chronological Annotations to 250 Letters of Thomas Moore." PUBLICATIONS OF THE BIBLIOGRAPHICAL SOCIETY OF AMERICA, 63 (1969), 105-17.

Corrects or refines the dating of 250 letters in Wilfred S. Dowden's edition (above).

Priestley, J[ohn] B[oynton], ed. TOM MOORE'S DIARY: A SELECTION. Cambridge: Cambridge University Press, 1925.

See Quennell, below.

@Quennell, Peter, ed. THE JOURNAL OF THOMAS MOORE, 1818-1841. London: B.T. Batsford, 1964.

Like J.B. Priestley's selection (above), this volume reprints passages thought to be of general interest from the (expurgated) version of Moore's journal included in Lord John Russell's edition of MEMOIRS, JOURNAL AND CORRESPONDENCE.

#Russell, Lord John, ed. MEMOIRS, JOURNAL, AND CORRESPONDENCE OF THOMAS MOORE. 8 vols. London: Longman, Brown, Green, and Longmans, 1853-56.

Valuable, but Moore's candid comments were often censored by Russell, and the index is inadequate (see Dowden, above).

Strong, Leonard Alfred George. THE MINSTREL BOY: A PORTRAIT OF TOM MOORE. London: Hodder and Stoughton, 1937.

White, Terence de Vere. TOM MOORE, THE IRISH POET. London: Hamish Hamilton, 1977.

d. CRITICISM

Birley, Robert. "Thomas Moore: LALLA ROOKH." In his SUNK WITHOUT TRACE: SOME FORGOTTEN MASTERPIECES RECONSIDERED. London: Rupert Hart-Davis, 1962. Pp. 136-71.

Brogan, Howard O. "Moore: Irish Satirist and Keeper of the English Conscience." PQ, 24 (1945), 255-76.

Broms, Wilbur Strong. "Thomas Moore and the Romantic Composers." MUSIC JOURNAL, 19 (March 1961), 36, 71-73.

Brown, Wallace Cable. "Thomas Moore and English Interest in the East." SP, 34 (1937), 576-88.

@De Ford, Miriam Allen. THOMAS MOORE. Twayne's English Authors Series. New York: Twayne, 1967.

> A balanced study of Moore's works.

Hennig, John. "Goethe and LALLA ROOKH." MLR, 48 (1953), 445-50.

#Jordan, Hoover H. "Thomas Moore: Artistry in the Song Lyric." SEL, 2 (1962), 403-40.

> An important defense of the IRISH MELODIES, with emphasis on their need for their accompanying music.

Stockley, W.F.P. "Moore's Satirical Verse." QUEEN'S QUARTERLY, 12 (1905), 229-346; 13 (1906), 1-13.

Tessier, Thérèse. LA POÉSIE LYRIQUE DE THOMAS MOORE (1779-1852). Paris: Didier, 1976.

> A substantial French thesis on the subject.

Trench, W.F. TOM MOORE: A LECTURE, NOW REVISED WITH ADDITIONS. Dublin: The Sign of the Three Candles, 1934.

> A spirited call for a positive reassessment of Moore's claims as a poet (especially in his IRISH MELODIES), and as a satirist, a biographer, a critic, and a political thinker. This pamphlet also contains notes on LALLA ROOKH and "Let Erin Remember."

9. Thomas Love Peacock (1785-1866)

Peacock's life and career are closely intertwined with PBS's. See Chapter 6, especially Section C, the chief biographical studies, including Cameron and Reiman, SHELLEY AND HIS CIRCLE (Sec. 6.C.3).

a. BIBLIOGRAPHY

Madden, Lionel. "A Short Guide to Peacock Studies." CRITICAL SURVEY, 4 (1970), 193-97.

 Helpfully annotated bibliographical overview.

#Read, Bill. "The Critical Reputation of Thomas Love Peacock, with an Enumerative Bibliography of Works by and about Peacock from February 1800 to June 1958." Ph.D. dissertation, Boston University, 1959.

 Available from Xerox's University Microfilms Division, Ann Arbor, Michigan, this and Eleanor L. Nicholes' section in NCBEL provide the fullest bibliographical listings. Nicholas A. Joukovsky is compiling a new bibliography.

#_____. "Thomas Love Peacock: An Enumerative Bibliography." BULLETIN OF BIBLIOGRAPHY, 24 (1963), 32-34; (1964), 70-72, 88-91.

b. EDITIONS

Brett-Smith, H[erbert] F.B., ed. PEACOCK'S FOUR AGES OF POETRY, SHELLEY'S DEFENCE OF POETRY, BROWNING'S ESSAY ON SHELLEY. The Percy Reprints. Oxford: Basil Blackwell, 1921; 2nd ed., 1923.

 A convenient edition. See also John E. Jordan's edition of PBS's and Peacock's essays (Chap. 6.B.4).

*Brett-Smith, H[erbert] F.B., and C.E. Jones, eds. THE WORKS OF THOMAS LOVE PEACOCK. Halliford Editions. 10 vols. London: Constable, 1924-34.

 Contains not only the most complete edition of the poems (in Vols. 6 and 7), but also one of the best biographical accounts in the 200-page "Biographical Introduction" (Vol. 1) and the only collected edition of Peacock's letters (Vol. 8).

Gallon, D.N. "T.L. Peacock's Later Years: The Evidence of Unpublished Letters." RES, n.s. 20 (1969), 315-19.

 See also Hawkins, below.

*Garnett, David. THE NOVELS OF THOMAS LOVE PEACOCK. London: Rupert Hart-Davis, 1948; 2 vols., paperback, 1963.

 The best edition of the novels, with excellent introductions and notes.

Hawkins, Peter A. "T.L. Peacock's Later Years." RES, n.s. 21 (1970), 338.

Johnson, R. Brimley, ed. THE POEMS OF THOMAS LOVE PEACOCK. London: George Routledge and Sons, 1906.

> The only volume attempting to collect all of the poetry from the novels as well as the published poetry (but not including the poems later published with the plays or remaining in MS).

Joukovsky, Nicholas A. "Thomas Love Peacock on Sir Robert Peel: An Unpublished Satire." MP, 73 (1975), 81–84.

> One among several important discoveries published in the 1970s by Joukovsky, a leading Peacock scholar.

Mills, Howard, ed. THOMAS LOVE PEACOCK: MEMOIRS OF SHELLEY AND OTHER ESSAYS AND REVIEWS. New York: New York University Press, 1970.

> A useful compilation for those who cannot consult the Halliford Edition (see Brett-Smith and Jones, above).

Scott, W[alter] S[idney], ed. NEW SHELLEY LETTERS.

> Contains letters to and from Peacock not in the Halliford Edition, (Brett-Smith and Jones, above), many of which are now being re-edited more accurately in Cameron and Reiman, SHELLEY AND HIS CIRCLE (Chap. 6.C.3).

Young, A[rthur] B[utton], ed. THE PLAYS OF THOMAS LOVE PEACOCK, PUBLISHED FOR THE FIRST TIME. London: David Nutt, 1910.

> Like the novels, Peacock's early prose plays contain some delightful songs.

c. BIOGRAPHICAL SOURCES AND STUDIES

Fain, John Tyree. "Peacock's Essay on Steam Navigation." SOUTH ATLANTIC BULLETIN, 35 (1970), 11–15.

> Verifies Peacock's authorship and comments on the form of a report to the government on the feasibility on steamer trade-routes to India.

@Felton, Felix. THOMAS LOVE PEACOCK. London: George Allen and Unwin, 1973.

> A substantial and sympathetic, but rather careless and unscholarly life of Peacock.

*Nicholes, Eleanor L. "Thomas Love Peacock: Life and Works." In SHELLEY AND HIS CIRCLE. Ed. Kenneth Neill Cameron and Donald H. Reiman. Cambridge: Harvard University Press, 1961. I, 90-114.

> This most accurate, though brief, biographical sketch is reprinted in ROMANTIC REBELS: ESSAYS ON SHELLEY AND HIS CIRCLE, ed. by Cameron (Chap. 2.E.1).

Van Doren, Carl. THE LIFE OF THOMAS LOVE PEACOCK. New York: E.P. Dutton, 1911.

> For several decades the fullest biographical source, this volume has been superseded by more recent studies, particularly those of Brett-Smith and Jones (Sec. B.9.b), and Eleanor L. Nicholes (above).

d. CRITICISM

Black, Sidney J. "The Peacockian Essence." BOSTON UNIVERSITY STUDIES IN ENGLISH, 3 (1957), 231-42.

Brogan, Howard O. "Romantic Classicism in Peacock's Verse Satire." SEL, 14 (1974), 525-36.

@Campbell, Olwen W[ard]. THOMAS LOVE PEACOCK. London: Arthur Barker, 1953.

> This brief study, emphasizing (as all critical studies do) Peacock's novels, also contains one of the best accounts of Peacock's relations with PBS.

*Dawson, Carl. HIS FINE WIT: A STUDY OF THOMAS LOVE PEACOCK. Berkeley: University of California Press, 1970.

> The best account of Peacock's artistic and intellectual development, lacking only in historical depth and perspective.

_____. THOMAS LOVE PEACOCK. Profiles in Literature. London: Routledge and Kegan Paul, 1968.

Dyson, A.E. "Peacock: The Wand of Enchantment." In his THE CRAZY FABRIC: ESSAYS IN IRONY. London: Macmillan, 1965. Pp. 57-71.

> Centered on the novels, but relevant to Peacock's thought.

Fain, John T. "Peacock on the Spirit of the Age (1809-1860)." In ALL THESE TO TEACH: ESSAYS IN HONOR OF C.A. ROBERTSON. Ed. Robert A. Bryan, A.C. Morris, A.A. Murphree, and A.L. Williams. Gainesville: University of Florida Press, 1965. Pp. 180-89.

A chronological overview, drawing on the early poems as well as the novels.

Freeman, A[lexander] Martin. THOMAS LOVE PEACOCK: A CRITICAL STUDY. London: Martin Secker, 1911.

Long considered one of the best critical studies of Peacock.

Hoff, Peter Sloat. "The Paradox of the Fortunate Foible: Thomas Love Peacock's Literary Vision." TSLL, 17 (1975), 481-88.

#Mayoux, Jean-Jacques. UN ÉPICURIEN ANGLAIS: THOMAS LOVE PEACOCK. Paris: Les Presses modernes, 1933.

The best study of Peacock's intellectual background.

#Mills, Howard. PEACOCK, HIS CIRCLE AND HIS AGE. Cambridge: Cambridge University Press, 1969.

Though generally inferior to Dawson's fine study (above), Mills's volume gives greater emphasis to Peacock's intellectual and social milieu.

#Priestley, J[ohn] B. THOMAS LOVE PEACOCK. English Men of Letters Series. London: Macmillan, 1927.

Long regarded as the best critical study of Peacock, this well-written work is now dated and largely superseded by the books of Campbell, Dawson, and Mills (all cited above).

Tedford, Barbara W. "A Recipe for Satire and Civilization." COSTERUS, 2 (1972), 197-212.

Tillyard, E[ustace] M.W. "Thomas Love Peacock." In his ESSAYS LITERARY AND EDUCATIONAL. London: Chatto and Windus, 1962. Pp. 114-29.

10. Samuel Rogers (1763-1855)

Though LB rated Rogers as one of the great poets of the age, Rogers is now chiefly remembered as a patron of the arts and an an anecdotalist. There has been virtually no modern scholarly work--bibliographical, editorial, or critical--published on Rogers' poetry.

a. BIBLIOGRAPHY

Blunden, Edmund. "Samuel Rogers." In NCBEL. Ed. George Watson. Cambridge: Cambridge University Press, 1969. III, 181-82.

Hinton, Percival F. "Samuel Rogers's POEMS, 1812." BOOK COLLECTOR, 13 (1964), 70-71.

b. EDITIONS

*POEMS OF SAMUEL ROGERS. London: Thomas Cadell and Edward Moxon, 1834.

> An illustrated standard edition of the period, reissued (with additions) by Moxon in 1838.

THE POETICAL WORKS OF SAMUEL ROGERS, WITH A MEMOIR. New York: Leavitt and Allen, 1857.

Sargent, Epes, ed. THE COMPLETE POETICAL WORKS OF SAMUEL ROGERS AND THOMAS CAMPBELL. Boston: Phillips, Sampson, 1857.

_____. THE COMPLETE POETICAL WORKS OF SAMUEL ROGERS, WITH A BIOGRAPHICAL SKETCH AND NOTES. Boston: Phillips, Sampson, 1854.

> This volume was combined with Sargent's edition of Campbell in 1857 (see above) into a single volume.

c. BIOGRAPHICAL SOURCES AND STUDIES

#Barbier, Carl Paul. SAMUEL ROGERS AND WILLIAM GILPIN: THEIR FRIENDSHIP AND CORRESPONDENCE. London: Oxford University Press, 1959.

Clayden, P[eter] W[illiam]. THE EARLY LIFE OF SAMUEL ROGERS. Boston: Roberts Brothers, 1888.

* _____. ROGERS AND HIS CONTEMPORARIES. 2 vols. London: Smith, Elder, 1889.

> A full Victorian biography with many amusing anecdotes but no particularly searching analysis of their significance.

#[Dyce, Alexander, ed.]. RECOLLECTIONS OF THE TABLE-TALK OF SAMUEL ROGERS. TO WHICH IS ADDED PORSONIANA. London: Edward Moxon, 1856; reissued, introd. Morchard Bishop, London, 1952.

> Contains livelier, less "proper" anecdotes than Sharpe's official version, below.

#Hale, J.R., ed. SAMUEL ROGERS' ITALIAN JOURNAL, WITH AN ACCOUNT OF ROGERS' LIFE AND OF TRAVEL IN ITALY IN 1814-1821. London: Faber and Faber, 1956.

*Powell, G[eorge] H[erbert], ed. REMINISCENCES AND TABLE-TALK OF SAMUEL ROGERS, BANKER, POET, AND PATRON OF THE ARTS, 1763-1855; COLLECTED FROM THE ORIGINAL MEMOIRS OF DYCE AND SHARPE, WITH INTRODUCTION AND INDEX. London: R.B. Johnson, 1903.

> Brings together the two chief sources of Rogers' gossipy anecdotes and indexes them.

Roberts, R. Ellis. SAMUEL ROGERS AND HIS CIRCLE. London: Methuen, 1910.

#[Sharpe, William, ed.]. RECOLLECTIONS BY SAMUEL ROGERS. London: Longman, Green, Longman, and Roberts, 1859.

> Rogers' official, authorized memoirs. See also Dyce, above.

d. CRITICISM

Bishop, Morchard. "Samuel Rogers, 1763-1855: A Centenary Tribute." CHARLES LAMB SOCIETY BULLETIN, No. 128 (January 1956), pp. 90-91.

Knieger, Bernard. "Samuel Rogers, Forgotten Maecenas." COLLEGE LANGUAGE ASSOCIATION JOURNAL, 3 (1960), 187-92.

> On Rogers as a patron of art and letters.

Weeks, Donald. "Samuel Rogers: Man of Taste." PMLA, 62 (1947), 472-86.

> Discusses Rogers as a connoisseur of art and an influential patron of poetry and art.

11. [Sir] Walter Scott (1771-1832)

Besides the works listed below, there exists a vast body of material by and about Scott as novelist, editor, and man of politics and letters that is not directly relevant to his role as a poet and is, therefore, omitted here but included in another volume in the Gale Information Guide series. For a general listing of materials to 1966 on all aspects of Scott's career, see J.C. Corson, "Sir Walter Scott," NCBEL, III, 670-92; and for a critical evaluation of such sources, see the article by James T. Hillhouse and Alexander Welsh in the second edition of Houtchens and Houtchens, THE ENGLISH ROMANTIC POETS AND ESSAYISTS (Sec. A.1, above).

a. BIBLIOGRAPHY

Burr, Allston. SCOTT: AN INDEX PLACING THE SHORT POEMS IN HIS NOVELS AND IN HIS LONG POEMS AND DRAMAS. Cambridge: Harvard University Press, 1936.

Indexes some 700 short poems and fragments by titles and first lines; unfortunately, many of the "poems" so indexed are quotations or adaptations from other poets.

*Corson, James Clarkson. A BIBLIOGRAPHY OF SCOTT: A CLASSIFIED AND ANNOTATED LIST OF BOOKS AND ARTICLES RELATING TO HIS LIFE AND WORKS, 1797-1940. Edinburgh: Oliver and Boyd, 1943.

An excellent bibliography listing approximately 3,000 secondary sources.

Hafter, Monroe Z. "The Spanish Version of Scott's DON RODERICK." SiR, 13 (1974), 225-34.

Translated (and altered) by Agustín Aicart, using his penname, "A. Tracia," and published in 1829.

Legouis, Emile. "La fortune littéraire de Walter Scott in France." ÉTUDES ANGLAISES, 24 (1971), 442-50.

Posthumous publication of a lecture given at the Sorbonne, 21 January 1933.

Ruff, William. "A Bibliography of the Poetical Works of Sir Walter Scott, 1796-1832." EDINBURGH BIBLIOGRAPHICAL SOCIETY TRANSACTIONS, 1 and 2 (Session 1936-37), 99-239. Edinburgh: R. and R. Clark, 1938.

The standard bibliography with twenty-three title pages in facsimile.

Ruff, William, and Ward Hellstrom. "Some Uncollected Poems of Sir Walter Scott: A Census." NOTES AND QUERIES, n.s. 14 (1968), 292-94.

*Van Antwerp, William C. A COLLECTOR'S COMMENT ON HIS FIRST EDITIONS OF THE WORKS OF SIR WALTER SCOTT. San Francisco: Gelber, Lilienthal, 1932.

The "Poems and Miscellaneous Works" are listed, collated (in some cases), and commented upon (pp. 3-68).

b. EDITIONS

The "Magnum Opus" edition of Scott's collected works published by Cadell began to appear in 1829 under Scott's supervision (the poems dated 1830 and 1831) and was completed by Lockhart's edition of twenty-eight volumes of collected prose (1834-40) and the ten-volume second edition of Lockhart's LIFE (1839)--for a total of ninety-eight volumes. Most of the many subsequent nineteenth-century editions of Scott's poems derive from his 1830-31 revised versions. There is no modern critical edition of his collected poems.

Dean, Dennis R. "Scott and Mackenzie: New Poems." PQ, 52 (1973), 265-73.

> The Prologue (by Scott) and Epilogue (by Mackenzie) to Joanna Baillie's THE FAMILY LEGEND (1810). See also Dean's "Four Notes on Scott." STUDIES IN SCOTTISH LITERATURE, 10 (1972), 51-53.

Henderson, Thomas Finlayson, ed. THE MINSTRELSY OF THE SCOTTISH BORDER. 4 vols. Edinburgh: William Blackwood and Sons, 1902.

> An excellent critical edition.

*THE POETICAL WORKS OF SIR WALTER SCOTT. 12 vols. Edinburgh: Robert Cadell, 1833-34.

> Often reprinted in editions of from one to twelve volumes.

*Robertson, J. Logie, ed. POETICAL WORKS. Oxford: Clarendon Press, 1894.

> The standard edition, reprinted at least as recently as 1951.

Rolfe, William J., ed. THE POETICAL WORKS. Boston: Houghton Mifflin, 1899.

> Claims to be "a careful revision of the text."

Ruff, William, and Ward Hellstrom. "Scott's Authorship of the Songs in Daniel Terry's Plays." STUDIES IN SCOTTISH LITERATURE, 5 (1968), 205-15.

Thompson, A[lexander] Hamilton, ed. SELECTIONS FROM THE POEMS OF SIR WALTER SCOTT. Cambridge: Cambridge University Press, 1922.

> About 200 pages of selections.

c. BIOGRAPHICAL SOURCES AND STUDIES

*Anderson, W.E.K., ed. THE JOURNAL OF SIR WALTER SCOTT. Oxford: Clarendon Press, 1972.

> The first complete text, with useful notes and maps, of the interesting journal Scott kept during the final six years of his life.

Clark, Arthur Melville. SIR WALTER SCOTT: THE FORMATIVE YEARS. Edinburgh: William Blackwood, 1969.

> Includes quotations from a wide variety of relatively obscure sources about Scott's schooling and early reading.

Crawford, Thomas. SCOTT, Edinburgh: Oliver and Boyd, 1965.

Daiches, David. SIR WALTER SCOTT AND HIS WORLD. London: Thames and Hudson, 1971.

French, Richard. "The Religion of Sir Walter Scott." STUDIES IN SCOTTISH LITERATURE, 2 (1964), 32-44.

Gell, Sir William. REMINISCENCES OF SIR WALTER SCOTT'S RESIDENCE IN ITALY, 1832. Ed. James C. Corson. Edinburgh: Nelson, 1957.

#Grierson, H[erbert] J.C. SIR WALTER SCOTT, BART: A NEW LIFE, SUPPLE-MENTARY TO AND CORRECTIVE OF LOCKHART'S BIOGRAPHY. London: Constable, 1938.

> The fullest corrective to Lockhart until the publication of Johnson's life (both below).

* _____, ed., assisted by Davidson Cook, W.M. Parker, et al. THE LETTERS OF SIR WALTER SCOTT. 12 vols. London: Constable, 1932-37.

> This important collection of approximately 4,200 letters to over 400 correspondents suffers from the absence of an index and must be supplemented by various later publications (see NCBEL, III, 677-78).

Hutton, Richard H. SIR WALTER SCOTT. English Men of Letters Series. London: Macmillan, 1878.

> A brief, sensible account of Scott's life derived entirely from Lockhart, below.

*Johnson, Edgar. SIR WALTER SCOTT: THE GREAT UNKNOWN. 2 vols. New York: Macmillan, 1970.

> A painstakingly researched and well-written biography; the standard authority on Scott's life.

*Lockhart, John Gibson. MEMOIRS OF THE LIFE OF SIR WALTER SCOTT. 7 vols. Edinburgh: Robert Cadell, 1837-38.

> The standard scholarly edition of Lockhart by A.W. Pollard (5 vols., 1900), adds material from Lockhart's papers.

Low, Donald A. "Walter Scott and Williamina Belsches." TIMES LITERARY SUPPLEMENT, 23 July 1971, pp. 865-66.

> Argues that Scott "never entirely recovered" from losing this early love to a rival.

#Quayle, Eric. THE RUIN OF SIR WALTER SCOTT. London: Rupert Hart-Davis, 1969.

> Especially useful for Scott's dealings with James and John Ballantyne.

Ratchford, Fannie E., and William M. McCarthy, Jr. THE CORRESPONDENCE OF SIR WALTER SCOTT AND CHARLES ROBERT MATURIN. Austin: University of Texas Press, 1937.

> Seventy-three hitherto unpublished letters. Other additions to Grierson's edition have since appeared in pamphlets and periodicals; see Corson and NCBEL.

Young, Douglas. EDINBURGH IN THE AGE OF SIR WALTER SCOTT. Norman: University of Oklahoma Press, 1965.

> A general background book on the "Athens of the North" during its heyday.

d. CRITICISM

In addition to the works listed below, see especially Kroeber, ROMANTIC NARRATIVE ART (Chap. 2.C), and Riese and Riesner, VERSDICHTUNG DER ENGLISCHEN ROMANTIK (Chap. 2.E.3).

#Bell, Alan, ed. SCOTT BICENTENARY ESSAYS. Edinburgh: Scottish Academic Press, 1974.

> Includes twenty-four papers on various subjects read at the Scott Bicentenary Conference, Edinburgh, in 1971.

Calder, Angus, and Jennie Calder. SCOTT. Literature in Perspective. London: Evans Brothers, 1969.

Crawford, Thomas. "Scott as a Poet." ÉTUDES ANGLAISES, 24 (1971), 478-91.

> One of a group of essays in a special Scott issue of ÉTUDES ANGLAISES.

Daiches, David. "Sir Walter Scott and History." ÉTUDES ANGLAISES, 24 (1971), 458-77.

> Refutes the view that "history" was an "antiquarian passion" for Scott, showing how Scott saw history as a way of understanding the present and future.

Davie, Donald. THE HEYDAY OF SIR WALTER SCOTT. London: Routledge and Kegan Paul, 1961.

> Davie's specific ideas on the poetry appear in his paper "The Poetry of Scott" in PROCEEDINGS OF THE BRITISH ACADEMY, 47 (1961).

Devlin, D.D., ed. WALTER SCOTT. Modern Judgments Series. London: Macmillan, 1968.

Easton, Charles C. "Sir Walter Scott--A Bi-Centenary Assessment." BURNS CHRONICLE AND CLUB DIRECTORY (Kilmarnock), 3rd Ser., 20 (1971), 48-71.

> Pages 14-20 of the same volume contain Donald A. Low's "Scott on Burns."

Emerson, O.F. "The Early Literary Life of Sir Walter Scott." JEGP, 23 (1924), 28-62, 241-69, 389-417.

> The most detailed record of Scott's writings to 1810.

Guest, Ann M., "Imagery of Color and Light in Scott's Narrative Poems." SEL, 12 (1972), 705-20.

#Hayden, John O., ed. SCOTT: THE CRITICAL HERITAGE. London: Routledge and Kegan Paul, 1970.

> Reprints reviews and comments on Scott's works from 1805 through 1883 (naturally concentrating on the novels).

Hillhouse, J.T. "Sir Walter's Last Long Poem." HUNTINGTON LIBRARY QUARTERLY, 16 (1952), 53-73.

> Studies the Huntington MS of HAROLD THE DAUNTLESS for evidence on the composition and revision of the poem.

Jeffares, A. Norman, ed. SCOTT'S MIND AND ART. Edinburgh: Oliver and Boyd, 1970.

Johnson, Edgar. "Scott and the Corners of Time." VIRGINIA QUARTERLY REVIEW, 49 (1973), 46-62.

> Defends Scott as "a Tory progressive, almost a Tory radical."

Lang, Andrew. SIR WALTER SCOTT AND THE BORDER MINSTRELSY. 1910; rpt. New York: AMS Press, 1968.

Larsen, T. "The Classical Element in Scott's Poetry." TRANSACTIONS OF THE ROYAL SOCIETY OF CANADA, 3rd Ser. 32, Sec. 2 (1938), 107-20.

Lauber, John. SIR WALTER SCOTT. Twayne's English Authors Series. New York: Twayne, 1966.

> A pedestrian general introduction to Scott's life and art.

McClatchy, J.D. "The Ravages of Time: The Function of the MARMION Epistles." STUDIES IN SCOTTISH LITERATURE, 9 (1972), 256-63.

@Mayhead, Robin. WALTER SCOTT. Profiles in Literature Series. London: Routledge and Kegan Paul, 1968.

Pikoulis, John. "Scott and MARMION: The Discovery of Identity." MLR, 66 (1971), 738-50.

Rubenstein, Jill. "The Dilemma of History: A Reading of Scott's BRIDAL OF TRIERMAIN." SEL, 12 (1972), 721-34.

_____. "Symbolic Characterization in THE LADY OF THE LAKE." DAL-HOUSIE REVIEW, 51 (1971), 366-73.

Smith, Janet Adam. "Scott and the Idea of Scotland." UNIVERSITY OF EDINBURGH JOURNAL, 21 (1964), 198-209, 290-98.

Stuart, Alice V. "Scott and Wordsworth: A Comparison." CONTEMPORARY REVIEW, 224 (1974), 251-54.

Wittig, Kurt. THE SCOTTISH TRADITION IN LITERATURE. Edinburgh: Oliver and Boyd, 1958.

> Important for all Scottish writers, including Scott and Hogg.

Zug, Charles G., 3rd. "Sir Walter Scott and the Ballad Forgery." STUDIES IN SCOTTISH LITERATURE, 8 (1970), 52-64.

12. Robert Southey (1774-1843)

a. BIBLIOGRAPHY

*Curry, Kenneth. "The Published Letters of Robert Southey: A Checklist." BNYPL, 71 (1967), 158-64.

_____. "Robert Southey." In THE ENGLISH ROMANTIC POETS AND ES-SAYISTS. 2nd ed. Ed. Carolyn Washburn Houtchens and Lawrence Huston Houtchens. New York: Published for the Modern Language Association by New York University Press, 1966. Pp. 157-82.

> This essay should be supplemented by the NCBEL bibliography, by Raimond (Sec. 12.c., below), by the "List of Southey's Works" in Simmons (Sec. 12.c, below), and by the annual bibliographies of English literature and Romanticism.

Curry, Kenneth, and Robert Dedmon. "Southey's Contributions to the QUAR-TERLY REVIEW." WC, 6 (1975), 261-72.

> A definitive list (1809-39) that modifies our conception of Southey's political stance (in a special issue of WC devoted to Southey).

Volz, Robert, and James Rieger. "The Rochester Southey Collection." WC, 5 (1974), 89-91.

> One of nine articles on Southey in a special issue of WC devoted to him.

b. EDITIONS

FitzGerald, Maurice H., ed. POEMS OF ROBERT SOUTHEY. Oxford Standard Authors Edition. London: Oxford University Press, 1909.

> A well-edited selection, including THALABA, MADOC, THE CURSE OF KEHAMA, RODERICK, and many shorter poems.

Griegson, Geoffrey, ed. A CHOICE OF SOUTHEY'S VERSE. London: Faber and Faber, 1971.

Merchant, Paul. "Southey's 'St. Patrick's Purgatory'--An Unpublished Manuscript." ALTA: THE UNIVERSITY OF BIRMINGHAM REVIEW, 2 (1969), 147-52.

*THE POETICAL WORKS OF ROBERT SOUTHEY, COLLECTED BY HIMSELF. 10 vols. London: Longman, Orme, Brown, Green, and Longmans, 1837-38.

> The nearest thing to a complete edition, though including much-revised texts of some of the early poetry.

c. BIOGRAPHICAL SOURCES AND STUDIES

#Braekman, W., ed. "Letters by Robert Southey to Sir John Taylor Coleridge." STUDIA GERMANICA GANDENSIA (Belgium), 6 (1964), 103-230.

Carefully annotates and indexes Southey's most important correspondence relating to the QUARTERLY REVIEW.

Brown, Simon. "Ebenezer Elliott and Robert Southey: Southey's Break with
the QUARTERLY REVIEW." RES, n.s. 22 (1971), 307-11.

Traces Southey's friendship with Elliott and attributes Southey's
break with the QUARTERLY to an article on Elliott.

Cabral, Adolfo, ed. ROBERT SOUTHEY: JOURNALS OF A RESIDENCE IN
PORTUGAL 1800-1801 AND A VISIT TO FRANCE IN 1838. Oxford: Clarendon Press, 1960.

The Portuguese journal is especially important as a guide to
Southey's intellectual and political development.

#Curry, Kenneth. "The Library of Robert Southey." In STUDIES IN HONOR
OF JOHN C. HODGES AND ALWIN THALER (TENNESSEE STUDIES IN LIT-
ERATURE, SPECIAL NUMBER, 1961). Pp. 77-86.

Surveys the growth and dispersal of Southey's 14,000-volume collection.

*_____, ed. NEW LETTERS OF ROBERT SOUTHEY. 2 vols. New York:
Columbia University Press, 1965.

The most important selection of Southey's correspondence, well
edited and indexed.

*Dowden, Edward, ed. THE CORRESPONDENCE OF ROBERT SOUTHEY WITH
CAROLINE BOWLES, TO WHICH ARE ADDED: CORRESPONDENCE WITH
SHELLEY, AND SOUTHEY'S DREAMS. Dublin: Hodges, Figgis; London:
Longmans, Green, 1881.

A very important volume of correspondence with the younger writer
who became Southey's second wife, as well as Southey's revealing
exchange with PBS and Southey's record of his own (often violent)
dreams.

FitzGerald, Maurice H., ed. LETTERS OF ROBERT SOUTHEY: A SELECTION.
London: Oxford University Press, 1912.

A representative selection, with a few notes at the end of the
volume (but no index).

#Haller, William. THE EARLY LIFE OF ROBERT SOUTHEY, 1774-1803. New
York: Columbia University Press, 1917.

Still the most detailed analysis in English of Southey's formative
years, but dated by more recent documents and contextual information (and attitudes).

@Simmons, Jack. SOUTHEY. London: Collins, 1945.

> Once the standard critical biography, now somewhat dated by
> more recent scholarship--especially that of Curry and Raimond.

#Southey, Charles Cuthbert, ed. THE LIFE AND CORRESPONDENCE OF
ROBERT SOUTHEY. 6 vols. London: Longman, Brown, Green, and Longmans,
1849-50.

> Later reissued in one large volume, this pious compendium of
> letters (carefully chosen and abridged) attempts to hide Southey's
> embarrassments, as well as to ignore his relationship with Caroline
> Bowles (see Dowden, above).

d. CRITICISM

Carnall, Geoffrey. ROBERT SOUTHEY. London: Published for the British
Council and the National Book League by Longmans, Green, 1964.

> A concise appraisal of the man and his work.

_____. ROBERT SOUTHEY AND HIS AGE: THE DEVELOPMENT OF A CON-
SERVATIVE MIND. Oxford: Clarendon Press, 1960.

> Though chiefly concerned with Southey's prose, this significant
> study is a key to the understanding of Southey's literary as well
> as his political development.

*Curry, Kenneth. SOUTHEY. Routledge Author Guide Series. London: Rout-
ledge and Kegan Paul, 1975.

> The best general introduction to the writer and his work.

Dowden, Wilfred S. "The Source of the Metempsychosis Motif in Southey's
THALABA." MLN, 66 (1951), 555-56.

Hoffpauir, Richard. "The Thematic Structure of Southey's Epic Poetry." WC,
6 (1975), 240-48.

> Treats JOAN OF ARC and THALABA--not all five "epics."

Jacobus, Mary. "Southey's Debt to LYRICAL BALLADS (1798)." RES, n.s.
22 (1971), 20-36.

> Discusses the impact of WW's LYRICAL BALLADS on Southey's sub-
> sequent verse.

Kaderly, Nat Lewis. "Southey's Borrowings from Celia Fiennes." MLN, 69
(1954), 249-55.

#Madden, Lionel, ed. ROBERT SOUTHEY: THE CRITICAL HERITAGE. London: Routledge and Kegan Paul, 1972.

> Includes contemporary reviews of Southey's publications, as well as comments from letters and general essays from 1794 through 1879.

Morgan, Peter F. "Southey on Poetry." TENNESSEE STUDIES IN LITERATURE, 16 (1971), 77-89.

> Surveys Southey's ideas on poetry and on the history of English literature, and claims a place for Southey as a significant critic.

#Raimond, Jean. ROBERT SOUTHEY: L'HOMME ET SON TEMPS--L'OEUVRE--LE RÔLE. Études Anglaises, No. 28. Paris: Didier, 1968.

> The most extensive modern scholarly study of Southey's life and works, with a full (though flawed) bibliography of primary and secondary materials to 1963, arranged chronologically. See also Curry's review in ELN, 7 1969, Supplement, 46-47.

Rammamurty, K. "Robert Southey: The Development of His Poetic Art." CALCUTTA REVIEW, n.s. 1 (1969), 305-20.

Runyan, William Ronald. "Bob Southey's Diabolical Doggerel: Its Influence on Shelley and Byron." WC, 6 (1975), 249-54.

> The impact of "The Devil's Thoughts" on PBS's "The Devil's Walk," and LB's "The Devil's Drive" and part of DON JUAN.

Sanderson, David R. "Robert Southey and the Standard Georgian Style." MIDWEST QUARTERLY (Pittsburg, Kans), 12 (1971), 335-52.

AUTHOR INDEX

In addition to authors this index includes editors, compilers, and contributors. References are to page numbers and alphabetization is letter by letter.

Author Index

Author Index

Author Index

Author Index

Author Index

Author Index

Author Index

TITLE INDEX

This index consists of all titles of books cited in the bibliography. Some lengthy titles have been shortened. This index is alphabetized letter by letter and references are to page numbers.

C

Title Index

Title Index

Title Index

Title Index

Title Index

S

Title Index

SUBJECT INDEX

Underlined numbers refer to main entries in the subject. This index is alphabetized letter by letter and references are to page numbers.

Subject Index

anthologies containing the poetry
of 186, 187
biography of 197
Gothic drama and 59
Ballads, poetic 44
of Coleridge 94
of Wordsworth 89, 90, 91, 93,
94, 97
Ballantyne, James and John, Scott's
dealings with 222
Balston, William 13
Bank of England 7
Banks and banking 13
Barbauld, Anna Laetitia, anthologies
containing the poetry of 186
Barclay's Bank, Ltd. 13-14
Barham, Richard Harris, literary
ballads of 44
Barnes, Thomas, contributions to the
REFLECTOR by 202
Barrett, Eaton Stannard, anthologies
containing the poetry of 187
Barthes, Roland 47
Barton, Bernard
anthologies containing the poetry
of 187
catalog of the library of 54
Baudelaire, Charles Pierre
opium use by 64
sado-masochism in the writings of
55
Bayly, Thomas Haynes, anthologies
containing the poetry of 187
Beck, Thomas, anthologies containing
the poetry of 187
Beddoes, Thomas Lovell 60, 188-90
anthologies containing the poetry
of 185, 186
bibliographies on 188
biographies of and sources of information for 189
editions of the works of 188-89
general criticism of 188, 190
in Germany 189
literary ballads of 44
narrative poetry of 70
themes and imagery in the poetry
of 190
Beerbohm, Max 9
Beethoven, Ludwig van 66

Bellow, Saul, pastoral form of 45
Belsches, Williamina, relationships
with Scott 221
Bentham, Jeremy
editing of the works of 50
social influence of 9
Berkeley, George, influence of on
the Romantics 21
Bible
influence of attitudes toward on
literature 21
literary analysis of 48
printing of in London 16
Shelley's knowledge and use of
165
Bibliography, descriptive and
analytical 50-52
Biographies 5-6
of architects 27
of artists 28
bibliography of 2
of British authors 40
of engineers 24
Greek and Roman 42
of printers and publishers 16
See also Autobiographies
Biological sciences, relationship to
poetic metaphor and symbolism 25
Birch, Walter, Landor's letters to
207
Bixby, W.K., Shelley collection of
151
Blackmur, R.P., analysis of the
criticism of 49
Blackwood, William 18
BLACKWOOD'S MAGAZINE, index
to 18
Blake, William xiii, 183
anthologies containing the poetry
of 57, 185
bibliographies on 54, 185
biography of 67
general criticism of 47, 48, 61,
68, 69, 70, 71
imagination in the works of 59,
95
impact of the Enlightenment on
70
love as a theme in the works of
58

mythology in the poetry of 23
relationship to Milton 46
religious trends in the poetry of
20, 23
role of social and personal change
in the writings of 8, 46, 60
satanic hero of 66
search for the hero in the epic
poetry of 62
"strangers and pilgrim" theme of 58
the sublime in the works of 62
Bland, Robert, anthologies containing
the poetry of 187
Blessington, Margaret Power (Lady)
catalog of the library of 54
relationships with Byron 129
Bloomfield, Robert 45
anthologies containing the poetry
of 185
catalog of the library of 54
Bodkin, Maud, analysis of the criticism of 49
Boehme, Jakob, influence of on
Wordsworth 87
Bonaparte, Napoleon 11
Book reviewers and reviewing 16
bibliography of 19
Coleridge's ambivalence toward
108
compilations of 18
Scottish 15
See also Literary criticism
Books and reading
analysis of best sellers 14
bibliographical analysis of 14-15,
16
bibliography of annuals and gift
books 16
Booksellers
checklist of London 17
history of 17
Booth, David, anthologies containing
the poetry of 187
Bowles, William Lisle, anthologies
containing the poetry of
186, 187
Bowles, Caroline, correspondence and
relationships with Southey
226, 227
Bradley, F.H., religion in the writings
of 20

Brawne, Fanny, letters of 172
Brontë, Emily, anthologies containing
the poetry of 186
Brontë, Patrick, anthologies contain-
ing the poetry of 187
Brooks, Cleanth, analysis of the
criticism of 49
Brooks, Van Wyck, analysis of the
criticism of 49
Brown, Charles Armitage, letters
of 172
Browning, Robert
Biblical criticism in the works of
21
dramatic monologues of 61
general criticism of 71
imagination in the works of 58
nature in the poetry of 63
opinions of Shelley by 145
the publisher of 17
Brummell, George Byron 8, 9
Brun, Friederike, influence of on
Coleridge 112
Bryant, Jacob, influence of on the
Romantics 21
Brydges, Samuel Egerton, anthologies
containing the poetry of
187
Buber, Martin, compared to Shelley
159
Burges, James Bland, anthologies
containing the poetry of
187
Burke, Edmund 72
political and social thought of 6
the sublime in the works of 62
Burke, Kenneth 49
Burney, Charles 29, 33
commentary of on Wordsworth's
ballads 97
Burns, Robert xv, 45
anthologies containing the poetry
of 57, 186
general criticism of 69, 71
impact of the Enlightenment on
70
love as a theme in the works of
58
religious trends in the poetry of
20

Subject Index

M

Subject Index

Peel, Robert, Peacock on 214
Peerage, British 5
Percy, Thomas, literary ballads of 44
Periodicals
  bibliographies of 16, 17, 19
  checklist of those concerned with
    the Romantics 55-56
  publishing of in London 16
  Romantic literature in 70
  See also names of periodicals (e.g.
    MONTHLY REVIEW, THE)
Persius, Aulus (Flaccus), Byron's
    imitation of 138
Peterborough Museum and Art Gallery.
    John Clare Collection, cata-
    log of 192
Peterloo Massacre 9
  Byron on 133
Pforzheimer (Carl H.) Library, MSS
    catalog of 156
Pharmacy, history of 13
Philology. See Language and
    linguistics
Philosophy 19-21
  of Byron 136
  of Coleridge 103, 111, 115-16,
    117
  influence of on Wordsworth 85,
    86, 92, 94
  of Keats 178, 181, 182
  of Shelley 158, 162, 164, 166
  See also schools of philosophy
    (e.g. Empiricism, English)
Pigot, Elizabeth, relationships with
    Byron 130
Plato
  Coleridge's literary relationship to
    111
  Shelley's use of the ideas of 163,
    164
Plotinus, influence of on Wordsworth
    87
Poe, Edgar Allan, opium use by 64
Poetry
  diction and 34
  effect of science on seventeenth
    century 26
  encyclopedias of 41
  Freudian interpretations of 42-43
  indexes to 40

influence of the poet's voice on
    his 34
  the primary language of 35
  theories of composition and style
    45
  See also Ballads, literary; Epic
    poetry; Lyric poetry; Narra-
    tive poetry; Romantic litera-
    ture; Sonnets; Structuralism
    in poetry; Syntax, poetic
Poetry, English 42
  criticism of 49, 50
  Elizabethan in the eighteenth
    century 46
  history of 39
  metrics and versification in 34,
    35, 36
  psychology of 25
  religion and 21
  treatment of nature in 45
  unlearned or "peasant" 45-46
  See also Romantic literature; names
    of poets (e.g. John Keats)
Poetry, Scottish vernacular 69
Polidori, John William, diary of 130
Politics, nineteenth century 6-10
  Byron and 122, 133-34, 136,
    138, 139
  Coleridge and 108, 113, 114,
    117
  the press and 14
  the Romantics and 57, 59, 62
  satire on 188
  Scott and 223
  Shelley and 148, 150, 162
  Southey and 225
  Wordsworth and 88
  See also Conservatism; Liberalism,
    English; Liberalism, French;
    Radicalism, British; Radical-
    ism, European; Revolution
Poole, Thomas, account of his friend-
    ship with Coleridge 106,
    109
Poor laws 9
Pope, Alexander 42, 69
  influence on Shelley 165
  relationships with Byron 139
Population. See Malthusianism
Portraiture. See Miniature painting

286

Subject Index

in Keats's poetry 179
literary analysis of 48
relationship of to the development
of the biological sciences
25
in Romantic poetry 60, 61, 68
in Scott's poetry 224
in Shelley's poetry 156-57, 160
in Wordsworth's poetry 90
Syntax, poetic, Shelley's 161

T

Taaffe, John 133, 156
Talfourd, Thomas Noon, the publisher
of 17
Tasso, Torquato, impact of on English
poetry 43
Tate, Allen, analysis of the criticism
of 49
Taxation 10
Taylor, John 15
relationships with Clare 194
Technology
bibliography of the history of 25
in the industrial revolution 26
See also Science
Tennyson, Alfred
dramatic monologues of 64
elegies of 45
imagination in the works of 58
nature in the poetry of 63
the publisher of 17
Terry, Daniel, Scott as author of the
songs in the plays of 220
Theater. See Drama
Thelwall, John
anthologies containing the poetry
of 187
comments on Coleridge by 106
Thom, William, anthologies containing
the poetry of 186
Thurlow, Edward, Lord, anthologies
containing the poetry of 186,
187
Ticknor, George, influence of Coleridge on 100
Tighe, Mary, anthologies containing
the poetry of 187
Tinker, Chauncey Brewster, catalog of
the library of 37

Tobin, John, Gothic drama of 59
Toleration, politics of 7
Tolstoi, Leo 166
Tooke, Horne 33
Torrey, Joseph, influence of Cole-
ridge on 100
Tragedy, critical theory of 42
Trials in the 1790s 7
Tucker, Abraham, influence of on
the Romantics 21
Turner, J.M.W. 30, 31, 162

U

United States
Byron and 123, 140
Campbell and 191
Keats and 168
Romanticism in 64, 65, 69
Shelley's reputation in 144, 145,
146
Wordsworth in the literary crit-
icism of 75
Utilitarianism
infiltration of into British official-
dom 12
social influences of 9

V

Valery, Paul, critical works on 48
Vallon, Annette, Wordsworth's relationships with 84, 86,
90
Versification. See Poetry, English,
metrics and versification in
Voice, effect of the poet's on his
poetry 34

W

Wages, minimum 9
Walker, William Sidney, anthologies
containing the poetry of
187
Walpole, Horace 29
Wandering Jew, legend of 21-22,
149
Warren, Robert Penn, analysis of the
criticism of 49
Water color painting 29, 30